Sickness and God

Sickness and God

Vinu V Das

Tabor Press

© 2025 Tabor Press. All rights reserved. No part of this publication may be reproduced, distributed, or transmitted in any form or by any means without the prior written permission of the publisher, except in the case of brief quotations embodied in critical reviews and certain other noncommercial uses permitted by copyright law.

ISBN 978-1-997541-28-8

Table of Contents

Chapter 1 – Shalom Shattered: Creation, Fall, and the Origin of Sickness 13

    1.0 Prologue – The Enigma of Suffering 13

    1.1 The Perfect Order (Gen 1:31) 15

    1.2 The Entrance of Corruption (Gen 3; Rom 5:12) . 18

    1.3 Cosmic Fallout and the Cursed Ground (Gen 3:17–19) 20

    1.4 Divine Justice and Mercy Intertwined 23

    1.5 Hope Prefigured Amid Ruin 25

    1.6 Pastoral and Scientific Reflections 27

    1.7 Transitional Summary and Reflection 30

Chapter 2 – Sin and Sickness: Personal, Corporate, Ancestral 32

    2.0 Prelude — Diagnosing the Link Between Sin and Sickness 32

    2.1 Individual Sin and Bodily Affliction 34

    2.2 Generational Brokenness 37

    2.3 National or Communal Sin 39

    2.4 The Silence of the Innocent: Job, the Man Born Blind, and Beyond 42

    2.5 Christological Fulfillment—The Sin-Bearer and the Sick-Healer 43

    2.6 Discernment and Pastoral Praxis 45

2.7 Worship, Sacrament, and Community Health 47

2.8 Epilogue — Toward Holistic Repentance and Societal Wholeness 49

Chapter 3 – Satan Tested, God Permitted: Spiritual Warfare and Bodily Trials 51

3.0 Prologue — Unseen Battlefields and Human Frailty 51

3.1 Job's Ordeal Revisited (Job 1–2) 53

3.2 Old-Testament Foreshadows of Deliverance 55

3.3 New-Testament Confrontations 57

3.4 Christological Center — The Cross as Cosmic Triumph 59

3.5 Discernment and Prayer Strategy 60

3.6 Pastoral Protocols for Deliverance Ministry.62

3.7 Suffering, Sanctification, and Redemptive Mystery 64

3.8 Communal Warfare — Intercession for Cities and Nations 66

3.9 Epilogue — Courageous Faith on Contested Ground 68

Chapter 4 – God's Redemptive Purposes in Affliction ..70

4.0 Prelude — The Alchemy of Suffering 70

4.1 Sickness as a Canvas for Glory (Jn 9:3) 72

4.2 Formation through Pain (2 Cor 12:7–10).....74

4.3 Preparation for Future Ministry 76

4.4 The Mystery of Delayed or Partial Healing .. 78

4.5 Communal Edification and Mutual Care 79

4.6 Eschatological Horizon of Wholeness 80

4.7 Pastoral and Practical Frameworks 82

4.8 Epilogue — From Wounds to Wellsprings ... 84

Chapter 5 – The Innocent Sufferer: Newborn Illness and Divine Compassion 86

5.0 Prelude — When the Cradle Becomes a Cross 86

5.1 Theological Tension of Infant Pain 88

5.2 Medical Advances as Providential Care 90

5.3 Liturgy of Lament and Hope for Families 92

5.4 Covenant Signs and Sacramental Consolation 94

5.5 Pastoral Presence in the NICU 96

5.6 Compassion-Driven Ethics and Advocacy ... 98

5.7 Testimonies and Missional Impact 100

5.8 Eschatological Comfort and the Hope of Reunion 101

5.9 Epilogue — Cradling Mystery in the Arms of Mercy 103

Chapter 6 – Bodily Ailments: Acute, Chronic, Curable, Incurable 104

6.0 Prelude — Our Common Frailty, God's Persistent Care 104

6.1 Taxonomy of Physical Diseases 106

6.2 Navigating Prognosis in Faith 108

6.3 Embodied Spiritual Practices 111

6.4 Integrative Medicine and Faith 113

6.5 Communities of Care and Accountability ... 115

6.6 Eschatological Vision and Present Resilience 117

6.7 Pastoral Tools for Diverse Diagnoses 119

6.8 Epilogue — Wholeness in Fractured Flesh 121

Chapter 7 – Mental and Emotional Disorders: Depression, Anxiety, Psychosis 122

7.0 Prelude — Sound Mind, Fragile Heart 122

7.1 Scriptural Windows into Inner Turmoil 124

7.2 Clinical Taxonomy and Symptomatology ... 127

7.3 Integrating Psychiatry and Pastoral Care .. 130

7.4 Congregational Practices for Mental-Health Flourishing 132

7.5 Suicide Prevention and Theological Hope . 134

7.6 Formation and Discipleship in the Dark Seasons 136

7.7 Eschatological Assurance and Present Endurance 139

7.8 Epilogue — A Church That Guards Minds and Hearts 140

Chapter 8 – Losing One's Self: Amnesia, Dementia, and

Identity in Christ 142
- 8.0 Prelude — When Memories Slip Through Fingers..142
- 8.1 Memory, Personhood, and the Imago Dei.144
- 8.2 Trajectories and Typologies of Memory Loss 146
- 8.3 Caregiving as Covenant Faithfulness.........149
- 8.4 Liturgical and Spiritual Tools for Memory Loss..152
- 8.5 Communities of Remembrance...................155
- 8.6 The Theological Mystery of Identity and Continuity 157
- 8.7 Eschatological Restoration of Memory.......160
- 8.8 Pastoral Resources and Training Modules162
- 8.9 Epilogue — God Remembers Our Frame .164

Chapter 9 – Lifestyle and Environment: Diet, Addiction, and Stewardship 166
- 9.0 Prelude — Bodies on Loan, Earth in Trust 166
- 9.1 A Theology of Nourishment 168
- 9.2 Daniel's Experiment Revisited (Dan 1) 171
- 9.3 Substance Abuse and the Temple Body (1 Cor 6:19–20)...173
- 9.4 Formation of Holy Habits.............................175
- 9.5 Environmental Justice and Public Health ..177
- 9.6 Creation Care as Preventive Medicine.......180
- 9.7 Integrative Medical Partnerships.................182

9.8 Global Perspectives on Lifestyle Disease .185

9.9 Epilogue — Taste and See: Toward a Kingdom Ecology of Health 187

Chapter 10 – Genetics, Mutation, and Evolution: A Theology of Biology..189

10.0 Prelude — Genes in the Light of Glory 189

10.1 DNA, Providence, and the Fall.................191

10.2 Evolution, Natural Selection, and Theological Horizons...193

10.3 Ethical Frontiers: Gene Therapy and Editing 195

10.4 Genetic Testing, Counseling, and Congregational Care 198

10.5 Hope Beyond Heredity (1 Cor 15:49–53) 200

10.6 Worship and Vocation in the Age of Genomics 201

10.7 Epilogue — From A-C-G-T to Alpha and Omega 203

Chapter 11 – Healing and Medicine: Prayer, Sacrament, Science...205

11.0 Prelude — Sickbeds and Sanctuaries: A Meeting Place for Grace 205

11.1 Historical Synergy of Faith and Medicine 207

11.2 Vocations of Healing....................................209

11.3 Prayer and the Sacramental Imagination 211

11.4 Charisms of Healing (1 Cor 12:9)..............214

11.5 Ethical Decision-Making at Life's Margins 216

11.6 Global Health, Justice, and Medical Missions 218

11.7 Formation and Resilience of Healers 220

11.8 Eschatological Horizons of Health............222

11.9 Epilogue — Toward a New Hippocratic Amen..224

Chapter 12 – Lament, Worship, and Formation Amid Suffering 225

12.0 Prelude — When Tears Become Theology 225

12.1 The Psalms of Lament as Spiritual Guide 227

12.2 Corporate Rhythms of Grief and Hope 229

12.3 Formational Outcomes of Suffering..........232

12.4 Joy and Gratitude Practices in the Furnace (Hab 3:17–19)..234

12.5 Discipling the Next Generation Through Honest Worship..237

12.6 Pastoral Care Architectures for Long-Term Sufferers...239

12.7 Eschatological Lament and Final Hallelujah 241

12.8 Epilogue — From Wailing Wall to Wedding Feast...244

Chapter 13 – The Church's Vocation: Compassionate

Community and Advocacy 246

    13.0 Prelude — Love with Skin On: Why Ecclesial Compassion Still Matters 246

    13.1 Pastoral Theology of Presence 248

    13.2 Congregational Care Ecosystems 251

    13.3 Formation of Compassionate Disciples ... 254

    13.4 Prophetic Voice in Public Health 258

    13.5 Missional Partnerships for Holistic Care .. 261

    13.6 Eschatological Imagination and Advocacy 264

    13.7 Epilogue — Hands Ready, Hearts Soft: Becoming a People of Embodied Mercy 267

Chapter 14 – The Eschatological Hope: New Creation and the End of Sickness 269

    14.0 Prelude — Longing for the Last Word 269

    14.1 Biblical Visions of Total Healing (Rev 21:4) 270

    14.2 Resurrection Theology and Bodily Redemption 271

    14.3 Living in Anticipation 273

    14.4 Pastoral and Practical Eschatology 274

    14.5 Apologetics of Hope in a Skeptical Age ... 275

    14.7 Epilogue — From Alpha to Omega: Embracing the Story's Happy Ending 276

Chapter 1 – Shalom Shattered: Creation, Fall, and the Origin of Sickness

From the very dawn of human history, sickness has shadowed our lives, prompting the deepest questions about pain, purpose, and the divine. Long before germs, genetics, or environmental toxins were understood, Scripture reveals that illness is woven into the story of creation and the human heart. In Eden's perfect harmony, every element—human, animal, and earth—functioned in seamless partnership under God's benevolent care. Yet when trust faltered and rebellion brewed, that original symphony of life fractured, and a new reality of decay and disease took root. This chapter traces that seismic shift from blessing into curse, exploring how moral choices unleashed cosmic consequences that extend even into our cells. As we journey through Genesis and beyond, we discover that sickness is not an afterthought or random misfortune but a mirror reflecting the breach between Creator and creature. At the same time, we encounter glimmers of divine compassion—promises of redemption that anticipate the great Physician who would enter our suffering world. By understanding the origin of sickness in the fall of creation, we equip ourselves to face suffering with both honesty and hope, recognizing that every ache carries the potential to draw us closer to the One who heals.

1.0 Prologue – The Enigma of Suffering

1.0.1 The Universality of Illness (Job 5:7)

Every human across time and culture confronts the fragility of body and mind, reminding us that suffering is woven into the human condition (Job 5:7). From infancy to old age, disease and injury mark the trajectory of life, shaping our stories in ways both small and profound. Even societies with the most advanced medicine cannot eradicate every ailment, testifying that illness transcends technological mastery. Ancient texts from Mesopotamia to Egypt lament plagues, fevers, and deformities, underscoring that no age enjoys perfect health. In the Bible, Job's lament over relentless pain illustrates the depth of human anguish and the search for meaning amid inexplicable suffering (Job 3). The universality of illness invites pressing questions: Why does a good God permit disease? Is sickness arbitrary or purposeful? These queries echo through hospital corridors, pastoral counseling sessions, and solitary moments of fear. Illness fractures routines, exposes dependency, and often drives us to consider eternity. Cultural responses range from demonizing sickness as divine retribution to reducing it to impersonal biochemistry. Yet the Christian narrative refuses simplistic answers; it acknowledges mystery while anchoring hope in a God who is both just and compassionate. Personal stories of survival and loss reveal how illness can deepen relationships, spark empathy, and cultivate spiritual maturity. Communities mobilize around the sick, forming support networks that reflect God's heart for the weak. The ubiquity of sickness also shapes theology: doctrines of sin, redemption, and eschatology must account for pain's pervasiveness. Medical vocations become callings in this light, where healing work reflects divine mercy at the bedside. Even those untouched by chronic illness bear its ripple effects in family caregiving and social policy. The pervasiveness of disease thus demands integrated responses—scientific, ethical, and spiritual. Recognizing its universality safeguards us against judging sufferers and fuels a posture of solidarity. It prepares hearts to explore deeper roots of sickness, beyond accident or randomness. As we turn toward the primeval narrative of Eden, we will see how this universal brokenness began and what it reveals about God's redemptive plan.

1.0.2 Why Begin in Eden? Method and Scope

Tracing sickness back to the Garden of Eden is not about antiquarian curiosity but about understanding root causes and ultimate resolutions. By examining the first fracture in perfect creation, we uncover patterns that reappear in every fevered brow and failing limb.

Our method combines careful exegesis of Genesis with insights from medical history, biology, and pastoral care. We engage both ancient narrative and contemporary research, recognizing that theology and science inform each other. Addressing the origin story shapes our approach to individual and communal healing: symptoms must be treated, but systemic restoration requires tackling underlying causes. Beginning in Eden also clarifies the nature of divine intention: God's design for shalom sets the standard against which all deviations are measured. This hermeneutical lens prevents reading modern diseases back into ancient texts anachronistically; instead, we discern how timeless truths illuminate present struggles. The scope of our study spans personal affliction, ancestral legacies, and cosmic redemption, reflecting the multifaceted dimensions of sickness. We will employ case studies, scriptural expositions, and practical applications, ensuring that theory translates into compassionate ministry. Scholarly dialogues—biblical theology, ethics, epidemiology—will be woven into accessible narratives for pastors, health workers, and lay readers alike. This interdisciplinary posture honors the complexity of human suffering without succumbing to reductionism. By starting in Eden, we affirm that every pandemic and personal ailment ultimately points back to relationship brokenness between Creator and creature. Yet our aim is not to leave readers in despair but to equip them for hope-filled engagement. As we proceed from the pristine garden through the Fall into redemptive history, we will chart a path that leads both downward into honest lament and upward toward Christ's healing work. In this way, our journey from Eden becomes a pilgrimage of insight, empathy, and transformative action.

1.1 The Perfect Order (Gen 1:31)

1.1.1 Original Blessing and Human Flourishing

God surveyed all that He had made and declared it "very good," a divine affirmation of perfect order and blessing that included humanity as its crowning jewel (Gen 1:31). In this original state, the human couple experienced flourishing in every dimension of their being—physical health, emotional well-being, relational harmony, and spiritual communion with their Creator. Their bodies functioned without pain or disease; every cell operated in sync with God's life-giving rhythm. Emotions were balanced by trust in God's provision, fostering joy, wonder, and restfulness without fear or anxiety. Relationships flowed in unbroken intimacy—Adam and Eve knew each other deeply, and both knew the Lord face to face, unhindered by shame or guilt (Gen 3:8). Their minds were clear and creative, able to reflect God's image in naming animals, cultivating the land, and exploring the mysteries of creation. Spiritually, they worshiped with unclouded devotion, offering gratitude in unison with all creation that praised its Maker (Ps 148). Environmental harmony meant a lush garden without thorns or thistles, abundant streams, and fruitful trees yielding sustenance—a habitat designed for delight. There was no decay; life extended seamlessly from seed to tree, from parent to child, in ongoing cycles of renewal. Work was not toil but vocation— meaningful stewardship under God's benevolent oversight (Gen 2:15). In this pristine ecology, food was both medicine and joy, untainted by pathogens or scarcity. Community with the rest of creation reinforced a sense of belonging in a well-ordered cosmos. The blessing of fertile ground extended to fruitfulness in marriage, art, and culture, prefiguring the fullness of life God would ultimately restore. Sabbath rest punctuated this order, teaching humans to trust God's sovereignty over time and productivity (Ex 20:8–11). No sickness marred their bodies; no inner turmoil unsettled their minds. Even mortality, though present in God's sovereignty, did not yet intrude upon their lived experience. This original blessing set a benchmark for human flourishing that still informs our deepest longings. It provides the theological horizon against which all subsequent brokenness is measured. From this vantage, we perceive how far creation has fallen—and how direly we need redemption.

1.1.2 Integrated Ecology of Body, Mind, Spirit, and Environment

In Eden, the human person was more than a soul inhabiting a body; body, mind, spirit, and environment formed a seamless whole crafted by God's wisdom. Physical health depended on soil fertility, water purity, and climate stability, all gifts that flowed from divine provision. Mental clarity was fostered by rhythms of work and rest, creative tasks, and natural rhythms aligned with the sun and seasons. Spiritual vitality emerged from direct fellowship with God, unimpeded by shame, fear, or distraction—a state our Lord called "walking in the cool of the day" (Gen 3:8). Emotional resilience thrived in unbroken relationships, both with fellow humans and with animals, each creature reflecting an aspect of God's glory. Environment and human flourishing were mutually reinforcing: a healthy ecosystem supported bodily health, while wise human stewardship maintained environmental balance. Disease-causing microbes and toxic substances did not yet disturb the garden; no virus lurked in the air, and no malformation tainted the womb. Health and healing were inseparable from worship and work, as every activity, from tilling soil to naming beasts, was an act of worshipful creativity. Every sense—sight, sound, smell, taste, touch—functioned to delight in creation and to glorify the Creator. This integrated ecology set a pattern for preventive wisdom: proper rest, balanced diet, meaningful labor, spiritual rhythms, and environmental care. Longevity and generational continuity were built into creation's fabric. There was no division between sacred and secular—every aspect of life was sacramental, pointing beyond itself to God. This holistic design offers enduring principles: physical exercise, mental stimulation, spiritual disciplines, and environmental ethics all contribute to shalom. Thus health becomes more than absence of disease; it is flourishing in every dimension of life. This vision stands in stark contrast to our fractured present reality. It prepares the way for seeing how the Fall disrupted each strand of this ecology.

1.1.3 Human Vocation, Dominion, and Preventive Health (Gen 2:15)

God placed humanity in Eden with a clear vocation: to "till" and "keep" the garden, implying both cultivation and careful guardianship (Gen 2:15). This dual responsibility illustrates preventive health—in Eden, humans were co-stewards ensuring soil health, balanced flora and fauna populations, and water sustainability. Such stewardship cultivated not only vegetables and fruits but also habits of observation, care, and timely intervention before minor issues became major problems. Dominion over the earth did not mean exploitation but benevolent leadership: guiding animal reproduction, managing natural resources, and maintaining ecological boundaries set by God. This vocation served as preventive medicine; keeping the garden healthy prevented malnutrition, injury, and environmental devastation. Human creativity applied to agriculture, construction, and community infrastructure demonstrated that work is part of God's healing design for creation. Rituals such as the Sabbath provided preventive respite, guarding against burnout, stress-related illnesses, and overwork. Laws governing diet and water use, though fully internalized in Eden, prefigure later Mosaic prescriptions that promoted health (Lev 11; Deut 23:12–14). The very act of caring for the garden disciplined the hands, minds, and hearts—an early model for holistic wellness. This vocational paradigm highlights that meaningful work and preventive practices are divine gifts, not burdens. It sets a standard that when humans neglect their vocation—through laziness or pride—health consequences inevitably follow. In highlighting preventive health, Eden's design foreshadows modern public health principles and the dignity of labor. The Fall's disruption of this vocation directly contributes to environmental degradation, food scarcity, and the spread of disease. Understanding our original calling to preventive care deepens our lament over present disorder and our hope for restored stewardship under Christ.

1.2 The Entrance of Corruption (Gen 3; Rom 5:12)

1.2.1 Deception, Disobedience, and the First Fracture

The serpent's cunning words sowed doubt about God's goodness, introducing deception as the catalyst for disobedience in Eden (Gen 3:1–5). Eve's decision to eat the forbidden fruit shattered the trust that undergirded the human-God relationship, fracturing the core of shalom. This first fracture was not a minor misstep but an existential breach that unleashed moral and physical corruption. In that moment, the human will turned away from God's life-giving command into self-determination, a choice whose effects radiated beyond the garden. Disobedience became the gateway through which sin entered the human heart, warping desires and inclining the flesh toward self-preservation rather than reliance on divine provision. Guilt and shame spontaneously arose, leading Adam and Eve to hide, evidencing immediate relational rupture—not only with God but with each other. The ground itself responded to this rebellion; what was once fertile soil became cursed, no longer wholly responsive to human care (Gen 3:17). This inaugural act of disobedience introduced the principle that moral death precedes physical decay. Genesis 3 illustrates that corruption begins in the will and mind, then manifests in the body and environment. Romans connects this personal act to a universal condition: through one man's trespass, sin and death spread to all (Rom 5:12). Thus every human inherits a predisposition toward disobedience, setting the stage for sickness. The serpent's lie in Eden finds echoes in every human culture that has sought answers in false gods, quick fixes, or self-reliance. The Fall reveals that true healing must address not only symptoms but the underlying rebellion against God. This disobedience opens the door to every subsequent twist of disease, pain, and environmental decay. Recognizing the first fracture helps us see why mere medical solutions are insufficient without spiritual restoration. It also underscores why Christ's obedience and reversal of Adam's sin is foundational to redeeming both body and soul.

1.2.2 Fragmentation of Wholeness: Relational, Ecological, Physiological

In the aftermath of Eden's breach, fragmentation rippled across every fabric of creation. Relational wholeness dissolved as fear and blame replaced openness; humans now viewed each other and God with suspicion. Marital harmony became tainted by power struggles and shame, marking the beginning of broken relationships (Gen 3:16). Ecologically, the curse on the ground introduced thorns, thistles, and unpredictable weather patterns, disrupting the integrated ecosystem humans once tended. Soil erosion, seasonal extremes, and invasive species emerged as symptoms of a creation groaning under sin (Rom 8:22). Physiologically, the body became vulnerable: pain entered childbirth, work turned to toilsome labor, and mortality became inevitable. Genetic integrity eroded over generations, giving rise to inherited weaknesses and susceptibilities. Mental and emotional disorders found their origin in fragmented inner life—anxiety, guilt, and despair replacing peace and trust. Every creature, from the lowliest insect to the largest beast, displayed signs of corruption: predators and prey coexisted in a cycle of violence. Water sources became potential carriers of disease; foods once safe grew molds and toxins. Humans, no longer protected by perfect immune systems, faced infections, inflammation, and degeneration. This fragmentation teaches that sickness is downstream from disorder at moral and ecological levels. The breakdown of shalom is holistic, requiring holistic redemptive work. Yet even amid ruin, God's sustaining grace preserved life—springs still flowed, seasons still turned, and family bonds endured despite pain. This fractured reality sets the context for Christ's mission: to reconcile all things, restoring relationships, healing bodies, and renewing creation (Col 1:20).

1.2.3 Birth of Disease Processes: From Cell Death to Global Decay

The cosmic fall inaugurated biological processes that once lay dormant or under divine restraint. Cellular aging commenced as programmed cell death mechanisms operated without perfect repair, leading to tissue degeneration, organ failure, and physical decline. At the molecular level, DNA replication errors accumulated over time, producing genetic mutations that manifest as congenital disorders, cancers, and metabolic syndromes. Pathogens that once lived in peaceful symbiosis with hosts turned virulent, exploiting compromised immune systems to spread disease. Inflammatory responses, designed to protect, grew dysregulated, causing autoimmune conditions and chronic pain. On a larger scale, environmental decay—deforestation, pollution, habitat loss—exacerbated the spread of zoonotic diseases, as animals and humans were forced into unnatural proximity. Public health crises, from pandemics to malnutrition, trace their roots to this post-Eden disorder. Medical interventions emerged in response—antibiotics, vaccines, surgeries—but they address symptoms of a deeper theological and ecological crisis. The global rise of lifestyle diseases—diabetes, heart disease, obesity—reflects patterns of broken stewardship over bodies and ecosystems. Even mental health epidemics mirror the fragmentation of soul and society: depression, anxiety, and addiction flourish amid relational vacuums and environmental stressors. This birth of disease processes is not random but follows biblical patterns: curse leads to decay, and decay to suffering. Yet God's common grace preserves life and spurs human ingenuity toward remedies. The presence of healing arts and scientific research testifies to a divine spark within human creativity. Understanding disease's origin invites humility before God's design and dependence on divine restoration. It also motivates integrated approaches that combine spiritual care, medical science, and ecological stewardship. Ultimately, the broken processes of disease anticipate the final healing that Christ will enact in a renewed heaven and earth, where "death shall be no more, neither shall there be mourning nor crying nor pain anymore" (Rev 21:4).

1.3 Cosmic Fallout and the Cursed Ground (Gen 3:17–19)

1.3.1 Disorder in Nature: Thorns, Thistles, Pathogens

The moment Adam and Eve disobeyed, the perfect harmony of the garden gave way to hostile elements that now challenged human flourishing. Thorns and thistles sprang up where once only edible plants grew, symbolizing nature's resistance to human cultivation. The soil, formerly pliable and life-affirming, became stubborn and unyielding, requiring sweat and toil to yield even a modest harvest. Toxic plants and invasive weeds began to compete with cultivated crops, forcing humanity into a constant battle to secure sustenance. Waters that once ran crystal clear now carried silt and decay, reflecting creation's groaning under the weight of sin. Microbial life, which God originally designed to maintain balance, mutated into disease-causing pathogens that could no longer be restrained by a flawless immune system. Skin infections, respiratory illnesses, and internal fevers emerged as daily threats, turning simple wounds into life-threatening emergencies. Animal interactions changed as well—

predatory instincts became more pronounced, and creatures that once lived in peaceful coexistence turned dangerous. Bites and scratches could now introduce lethal toxins, a tragic echo of cosmic disorder. Even the weather patterns shifted unpredictably, with sudden storms, droughts, and frosts that devastated fields and homes. Earthquakes and floods entered the realm of human experience, reminding humanity of its vulnerability to forces beyond control. The very air seemed to carry unseen dangers, as airborne spores and viruses found fertile hosts among weakened bodies. Foodborne illnesses became common as spoilage accelerated in corrupt creation. This proliferation of hazards shattered the sense of security that characterized Eden, forcing humans to invent tools, shelters, and early pharmacopoeias in a desperate attempt to survive. These innovations, though helpful, could never fully counteract the fundamental disharmony between human intent and a creation now bent by sin. The natural world, designed as a partner for human stewardship, became a relentless adversary that highlighted the seriousness of the Fall. Yet in this adversity, human ingenuity and compassion began to flourish, sowing seeds of medical knowledge and community care. This grim transformation in nature set the stage for understanding disease not merely as random misfortune but as a theological statement about the cost of rebellion. As we grasp how thoroughly corruption infiltrated soil, plant, animal, and microbe, we recognize the vast scope of God's redemptive work needed to restore creation.

1.3.2 Entropy, Genetic Degeneration, and the Long Shadow of the Fall

Beyond the visible thorns and pathogens lies the insidious reality of entropy: the gradual decline of order over time. Cells that once replicated with flawless precision now accumulate errors in DNA transcription, giving rise to genetic mutations. These mutations manifest as a spectrum of disorders, from minor cosmetic defects to life-threatening congenital diseases. Telomeres, the protective caps on chromosomes, shorten with each cell division, heralding the onset of aging, organ failure, and ultimately death. Mitochondria, once robust energy centers, become less efficient, producing harmful free radicals that damage proteins, lipids, and nucleic acids. This cellular wear-and-tear contributes to degenerative diseases such as osteoarthritis, Alzheimer's, and cardiovascular decline. The endocrine system, which coordinates growth and repair, begins to falter, leading to hormonal imbalances that affect metabolism, mood, and immunity. The immune system itself becomes overactive in some instances, attacking healthy tissue as in autoimmune diseases, or underactive in others, leaving the body vulnerable to infection. Genetic degeneration is compounded by environmental toxins—industrial pollution, chemical runoff, and radiation—that exacerbate DNA damage beyond its original post-Fall trajectory. As mutated genes pass from parent to child, inherited disorders find new footholds in each generation, underscoring how the Fall's effects magnify over time. Epigenetic changes, influenced by stress and lifestyle, further distort gene expression, weaving a complex tapestry of inherited weakness and environmental impact. This dynamic interplay between inherited corruption and external pressures illustrates the long shadow of sin on human biology. Entropy not only degrades individual bodies but also undermines societal resilience, as increasing numbers of chronically ill individuals strain community resources. Medical breakthroughs—gene therapy, regenerative medicine, and precision pharmaceuticals—offer hope but also reveal the depth of the problem. We perceive that the Fall touches us at the very blueprint of life, demanding both scientific innovation and divine intervention. The knowledge of entropy and degeneration invites humility before God's creative wisdom and fuels longing for the ultimate reversal promised in Christ. Meanwhile, researchers and clinicians labor under the conviction that true healing must address both genetic roots and environmental triggers. Recognizing the Fall's imprint on our DNA shapes our approach to medicine and our dependence on God's future restoration.

1.3.3 Groaning Creation Awaiting Liberation (Rom 8:19–22)

Scripture paints a vivid portrait of creation itself as eager for the day of redemption, groaning in labor pains until the full restoration arrives (Rom 8:22). This personification underscores that the Fall's consequences extend far beyond humanity, enveloping mountains, rivers, forests, and even the hidden microbial world. Creation's frustration manifests in natural disasters—volcanic eruptions, typhoons, earthquakes—that reflect the cosmos's cry for liberation. Ecosystems once stable now endure cycles of devastation and slow recovery, as if creation itself is anxious for a healer. The recurring pattern of destruction and renewal hints at the resurrection life Christ offers, where decay gives way to endless flourishing. Humanity participates in creation's groan through personal suffering—physical pain, psychological distress, and social upheaval—binding our stories to the larger narrative of redeemed cosmos. Yet the promise of adoption echoes here: just as believers await bodily resurrection, so the planet awaits the reversal of entropy and decay. Prophetic visions of new heavens and a new earth (Isa 65:17; Rev 21:1) reveal that God's redemptive scope is cosmic in scale. The cosmic groaning also fuels missionary zeal, as caring for the environment becomes an act of worship and anticipation of God's coming kingdom. Churches engage in creation care initiatives—reforestation, clean energy, conservation—as foretaste of the world to come. Scientific endeavors, likewise, participate in this redemption narrative when they aim to heal ecosystems and reverse pollution. This perspective reshapes our understanding of environmental stewardship: it is not optional but integral to Christian hope. The present sufferings of creation and human bodies alike are transient, pointing to a future where "the former things have passed away" (Rev 21:4). In the meantime, solidarity with groaning creation calls believers to lament, intercede, and act. As we look forward to the liberation of our bodies and planet, we embrace a theology that sees every healed river, every restored forest, and every cured disease as a token of the coming age. This vision seamlessly leads us into exploring how divine justice and mercy interweave in the grand tapestry of redemption.

1.4 Divine Justice and Mercy Intertwined

1.4.1 Justice in Allowing Consequences (Gal 6:7)

God's justice demands that moral choices bear real consequences—in the divine economy, sin cannot be ignored without undermining God's holiness. The principle "you reap what you sow" (Gal 6:7) reflects a foundational truth: actions aligned against God's will generate outcomes that uphold cosmic order. When Adam and Eve ate of the forbidden fruit, they triggered a cascade of penalties—pain in childbirth, toil in labor, and ultimately, death—all of which testify to God's commitment to justice. These consequences are not arbitrary punishments but intrinsic effects of departing from life-giving commands. Justice in this sense is akin to natural law: breaking the moral order yields disharmony. From a theological perspective, such justice reveals the seriousness with which God treats human freedom and responsibility. Far from capricious, divine justice maintains the coherence of creation, ensuring that choices matter. In the broader Biblical narrative, the justice of Yahweh surfaces in covenants, prophecies, and law codes—each reinforcing that betrayal of divine instruction brings repercussions. This pattern is visible in Israel's history: when idolatry spread, foreign oppression followed; repentance brought deliverance. Seen through this lens, sickness often reflects the unyielded consequences of systemic sin rather than isolated maladies. Yet justice never operates in a vacuum; it exists alongside mercy. Recognition of justice deepens our understanding of how mercy must be divinely integrated to restore broken order without annihilating the sinner.

1.4.2 Mercy Foreshadowed in the Proto-Evangelium (Gen 3:15)

Even as judgment loomed in Eden, the very first promise of redemption emerged: the Proto-Evangelium in Genesis 3:15 heralded the coming of One who would crush the serpent's head. This promise manifests God's mercy intertwined with justice, offering a path of reconciliation before full punishment is executed. God's provision of animal skins for Adam and Eve's clothing (Gen 3:21) further illustrates merciful care; a life sacrifice anticipates the atoning work of Christ. Mercy thus enters the story at the earliest juncture, demonstrating that divine love never retreats from a fallen world. Throughout the Old Testament, mercy resounds in God's patience with Israel, as He forgives again and again despite persistent rebellion. The sacrificial system, though imperfect, foreshadows ultimate mercy, pointing forward to the once-for-all sacrifice of Jesus. The prophets declare God's willingness to heal, restore, and forgive those who turn back to Him (Isa 1:18). This pattern teaches that mercy does not negate justice but transfigures it, absorbing penalties in a substitute. The incarnation of Christ embodies this divine merciful justice: He who knew no sin became sin for us (2 Cor 5:21), taking our sickness and curse upon Himself. Mercy's foothold in Eden assures us that God's redemptive plan was never a secondary thought but integral from creation's first breath. Recognizing this foreshadowing helps believers see sickness as an occasion for divine compassion rather than mere penal correction. In the unfolding story, mercy moves decisively toward the cross, transforming God's justice into restorative power.

1.4.3 Common Grace: Sustaining Life in a Broken World (Matt 5:45)

While special mercy secures redemptive breakthroughs, God's common grace sustains every living being under judgment. Jesus taught that the Lord "makes his sun rise on the evil and on the good, and sends rain on the just and on the unjust" (Matt 5:45). This universal provision tempers the severity of justice, preserving life even amid corruption. Food production continues, medical discoveries emerge, and seasons still turn, reflecting God's ongoing care for creation. The talents of physicians, the diligence of farmers, and the ingenuity of engineers all spring from this common grace. Sunlight, rain, and fertile soil remain available to sinner and saint alike, illustrating that God's patience extends broadly. In the context of sickness, common grace equips communities to devise hospitals, sanitation systems, and vaccines before the arrival of special mercy. It also empowers non-believers to collaborate in alleviating suffering, revealing God's benevolent work through diverse hands. This grace underscores the dignity of secular endeavors in science and public health, affirming that such efforts align with God's sustaining purpose. Human creativity and compassion flourish under this protective umbrella, testifying to God's goodness despite widespread corruption. Yet common grace also reminds us that ultimate healing requires more than temporal provision—it awaits the special grace of the gospel. Understanding common grace encourages cooperation between church and world in caring for the sick, while pointing to the limit of merely human remedies. This perspective paves the way for exploring how glimmers of redemptive hope shine even amid ruin.

1.5 Hope Prefigured Amid Ruin

1.5.1 Animal Skins and the First Atonement Sign (Gen 3:21)

After the Fall, God provided animal skins to clothe Adam and Eve, an act rich in theological meaning and cinematic in its compassion. The requirement of a blood-shed substitute prefigured the sacrificial system and ultimately the atonement of Christ, who would offer His life blood for humanity's redemption. This first act of covering sinners' shame underlines that God envisages reconciliation rather than destruction, even when justice demands payment. The provision of skins implies the death of an innocent creature, drawing a symbolic parallel to the Lamb of God who takes away the sin of the world (Jn 1:29). Through this gesture, God teaches that mercy emerges from judgment and that reconciliation involves cost. The imagery of clothing also communicates dignity restored; however fallen, humans remain bearers of God's image warranting care and honor. This early atonement sign resonates throughout Scripture—Abraham's ram in the thicket, the Passover lamb, Day of Atonement sacrifices—all pointing beyond themselves to Christ's once-for-all offering. The skins not only covered physical nakedness but initiated a divine pattern of substitutionary provision, foreshadowing believers' future robe of righteousness (Rev 7:14–17). This scene in Eden reveals God's heart for healing shame, a theme that echoes in every Gospel account of Jesus restoring outcasts. Even before formal revelation, God's mercy reached into the darkest moment of human history, lighting a beacon of hope. The first atonement sign assures us that tragedy need not be the final word; through divine initiative, restoration begins at the point of deepest loss. As we reflect on this primordial act, we glimpse the intersection of wrath and love, law and grace, death and life.

1.5.2 Archetypes of Healing in the Old Testament (Num 21:8–9)

The wilderness account of the bronze serpent in Numbers 21 offers another powerful archetype of healing amid divine judgment. When venomous snakes inflicted Israel for idolatry, Moses fashioned a bronze serpent and lifted it on a pole; those who looked were healed (Num 21:8–9). This remedy, prescribed by God Himself, underscores that deliverance can arise from the very symbol of death. The healing through a lifted serpent anticipates Christ's crucifixion, where He is lifted up to draw all people to Himself (Jn 12:32). The paradox of salvation through a representation of sin's curse underscores the depth of divine wisdom. As Israel gazed at the bronze image, faith encountered grace; their obedience to God's provision brought immediate relief. This event illustrates that healing often comes through divine-appointed means rather than human ingenuity alone. It also reveals that redemption is relational: people must look in faith rather than merely administer a remedy. The healing archetype recurs in prophetic literature—sermons about broken bones bound up, lepers cleansed, and blind eyes opened—each pointing toward holistic renewal. These stories teach that physical healing intertwines with spiritual restoration; as bodies are healed, hearts turn back to the Giver of life. The recurring motif of God's weapon of judgment becoming His means of healing offers profound comfort: our greatest wounds become the canvas for divine glory. For Christians, the bronze serpent narrative affirms that no sickness lies beyond Christ's restorative reach. In medical practice, this principle reminds caregivers to honor divinely ordained processes, including prayer, sacraments, and scientific methods. The archetypes of healing in the Old Testament encourage integration of faith and medicine, trusting God's sovereignty in every cure.

1.5.3 Messianic Promises of Ultimate Restoration (Isa 53:4–5)

The prophet Isaiah vividly foreshadows the suffering Servant whose wounds would secure our healing: "Surely he has borne our griefs and carried our sorrows… with his stripes we are healed" (Isa 53:4–5). This Messianic promise reaches beyond temporary relief to ultimate restoration of body, soul, and creation. The Servant's vicarious suffering aligns divine justice with mercy, for He endures punishment so that sinners may live. In His resurrection, Christ inaugurates a new age where sickness, pain, and death lose their sting. The early church witnessed healings that pointed to this truth, as apostles prayed over the sick, demonstrating that the kingdom's power overcomes every infirmity. New Testament writers reaffirm that believers who trust in Christ anticipate resurrection bodies free from disease (1 Cor 15:42–44). The future promise extends even to transformed creation: deserts bloom, deserts cry out, and waters flow in parched lands (Isa 35). In Revelation, the vision of the new Jerusalem includes life-giving water and leaves that bring healing to the nations (Rev 22:1–2). These promises assure us that every instance of restoration now is a foretaste of the age to come. Our present sufferings, difficult as they are, testify to pending glory—Christ's second coming will complete the work begun on the cross. This eschatological hope infuses our ministry to the sick with endurance, compassion, and confident expectation. As we engage in healing practices, we represent not merely the alleviation of symptoms but participation in God's grand narrative of redemption. Messianic promises thus form the capstone of hope prefigured amid ruin, leading us into a journey of faith that integrates present care with future consummation.

1.6 Pastoral and Scientific Reflections

1.6.1 Theological Anthropology and Modern Medicine

The study of the human person in theology reveals that every illness is not merely a physical malfunction but touches the imago Dei, the divine image stamped on each life. Pastoral theology reminds caregivers that bodies are sacred vessels, deserving of both medical intervention and prayerful presence. Modern medicine, with its advanced diagnostics and treatments, unfolds as a gift of common grace, reflecting God's ongoing care for a broken world. Physicians and chaplains alike bear witness to the mystery of suffering, where mechanical explanations of disease intersect with questions of purpose and meaning. Theologians propose that sickness can prompt existential reflection, inviting patients to consider their dependence on God even as they rely on scientific expertise. Medical ethics dialogues echo biblical mandates to love neighbor, compelling institutions to balance cutting-edge treatments with compassionate end-of-life care. Pastors learn from epidemiologists that public health measures—vaccination, sanitation, education—mirror the preventive stewardship of Eden's garden. In turn, medical practitioners benefit from pastoral insights into the power of hope, narrative, and community in promoting healing. When a patient receives a diagnosis, theology offers frameworks for understanding suffering as potentially redemptive, while medicine provides concrete pathways to extend and enhance life. Both fields face the challenge of technological hubris, for innovations such as gene editing raise profound questions about the limits of human dominion. Theologians caution that playing God with embryos or DNA demands humility before the Creator's wisdom. Pastoral care encourages dialogue about moral boundaries, urging believers to seek guidance from Scripture alongside scientific counsel. Conferences that bring together bioethicists, physicians, and clergy demonstrate how integrative approaches yield more holistic care plans. Such partnerships foster interdisciplinary training programs where seminarians learn basic physiology and medics gain exposure to spiritual care. This mutual enrichment resists the false dichotomy that separates body and spirit, honoring the biblical witness that God heals both flesh and soul (Psalm 103:3). Ultimately, theological anthropology insists that humans are embodied souls, and medical interventions must respect this duality. As we reflect on these dynamics, we turn our attention next to environmental stewardship, showing how caring for creation after Eden also contributes to human health.

1.6.2 Environmental Stewardship after Eden (Ps 24:1)

The psalmist declares that the earth is the Lord's and all that fills it, reminding us that environmental care is an essential dimension of human vocation (Psalm 24:1). After the Fall, creation suffers under the weight of entropy and pollution, directly impacting public health through contaminated water, poor air quality, and climate change. Pastoral leaders emphasize that environmental justice is inseparable from social justice, for marginalized communities often bear the brunt of ecological degradation. Scientific research confirms that exposure to toxins increases rates of cancer, respiratory disease, and birth defects, illustrating how sin's ripples extend from moral failure into environmental harm. Faith communities pioneer green initiatives—tree planting, clean-up drives, advocacy for clean energy—demonstrating sacrificial love for neighbors and future generations. These efforts stem from the Edenic mandate to "till and keep" creation (Genesis 2:15), translated today into fossil fuel reduction and regenerative farming practices. Environmental theology explores how the groaning of creation (Romans 8:22) calls the church to lament and intercede, coupling prayer with policy engagement. Medical professionals collaborate with environmental scientists in "planetary health" movements, recognizing that human disease cannot be separated from ecological systems. Hospitals adopt eco-friendly practices, reducing waste and energy consumption, as practical expressions of stewardship. Seminaries integrate creation care into their curricula, equipping pastors to preach responsibly on climate ethics. Congregations host educational series on healthy diets tied to sustainable agriculture, encouraging plant-based options that lower carbon footprints and reduce lifestyle diseases. As believers learn to view environmental action as worship, scientific data on ecosystem services becomes a tool for faithful living. These interdisciplinary partnerships reveal that healing the planet contributes to healing human bodies. With this holistic vision of vocation in place, we are led to explore how awareness of the Fall shapes our spiritual formation.

1.6.3 Spiritual Formation through Awareness of the Fall

Awareness of the Fall's pervasive impact offers fertile ground for spiritual growth, prompting humility, repentance, and deeper dependence on God's grace. When Christians recognize that every ache, every cellular mutation, and every ecological crisis stems from sin's rupture, they are invited to turn toward the cross where redemption begins. Spiritual disciplines such as confession and lament become essential practices, acknowledging personal and corporate complicity in creation's brokenness. Prayer for healing rises alongside prayers for forgiveness, creating an integrated posture before God that seeks restoration both bodily and relational. Retreats that combine solitude with contemplative reading of Genesis 3 can help believers lament what was lost and rehearse the hope of future renewal. Pastors guide congregations through the liturgy of lament found in the Psalms, teaching that honesty before God paves the way for authentic healing (Psalm 13). Small-group studies on the theme of Eden's loss foster mutual support, as members share burdens and intercede for one another's physical and emotional needs. Spiritual formation curricula incorporate environmental service projects, reinforcing the conviction that formation involves caring beyond church walls. Journals prompt participants to trace the arc from Eden to Calvary, recognizing that Christ's work addresses both sin's penalty and its pervasive effects in creation. Art and worship may feature images of Eden and the new creation, helping the imagination grasp the scope of redemption. Fasting from comforts draws attention to the fragility of life and spurs gratitude for God's sustaining provision. As believers internalize the narrative of shalom shattered and promised restoration, they develop resilience when facing personal or communal suffering. This growing awareness transforms theological concepts into lived realities, infusing every act of compassion with eschatological hope. As these reflections on pastoral and scientific integration, environmental stewardship, and spiritual formation conclude, we now turn to a transitional summary that will distill key insights and prepare the way for Chapter 2.

1.7 Transitional Summary and Reflection

1.7.1 Key Theological Insights on Sickness's Origin

The journey from Eden to the present reveals that sickness is not a random anomaly but the result of humanity's departure from divine design. Sin's emergence introduced corruption at relational, physiological, and ecological levels, fracturing the integrated wholeness God intended. The curse on the ground and the onset of entropy demonstrate that decay is woven into creation's fabric as a consequence of rebellion (Genesis 3:17–19). Yet divine justice did not leave sinners without hope; mercy appeared in the Proto-Evangelium and animal coverings, prefiguring the atonement of Christ (Genesis 3:15; 3:21). God's common grace sustains life and fuels human ingenuity in medicine, affirming that scientific pursuit aligns with divine provision (Matthew 5:45). Theological anthropology underscores that treating the body must involve addressing the soul and acknowledging imago Dei in every patient. Environmental stewardship emerges as a form of obedience to the Edenic mandate and a practical strategy for preventing disease. Spiritual formation through confession, lament, and hope binds individual healing to the grand narrative of redemption. Taken together, these insights form a comprehensive framework: sickness arises from cosmic rebellion, but it also opens avenues for divine compassion and human responsibility. This theological framework guards against reductionist views that see disease solely through biological or moral lenses, insisting instead on a holistic approach. As readers prepare to examine personal and communal dimensions of sin and sickness in Chapter 2, they carry forward an integrated vision rooted in Scripture and informed by science.

1.7.2 Questions for Personal Meditation and Small-Group Discussion

How does recognizing Eden's original design shape your understanding of your own health habits and environmental impact? In what ways might acknowledging personal sin influence how you receive medical care or pastoral support? Reflect on a time when a medical breakthrough or scientific discovery felt like an echo of God's sustaining grace; how did that experience affect your faith? Consider areas where you may have over-relied on human ingenuity rather than prayerful dependence on God. Discuss in your group how the curse on creation might inform Christian responses to climate change and public health crises. Share stories of communal lament or confession that led to personal or corporate healing. Explore the tension between God's justice and mercy in your own experience of suffering. How have practices of lament and thanksgiving shaped your resilience in trials? Identify spiritual disciplines that could help integrate awareness of the Fall into daily life. What responsibilities do Christians bear in promoting holistic health in their churches and neighborhoods? These questions aim to move theology from the page into relationships, action, and transformation.

Conclusion

Our exploration of Eden's pristine design and the Fall's far-reaching impact reveals that sickness is deeply rooted in the fabric of creation and the human condition. What began as harmonious flourishing has given way to entropy, genetic degeneration, and the emergence of formidable foes—be they microbial, environmental, or moral. Yet even amid this brokenness, God's justice and mercy dance together, foreshadowing the redemptive work of Christ and sustaining life through common grace. The theological insights and scientific reflections we have gathered here form a solid foundation for grappling with personal and communal afflictions. As we move forward, we carry with us a holistic vision that neither denies the gravity of disease nor overlooks the divine initiatives of healing already at work in our world. In the next chapter, we will turn our attention from the cosmic origins of sickness to its personal and social dimensions, learning how sin and responsibility intersect in the tapestry of human health. With eyes fixed on both Scripture's promises and Christ's compassion, we press onward toward wisdom that brings wholeness to body, mind, and spirit.

Chapter 2 – Sin and Sickness: Personal, Corporate, Ancestral

Sickness often wears many masks—personal affliction, inherited vulnerability, or societal collapse—yet each bears the imprint of humanity's separation from God's life-giving purposes. In this chapter, we explore how individual choices, family legacies, and communal dynamics intersect with physical and mental health. The biblical narrative offers both cautionary examples and corrective insights, revealing that while personal sin can open the door to suffering, disease also transcends simplistic cause-and-effect. Generational brokenness and national failings carry their own weight of consequence, yet through Christ's life-changing work, freedom emerges for individuals, families, and nations. As we weave together ancient wisdom and modern understanding, we learn how repentance, intercession, and corporate renewal unlock God's restorative power. This journey will equip us to navigate the complexities of blame and grace, responsibility and mercy, as we seek holistic healing under the banner of God's redeeming love.

2.0 Prelude — Diagnosing the Link Between Sin and Sickness

2.0.1 Scriptural Principles of Cause, Consequence, and Mystery (Deut 28; Jn 9:3)

The Bible teaches that God's law carries inherent consequences: obedience brings blessing and disobedience invites correction, a pattern made explicit in Deuteronomy's covenant promise of health for faithfulness and illness for rebellion. Across Israel's history, prophetic warnings link moral failure—idolatry, injustice, covenant breach—with national calamities that include pestilence and famine. Yet Scripture also insists on God's inscrutable purposes, as when Jesus tells His disciples that the man born blind suffered neither his own sin nor that of his parents, but so that God's works might be displayed (Jn 9:3). This tension—between clear cause-and-effect and divine mystery—recurs throughout redemptive history, demanding humility in our theological reflections on illness. We learn that not every ailment is punitive nor every healing a reward for holiness. Wisdom literature, including Proverbs, affirms that righteousness brings life, while folly brings death, yet also acknowledges times when the godly suffer without apparent cause. In prophetic visions, the righteous remnant suffers for the sins of the many, while the proud perish by their own devices, illustrating layered dimensions of consequence. New Testament letters add nuance, reminding believers that suffering can discipline, refine, or produce endurance, not simply punish wrongdoing. Paul's thorn in the flesh, for instance, serves as a divine mercy that keeps him dependent on Christ, not as a penalty for sin. When illness strikes the innocent, the church must resist the temptation to preach simplistic sermons that equate disease with divine wrath. Instead, faith communities hold together the biblical certainties of God's moral order and the profound mysteries of His sovereign will. Ministry must reflect both justice and compassion, acknowledging that medical science often uncovers natural causes, while pastoral care invites trust in God's benevolent purposes beyond our comprehension. As we explore the covenantal link between sin and sickness, we carry forward this balance of principle and paradox, recognizing that diagnosis requires both empirical investigation and prayerful discernment. This foundation prepares us to trace how the Old Covenant's patterns both continue and transform in the light of Christ.

2.0.2 Continuity and Discontinuity from Old Covenant to New (Jer 31:29–30; Gal 3:13)

The Old Covenant's teaching that children bear the consequences of their parents' iniquities finds a profound reorientation in Jeremiah's promise of a new covenant, where each person "shall die for his own sin" rather than inherit ancestral guilt (Jer 31:29–30). This prophetic shift underscores God's escalating grace, moving from collective corporate identity toward individual responsibility. Under Moses, plagues could strike entire communities for collective sin, but

Jeremiah envisions a day when divine judgment attends personal choice rather than family lineage. Centuries later, Paul proclaims that Christ redeemed us from the curse of the law by becoming a curse for us, liberating believers not only from sin's penalty but also from inherited spiritual liabilities (Gal 3:13). This New Covenant announcement does not abolish the reality that our actions bear consequences, but it reframes consequences in the context of Christ's atonement and the Spirit's power to create a new heart. The sacrificial system of Moses, with its prescribed remedies and atonements, prefigures the ultimate remedy in Jesus, who heals body and soul simultaneously. Yet some patterns persist: believers still experience the fallout of poor choices, communal failures, and systemic injustices, pointing to the ongoing relevance of covenant principles. The continuity lies in God's commitment to holiness and the moral order of creation; the discontinuity lies in the means of healing, shifting from animal sacrifices and ritual cleansings to the once-for-all sacrifice of Christ and the ministry of the Spirit. In practical ministry, this means pastors teach that forgiveness in Christ precedes deliverance from sickness, offering confidence that restorative grace reaches deeper than any symptom. Churches are called to uphold moral standards while proclaiming release from the law's curse through faith. As we navigate between covenantal continuity and transformative newness, we gain a holistic framework for understanding sin and sickness in both Testaments, leading into the more detailed exploration of worship, sacrament, and community health.

2.1 Individual Sin and Bodily Affliction

2.1.1 Biblical Case Studies of Cause and Effect

Scripture presents several vivid examples where personal sin correlates with physical suffering, challenging us to discern God's purposes without oversimplifying divine activity. Miriam's leprosy after speaking against Moses demonstrates that unchecked criticism of God's chosen servant brought about a visible and painful curse (Num 12). King David's adultery and its aftermath illustrate how moral failure unleashed family turmoil, and although the child born of Bathsheba eventually died, David's own grief conveyed the weight of sin's consequences (2 Sam 12). Uzzah's death for touching the ark improperly reminds us that reverence and obedience guard life even amid well–intentioned zeal (2 Sam 6). In the New Testament, Ananias and Sapphira fell dead when they lied to the Holy Spirit, showing that hypocrisy in the community of faith can bring immediate physical judgment (Acts 5). These examples teach that divine response to sin can sometimes be direct and severe. Yet not every sin produces immediate sickness, nor does every sickness stem from obvious wrongdoing. Psalm 32 celebrates forgiveness after David confessed his transgression, linking restored health to divine pardon: "When I kept silent, my bones wasted away" (Ps 32:3–4). In Corinth, Paul attributes some believers' sickness and even death at the Lord's Supper to their lack of discerning Christ's body, warning that spiritual negligence carries somatic risk (1 Cor 11:30). These cases show that the boundary between moral and medical realms can blur when God uses physical affliction to instruct, warn, or restore. We must learn from them without turning every headache or chronic illness into a moral indictment. The biblical authors invite us to probe our hearts, confess sin, and seek reconciliation, while also recognizing that God's redeeming purposes sometimes unfold through suffering rather than in spite of it. As we move to pastoral cautions, we will see how these case studies, while instructive, must be handled with humility and care.

2.1.2 Pastoral Cautions Against Simplistic Blame

Though the Bible records instances where sin and sickness intersect, pastoral wisdom demands restraint before attributing every illness to personal fault. The disciples' question about a man born blind—"Who sinned, this man or his parents?"—elicited Jesus's corrective response that neither was to blame, but that the man's condition might serve to display the Father's works (Jn 9:2–3). This teaches that disease can have purposes unrelated to individual guilt, and that casting blame can alienate sufferers from God's love. Early church leaders cautioned against spiritual arrogance that links every misfortune to specific sins, because such attitudes can drive people away rather than toward Christ. The healing ministry of Jesus often involved accompanying compassion rather than accusatory discourse; He touched lepers without condemning them, demonstrating that care must precede correction (Mk 1:41). Pastoral responses rooted in love recognize that guilt can exacerbate physical and emotional pain, trapping sufferers in cycles of shame. When counselors rush to moral explanations, they risk imposing burden rather than offering grace, echoing the Pharisees' judgmental spirit rather than Christ's mercy. Effective pastoral care listens deeply, providing safe spaces for confession while affirming God's unconditional presence amid suffering. It distinguishes between speaking the truth in love and wielding scripture as a weapon to shame. Pastors equipped with medical knowledge can gently challenge unhelpful beliefs while referring congregants to qualified professionals. By walking alongside the sick, ministers embody Christ's solidarity with human frailty. This posture of humble accompaniment paves the way for deeper discipleship, where correction arises organically from trust rather than from fear of condemnation. As we proceed to discern between divine discipline and demonic attack, these pastoral principles will guide our discernment.

2.1.3 Divine Discipline versus Demonic Attack: Discernment Markers

The New Testament draws a distinction between suffering as divine discipline and suffering as the result of demonic activity, instructing believers to test spirits and discern underlying causes. Hebrews 12 speaks of God disciplining His children so they "may share in his holiness," indicating that certain sufferings refine character rather than punish rebellion (Heb 12:10–11). By contrast, demonic affliction, such as the man possessed in Mark 5, manifests in destructive behaviors, supernatural phenomena, and a stark sense of evil oppression that exceeds normal human struggle. Discernment requires attentiveness to patterns: divine discipline often leads to repentance, humility, and renewed intimacy with God, whereas demonic attack aims to isolate, deceive, and drive believers into despair. Prayerful observation of symptoms, long-term life patterns, and responses to spiritual intervention helps distinguish between the two. Christian communities employ practices like anointing with oil and laying on of hands to test whether healing is accompanied by freedom from evil forces (Jas 5:14–15). Pastoral teams trained in deliverance ministries look for affirmations of Christ's lordship in the afflicted person's life as evidence of genuine spiritual conflict rather than psychosomatic distress. Yet caution is essential; attributing mental illness solely to demonic influence can hinder people from seeking psychiatric care. Discernment integrates scriptural insight, clinical knowledge, and community prayer, avoiding extremes of neglecting spiritual warfare or ignoring medical realities. When discipline is at work, it often follows persistent sin patterns and yields fruit of repentance and spiritual growth. In cases of demonic oppression, deliverance is pursued alongside pastoral care, spiritual edification, and sometimes medical support. Understanding these markers equips believers to navigate complex situations without falling into simplistic explanations. As we turn to practices of repentance, forgiveness, and somatic restoration, this discernment foundation ensures that healing efforts honor both God's sovereignty and human responsibility.

2.1.4 Repentance, Forgiveness, and Somatic Restoration

Throughout Scripture, the path to physical restoration often begins with repentance and confession, linking inner transformation with outward healing. King Manasseh's repentance after leading Judah into idolatry brought temporal deliverance, illustrating that the health of the body politic correlates with the moral posture of its leaders (2 Chr 33). James instructs believers to confess sins to one another so that prayer might lead to healing of both soul and body (Jas 5:16). This connection does not guarantee automatic cure, but it ensures that suffering is attended by spiritual renewal. The sacrament of confession in many traditions embodies this principle, as forgiveness communicates divine grace that can alleviate guilt-induced stress and psychosomatic symptoms. In a pastoral setting, guiding individuals through structured repentance can lower cortisol levels, improve sleep, and foster healthier lifestyles. Forgiveness from God and others often releases emotional burdens that physically manifest as tension, headaches, or digestive issues. Community rituals of reconciliation—public confession, shared anointing services—demonstrate the power of collective intercession for bodily restoration. Historically, medieval hospitals established by religious orders combined sacramental confession with herbal remedies, reflecting an integrated approach to healing. Modern studies confirm that feelings of spiritual peace correlate with improved immune function and accelerated recovery from surgery. Such data underscore that somatic restoration involves more than pharmaceutical interventions; it engages the whole person. Pastors and medical professionals collaborating can design care plans that incorporate spiritual practices—psalm singing, prayer, sacrament—with evidence-based treatments. This holistic model affirms that while not every illness results from sin, repentance and forgiveness can unlock channels of God's restorative blessing. As we conclude our study of individual dimensions of sin and sickness, we turn now to explore how ancestral patterns influence bodily affliction.

2.2 Generational Brokenness

2.2.1 The Concept of Inherited Consequences—Covenant and Family Systems

The notion that the sins of one generation affect subsequent ones finds support in Old Testament covenants, where corporate identity binds families in shared destiny. Exodus 34 speaks of God "visiting the iniquity of the fathers on the children to the third and the fourth generation," indicating that brokenness transmits through social and spiritual structures (Ex 34:7). In ancient Israel, family units functioned as economic and religious cells, so a patriarch's rebellion could compromise land fertility, communal health, and covenant fidelity. This collective dimension helps explain why certain diseases cluster in lineages, even apart from genetic disorders. Tribal and clan obligations meant that blessings or curses applied broadly, teaching descendants to heed ancestral patterns. The story of Achan illustrates that one person's hidden sin brought military defeat and plague upon the entire camp (Jos 7). Such narratives warn communities against isolating identity from responsibility. Anthropological studies of kinship systems confirm that family secrets, trauma, and maladaptive behaviors often embed in generational dynamics, shaping health outcomes through epigenetic mechanisms and learned coping strategies. Recognizing this covenantal matrix does not justify fatalism but calls for communal repentance and systemic transformation. In pastoral counseling, mapping family histories can reveal recurring themes of addiction, abuse, or illness that inform targeted prayers and interventions. The theology of inherited consequences thus bridges biblical teaching with practical tools for breaking cycles of dysfunction. As we move to the liberating work of Christ, we see how this heavy heritage gives way to new beginnings.

2.2.2 Freedom in Christ from Ancestral Patterns (Ezek 18; 2 Cor 5:17)

Ezekiel confronts the determinism of inherited sin by declaring that each person bears responsibility for their own choices, not those of their forebears (Ezek 18:20). This prophetic correction shifts the focus from ancestral guilt to individual accountability, opening space for divine grace to break familial cycles. In the New Testament, Paul's declaration that anyone "in Christ is a new creation" underscores that belonging to Jesus severs the ties of past brokenness (2 Cor 5:17). This spiritual re-covenanting empowers believers to live above hereditary patterns that once dictated health and behavior. Communities that welcome conversion testimonies often witness radical shifts in family dynamics, as repentant individuals refuse to perpetuate curses. Churches practicing "genealogical confession" publicly renounce ancestral sins—violence, witchcraft, and injustice—inviting collective healing. In such services, pastors call out specific generational strongholds by name, while the congregation prays declarations of freedom in Christ. Psychological research into intergenerational trauma shows that naming hidden patterns reduces their subconscious power, aligning well with biblical practices of confession and proclamation. Freedom in Christ does not erase history but reframes it, offering a future unbound by genetic and cultural legacies. Small-group discipleship that includes Scripture study, accountability, and prayer equips individuals to resist ancestral temptations. Bioethicists see parallels in gene therapy: while DNA mutations persist, activating or silencing certain genes can alter disease trajectories. Similarly, spiritual interventions can modulate inherited tendencies toward despair or addiction. Recognizing this transformative potential, believers partner with therapists, coaches, and spiritual mentors to reinforce new life patterns. As this chapter transitions to modern scientific correlates, we acknowledge that God's liberation works through both grace and wisdom.

2.2.3 Epigenetics, Trauma, and Spiritual Formation—Modern Corroborations

Recent discoveries in epigenetics reveal that environmental influences can switch genes on or off, transmitting trauma and resilience across generations without altering DNA sequence. Studies of descendants of Holocaust survivors, for instance, show heightened stress hormone responses, suggesting that severe trauma imprints biological marks on progeny. These findings resonate with biblical insights into inherited consequences, demonstrating that family histories of abuse, neglect, or war leave tangible imprints on physiology. Trauma-informed spiritual formation programs integrate this science with soul care, teaching practices that promote neuroplasticity and epigenetic healing—mindfulness, gratitude journaling, and community worship. Pastors trained in trauma ministry understand that inner-healing prayer and guided imagery can release epigenetic burdens, inviting God's renewal at cellular levels. Congregational retreats focusing on ancestral healing use liturgical acts—burning lists of inherited curses, anointing family birthrights with oil—to accompany scientific interventions like stress-reduction techniques. The correlation between spiritual transformation and measurable health improvements exemplifies God's design for holistic restoration. As neuroscience confirms that neurochemical balance improves with forgiveness and community support, the church's role in epigenetic recovery becomes increasingly vital. By weaving together biblical promises of new creation and scientific evidence of genetic adaptability, faith communities underscore that healing is both divine gift and human responsibility. This integrative approach prepares us to examine how entire nations and peoples experience brokenness and healing.

2.3 National or Communal Sin

2.3.1 Corporate Responsibility in Scripture—Famine, Plague, Exile

Scripture recounts how communal sin can trigger large-scale judgments affecting entire nations, reminding leaders that corporate ethics undergird societal health. In 2 Samuel 24, Israel's census—driven by pride—provoked a plague that killed seventy thousand people, illustrating that national decisions have corporeal consequences. The book of Judges recounts cycles of peace and oppression, where idolatry and injustice ushered in foreign domination, famine, and disease as instruments of divine correction. Jeremiah's prophecies link Jerusalem's moral decay—social oppression, false worship—to looming exile and economic collapse (Jer 5:25; 6:19). Ezekiel saw plagues on Tyre for its pride and cruelty, demonstrating that commercial and military arrogance invite biological and economic ruin. In the exile, Babylon's harsh conquest fulfilled prophetic warnings that collective rebellion against God breaches covenantal protection, exposing entire populations to violence, displacement, and hardship. New Testament parallels appear when Corinth's licentious culture led to internal divisions and spiritual maladies, requiring Paul to summon communal discipline and purification. Thus, corporate responsibility affirms that health and wholeness extend beyond individual piety to public policy, justice systems, and cultural values. Modern parallels—rising opioid epidemics in regions of socioeconomic despair, pandemics spreading through urban density—underscore that social sin bears physical fruit. Public health scholars note that racism, poverty, and environmental injustice correlate strongly with disease prevalence, echoing biblical patterns. Governments and churches share responsibility to create conditions that foster health: clean water, equitable access to care, honest leadership, and moral education. As we explore intercession and communal healing, these examples remind us that corporate repentance can unlock national renewal.

2.3.2 Intercession and Communal Healing (2 Chr 7:14; Joel 2:12–17)

The pathway to communal restoration frequently involves corporate repentance and intercession, as demonstrated when Solomon's dedication prayer invited God to forgive if His people humbled themselves (2 Chr 7:14). In Joel, the prophet calls Israel to turn with fasting, weeping, and mourning so that God might relent from sending further calamity (Joel 2:12–17). These passages establish a biblical pattern: acknowledging national sin together, seeking God's face, and committing to transformative action can avert or reverse collective judgments. Early church gatherings often included prayer for entire cities, fasting on behalf of communities experiencing persecution or disaster. In modern contexts, churches organize days of lament and prayer during epidemics, standing in the gap for overwhelmed hospitals and grieving families. Liturgical services incorporate prayers for civic leaders, health workers, and vulnerable populations, embodying Jeremiah's call to seek the welfare of the city (Jer 29:7). Historians note that during the 1918 flu pandemic, faith communities that engaged in organized intercession experienced stronger social cohesion and more effective mutual aid. Intercession fosters empathy across socioeconomic divides, mobilizing resources for feeding programs, mobile clinics, and mental-health initiatives. Pastoral coalitions partner with NGOs to advocate for public health policies—vaccination campaigns, pollution controls, and equitable health coverage—as expressions of communal confession. These collaborative efforts demonstrate that prayer and action go hand in hand, reflecting God's dual injunctions to repent and to do justice. As communities experience incremental healing—reduced mortality rates, restored public trust, revitalized neighborhoods—confidence grows that God honors collective turning toward Him. Building on this model, we now turn to the prophetic voices that challenge social injustice and promote holistic well-being.

2.3.3 Prophetic Voices, Social Justice, and Public Health (Amos 5:24)

Prophets like Amos thundered against empty ritual disconnected from justice, insisting that "let justice roll down like waters, and righteousness like an ever-flowing stream" (Amos 5:24). This vivid metaphor links spiritual integrity with societal health, suggesting that genuine worship and social reform go hand in hand. Isaiah similarly decried religious hypocrisy while the vulnerable suffered tyranny, connecting true fasts to feeding the hungry and sheltering the oppressed (Isa 58). These prophetic calls serve as blueprints for contemporary engagement in social determinants of health: poverty alleviation, safe housing, fair wages, and anti-discrimination measures. Churches embracing prophetic ministry speak into policy debates on issues like healthcare access, environmental regulation, and criminal justice reform. Public theologians draw on Amos and Isaiah to articulate an ethic that places human dignity at the center of legislative priorities. Epidemiological data confirm that communities practicing equitable social policies experience lower rates of chronic disease, violence, and mental illness. Faith-based NGOs implement programs that reflect prophetic imperatives: mobile health clinics in underserved areas, legal clinics for refugees, and advocacy for health equity. These initiatives exemplify how prophetic witness catalyzes systemic change, mediating God's justice in concrete improvements in public health. By aligning spiritual fervor with empirical research, churches become agents of transformation, demonstrating that faith without works is dead (Jas 2:17). As we conclude this chapter, we recognize that sin's reach extends from individual bodies to entire nations, but so does God's power to heal through repentance, intercession, and prophetic action. In the next chapter, we will explore how spiritual warfare and divine permission intersect in the complex landscape of bodily trials.

2.4 The Silence of the Innocent: Job, the Man Born Blind, and Beyond

2.4.1 The Righteous Sufferer Paradigm (Job 1–2; Ps 73)

The story of Job confronts us with a man who was "blameless and upright, fearing God and turning away from evil," yet he endures staggering losses of health, wealth, and family (Job 1:1). His unexplained suffering shatters any simplistic formula that equates righteousness with personal blessing. In the vast dialogues of Job, friends attempt to rationalize his pain by attributing it to hidden sin, but their well-meaning arguments collapse under the weight of his protestations of innocence (Job 16–17). Job's lament and questioning of divine justice highlight the agony of the innocent who find no answers in conventional wisdom (Job 23:3–7). God's ultimate response from the whirlwind does not offer neat moral explanations but reminds Job of divine transcendence, inviting him to trust beyond his limited understanding (Job 38–41). Similarly, Psalm 73 records Asaph's crisis of faith as he observes wicked people thriving while the righteous suffer. His honest confession of envy and confusion gives way to renewed perspective when he enters "the sanctuary of God" and grasps the temporary nature of prosperity apart from divine presence (Ps 73:16–17). These biblical portraits underscore that suffering often befell the innocent, serving purposes beyond moral retribution—purifying faith, cultivating perseverance, and deepening dependence on God. The righteous sufferer paradigm reminds pastors and counselors to hold space for lament and mystery, resisting the urge to explain away pain. In community worship, time must be made for honest cries of "Why?" alongside hymns of trust. Liturgies of lament, drawing on Job and the psalms, allow congregants to bring raw grief before God without fear of judgment. The narrative of innocent suffering also foreshadows Christ's own experience on the cross, where the perfect and blameless One endured agony for purposes of redemption (Isa 53). As we consider the limits of human explanation, we prepare to address how blame culture distorts our understanding of suffering and to explore corrective pastoral practices.

2.4.2 Correcting Blame Culture in Faith Communities (Jn 9:2–4)

When the disciples ask Jesus whose sin caused a man's blindness, they reveal a common tendency to link every misfortune to personal guilt (Jn 9:2). Jesus's reply—"neither this man nor his parents sinned...but that the works of God might be displayed"—shifts the focus from blame to purpose (Jn 9:3). This teaching dismantles a culture that equates suffering with divine punishment and calls communities to resist shaming the afflicted. In many congregations, sermons that insist on health as a reward for righteousness create an atmosphere where the sick feel excluded or judged. Blame culture fuels spiritual doubt, driving sufferers away rather than toward the love of Christ. Corrective pastoral ministry emphasizes that blessing and affliction coexist in the people of God, and that trials can serve sanctifying purposes without pinpointing individual fault. Training for lay caregivers and leaders must include sensitivity to language, avoiding phrases like "you must have unconfessed sin" when visiting the ill. Instead, ministry teams learn to ask open-ended questions about needs and hopes, offering prayer without presumption. Testimonies of healing should celebrate God's mercy without implying that healed individuals were holier or more faithful. Church teaching can incorporate Jesus's solidarity with the suffering, modeling empathy rather than judgment (Heb 4:15). Small-group curricula on theodicy explore biblical narratives of innocent suffering, helping believers wrestle with complexity. In youth and children's ministries, leaders teach that illness is not a sign of God's displeasure, protecting vulnerable hearts from guilt. Worship services that include psalms of lament affirm that grief and faith can coexist. When a congregation corrects blame culture, it cultivates a community where the broken feel safe to seek pastoral care and where lament transforms into trust. Having addressed the pitfalls of simplistic explanations, we now turn to how Christ's atoning work fulfills our deepest needs for both sin-bearance and healing.

2.5 Christological Fulfillment—The Sin-Bearer and the Sick-Healer

2.5.1 Atonement and Physical Healing in the Gospels (Mt 8:16–17; 1 Pet 2:24)

Matthew's Gospel links Jesus's healing ministry directly to Isaiah's prophecy: "He Himself took our infirmities and bore our diseases" (Mt 8:17), showing that Christ's atoning work encompasses bodily restoration. In numerous accounts, Jesus touches the leper, lays hands on the paralyzed, and speaks healing words to the infirm, demonstrating that physical cures are signs of the kingdom's inbreaking. His miracles function as foregleams of the full reconciliation inaugurated by the cross. Peter's epistle further unites atonement and healing: "by His wounds you have been healed" (1 Pet 2:24), indicating that Jesus's suffering carries restorative power for both sin and sickness. The overlap of sin-bearing and sick-healing in Christ's person and work invites believers to approach Him for holistic salvation. Gospel narratives emphasize that faith—expressed through touching Jesus's garment or believing His word—is the conduit for healing (Mk 5:28; Lk 17:19). Yet Jesus also warns against presuming entitlement to miracles, calling for faith that trusts Him even without visible results. He refuses to perform signs for skeptical onlookers (Lk 4:23–24), underscoring that healing serves redemptive goals rather than spectacle. The blending of forgiveness and cure in stories like the paralytic lowered through the roof illustrates that spiritual renewal and physical health are intertwined in the kingdom. Early Christians witnessed continued healings through apostolic ministry, with sick-beds becoming arenas of prayer and expectation (Acts 5:16). Liturgically, the church inherited these themes in anointing services and Eucharistic petitions for the sick. The integration of atonement and healing shapes Christian understanding of sacraments, prayer, and mission. As we trace Christ's example, we find a model for the church's calling to embody both proclamation of forgiveness and compassionate care for the afflicted.

2.5.2 The Cross as Victory over Generational and Corporate Sin (Col 2:14–15)

At the cross, Christ canceled the record of debt that stood against us in its legal demands, nailing it to the tree (Col 2:14). This decisive act eradicates the power of ancestral curses and communal guilt, granting believers freedom from generational shackles. By disarming rulers and authorities, Christ triumphed over spiritual forces that perpetuate corporate brokenness (Col 2:15). The victory manifests not only in personal justification but also in the liberation of families and nations from cycles of sin and sickness. Believers enter into this victory through baptism, symbolizing participation in Christ's death to old structures and resurrection to new life (Rom 6:4). Churches that teach the cross's cosmic scope encourage congregants to renounce inherited patterns of injustice, addiction, and trauma. Testimonies of families experiencing breakthrough—reconciliation across estrangements, deliverance from addictions—illustrate the cross's power in practical terms. In missional engagement, communities apply this truth by challenging social systems that perpetuate poverty and disease, advocating for policy reform and restorative justice. The corporate dimension of atonement underscores that Christ's triumph extends to every realm—spiritual, social, ecological—anticipating the new creation where death and tears are no more (Rev 21:4). As we integrate this robust Christology into ministry models, we prepare to explore practical frameworks for pastoral discernment and care.

2.6 Discernment and Pastoral Praxis

2.6.1 Diagnostic Questions and Prayerful Listening

Effective pastoral care for the sick begins with asking discerning questions that honor both spiritual and medical realities. Open-ended inquiries—such as "How has this illness affected your faith journey?"—invite honest sharing without presuming guilt or psychological causation. Pastors learn to listen prayerfully, attuning ears to unspoken needs and to the movement of the Spirit in conversations. In pastoral training, case studies highlight how failing to ask sensitive questions can drive individuals into isolation or exacerbate shame. Diagnostic dialogues include exploring lifestyle factors, family history, and spiritual practices, while carefully distinguishing between medical risk factors and theological interpretations. Prayerful listening integrates silence, compassionate touch, and Scripture reading, creating a sacred space for sufferers to express grief, anger, or doubt. Counselors avoid rushing to solutions, recognizing that presence often trumps advice. Regular supervision and peer consultation equip pastors to handle complex cases without overstepping professional boundaries. When indicators suggest deeper issues—such as suicidal ideation or severe trauma—pastors refer to mental-health professionals while continuing spiritual support. This collaborative model honors the expertise of clinicians and the calling of the church. Structured tools—intake forms, listening guides, and consent protocols—help ensure ethical practice and confidentiality. Ongoing reflection through journaling and group debriefings enables pastoral caregivers to discern patterns, avoid burnout, and remain sensitive to the Lord's leading. As caregivers sharpen their diagnostic and listening skills, they foster environments where healing—spiritual, emotional, and sometimes physical—can flourish.

2.6.2 Integrating Medical Referral with Spiritual Care (Sir 38:1–12)

The wisdom of Sirach exhorts believers to honor physicians for their skill, since "the Lord created medicines out of the earth" (Sir 38:4). Integrating medical referral with spiritual care acknowledges that God works through both prayer and professional expertise. Pastors encourage congregants to seek medical assessment for symptoms that may have physical causes, emphasizing that faith in God complements, not replaces, medical treatment. Churches partner with local clinics to host health fairs, screenings, and educational seminars, reducing barriers to care. Spiritual care teams build relationships with healthcare providers, facilitating warm handoffs and coordinated follow-up. In hospitalization visits, pastors pray at the bedside while also verifying that patients understand treatment plans and have support systems in place. Sermons on the goodness of God's created order include reminders that doctors, nurses, and researchers participate in divine service. Training sessions for lay ministers cover the basics of common illnesses, red flags for emergency care, and respectful language when discussing medical issues. Ethical guidelines ensure that confidentiality and informed consent guide every referral and prayer request. Pastoral care resources—prayer cards, Scripture bookmarks, anointing oil—accompany medical visits, blending spiritual encouragement with clinical interventions. Testimonies of collaborative care, where prayer and medicine intersected in God's healing work, build trust in this integrated model. As congregations embrace this holistic approach, the gap between spiritual ministry and healthcare narrows, honoring the full spectrum of God's provision for body and soul.

2.6.3 Ethical Boundaries in Deliverance and Inner-Healing Ministry

Ministries focused on deliverance and inner-healing walk a fine line between spiritual intervention and psychological care. Ethical practice requires clear boundaries: practitioners must obtain informed consent, clarify their role, and avoid making medical diagnoses. Training programs emphasize humility before God's sovereignty and respect for individual agency, steering clear of coercive or manipulative techniques. Deliverance sessions incorporate prayer, Scripture, and pastoral counsel but refer cases of complex trauma or mental illness to licensed professionals. Inner-healing retreats offer guided reflection on past wounds, employing practices like the "Prayer of Examen" and imaginal dialogues, while cautioning participants not to bypass needed therapy. Accountability structures—mentorship, peer supervision, and continuing education—guard against spiritual abuse and burnout. Churches establish written policies outlining when and how deliverance ministry occurs, including safety protocols for vulnerable participants. Pastors collaborate with Christian counselors to integrate spiritual insights with evidence-based therapies, creating referral networks that honor both domains. Confidentiality agreements protect personal disclosures, and group facilitators monitor emotional climates to prevent retraumatization. Ethical deliverance recognizes that evil spirits cannot violate a person's free will; thus, ministry always includes teaching on personal responsibility and God's enabling grace. Success is measured not by dramatic manifestations but by lasting fruit: increased peace, restored relationships, and freedom from destructive patterns. By upholding these ethical boundaries, deliverance and inner-healing ministries demonstrate the church's commitment to holistic care—addressing spiritual strongholds while respecting medical and psychological complexities. This balanced approach prepares us to conclude Chapter 2 with reflections on worship, sacrament, and community health in the next section.

2.7 Worship, Sacrament, and Community Health

2.7.1 Eucharist as "Medicine of Immortality" (Jn 6:54–56)

Early Christians called the Lord's Supper the "medicine of immortality," reflecting belief that partaking of Christ's body and blood nourishes both soul and body. In John 6, Jesus declares that whoever eats His flesh and drinks His blood has eternal life, suggesting that the Eucharist transcends mere symbolism to become a conduit of divine life. Patristic writers like Ignatius of Antioch emphasized that this sacred meal heals believers, uniting them to the living Christ and strengthening them for bodily trials. When congregations gather, the simple elements of bread and wine form a visible link between earthly fragility and heavenly restoration. The Eucharist reminds participants that their physical bodies matter to God, just as their spiritual souls do. Liturgical prayers for the sick often incorporate petitions for the Eucharistic life to flow into wounded bodies, manifesting grace that sustains human weakness. The communal aspect of the sacrament fosters unity, encouraging church members to bear one another's burdens in health and sickness. Modern science confirms that communal rituals increase oxytocin, reduce stress, and promote psychosomatic well-being—effects that resonate with the early church's intuition about Eucharistic healing. Pastors who administer the sacrament in hospital chapels or at homebound patients' doors witness how simple participation can bring calm, hope, and even unexpected physical relief. The theology of the Eucharist therefore extends beyond forgiveness of sins to include strengthening for the journey through suffering. In seminaries and theological colleges, courses on liturgical theology now integrate pastoral care modules that emphasize sacramental ministry to the chronically ill and terminally sick. These developments honor ancient wisdom while engaging contemporary insights, demonstrating that the Eucharist remains central to holistic health. As we consider fasting and confession, we will see how other worship practices similarly shape body and community.

2.7.2 Fasting, Confession, and Congregational Renewal (Isa 58; 1 Jn 1:9)

Fasting in Scripture is portrayed as a means of spiritual breakthrough that often intersects with physical and communal well-being. Isaiah 58 contrasts hollow fasts with genuine fasting that loosens bonds of wickedness, feeds the hungry, and shelters the oppressed, promising that such practices will bring healing and restoration to "your broken bones" (Isa 58:8). By denying the flesh, believers express solidarity with the suffering and sharpen spiritual sensitivity to the needs of others. Congregations that adopt corporate fasts for months plagued by disease or social unrest have reported increased unity, charitable action, and measurable declines in local crime and conflict. These outcomes reflect ancient promises that true fasting aligns human will with divine mercy, unleashing transformative power in society. Confession, another vital worship act, cleanses relationships both vertical and horizontal. John's assurance that if we confess our sins, God is faithful and just to forgive us, purifying us from all unrighteousness (1 Jn 1:9), highlights the emotional and spiritual release that confession offers. Pastoral groups led confession services before administering healing prayers, noting that participants often experience reductions in anxiety, improved sleep, and better immune response. The discipline of regular confession—whether private, pastoral, or communal—prevents the accumulation of spiritual burdens that can manifest as psychosomatic illnesses. In many traditions, confession is followed by anointing with oil, symbolizing God's healing presence. When churches incorporate rhythmic fasting and confession into their liturgical calendar—during

Lent, Advent, or special seasons—they create sustained opportunities for congregational renewal. These practices invite the body, mind, and spirit into alignment, reminding believers that personal and social repentance are essential to God's desired shalom. As this chapter concludes, we will draw together the insights gained and chart a course toward the spiritual warfare and divine permission that frame bodily trials in Chapter 3.

2.8 Epilogue — Toward Holistic Repentance and Societal Wholeness

Chapter 2 has shown that sin and sickness interweave at personal, ancestral, and communal levels, revealing a tapestry of moral, spiritual, and biological threads. Individuals are called to examine personal choices in light of biblical case studies, resisting simplistic blame yet acknowledging that repentance can unlock pathways to healing. Families benefit from understanding inherited consequences, leveraging the freedom offered in Christ to break generational cycles of dysfunction and disease. Nations and communities must heed prophetic warnings, recognizing that policies and cultural practices bear direct consequences for public health. Worship and sacrament emerge as primary vehicles for spiritual and somatic restoration, with practices like the Eucharist, fasting, and confession serving as divine remedies woven into church life. Pastoral responses grounded in diagnostic listening, medical collaboration, and ethical deliverance build trust and open doors for integrated care. Recognizing both God's justice and mercy fosters a balanced theology that honors divine holiness while embracing grace. The epilogue highlights that no sphere of life—individual, familial, or societal—escapes the impact of sin, nor lies beyond the reach of Christ's redeeming work. These key takeaways form a practical blueprint for churches, healthcare workers, and policymakers to collaborate in fostering holistic wholeness. Equipped with this framework, readers can move forward into deeper engagements with spiritual warfare in Chapter 3, prepared to address the stubborn realities of bodily trials within the broader narrative of redemption.

Conclusion Our examination of how sin shapes bodies and societies has shown that affliction is rarely a neutral occurrence. Whether born of personal choices, ancestral patterns, or national failures, sickness serves both as a stark reminder of humanity's brokenness and as an invitation to God's transformative mercy. We have discovered that God's justice demands accountability, yet His grace pioneers fresh starts—breaking free lineages of pain and renewing communities through repentance and worship. The convergence of Christ's atoning work and Spirit-empowered living offers pathways to profound healing that encompass soul, body, and society. With these insights in hand, we stand ready to engage the next dimension of suffering—spiritual warfare and divine permission—confident that our God, who redeems every wound, guides us through every trial toward ultimate restoration.

Chapter 3 – Satan Tested, God Permitted: Spiritual Warfare and Bodily Trials

In the hidden recesses of everyday life, an invisible battle rages— one that touches our bodies as much as our souls. From the courtroom drama in heaven's council to the demonic hold that bends the broken, Scripture reveals that sickness can be more than a biological malfunction; it may carry the fingerprints of spiritual conflict and divine testing. This chapter invites readers to peer behind the curtain at the adversary's assaults and the sovereign Lord's permission, learning how God sets boundaries even as He allows trials. We will encounter the ancient archetype of Job, explore deliverances in both Testaments, and center our hope on Christ's cosmic victory. Through careful discernment and earnest intercession, the church is called to engage both prayer and practical care, distinguishing natural maladies from spiritual strongholds and wielding the armor of God with humility and faith. By understanding these dynamics, believers gain confidence to stand firm when affliction presses in, assured that the same power that raised Jesus from the dead sustains us in every conflict.

3.0 Prologue — Unseen Battlefields and Human Frailty

3.0.1 Biblical Cosmology of Conflict (Rev 12; Eph 6)

The Bible unveils a vast spiritual realm in which angels and demons engage in continual conflict, invisible to our natural eyes but deeply affecting human affairs. Revelation 12 portrays a cosmic struggle: a great red dragon pursues the woman clothed with the sun, symbolizing Satan's unrelenting assault on God's people and purposes. This imagery reminds us that behind earthly events lies a heavenly courtroom and battlefield where spiritual powers vie for dominion. Ephesians 6 calls believers to don armor—truth, righteousness, the gospel, faith, salvation, and the Spirit's word—because our true adversary is not flesh and blood but "the rulers, authorities, and cosmic powers of this present darkness." The apostle's injunction underscores that spiritual reality informs every human encounter, including sickness. By framing conflict in cosmic terms, Scripture warns against reductionist explanations that ignore the unseen. The patriarchs, prophets, and apostles all operated within this worldview, interpreting plagues, famines, and personal afflictions through the lens of spiritual combat. Even Jesus, when casting out demons, claimed authority over spirits that inflict physical maladies. The New Testament writers assume this cosmic conflict as backdrop when describing Christian life as a battlefield requiring vigilance. As we explore bodily trials, we must remember that medical and spiritual dimensions interlock in a world where both God's and Satan's agendas intersect. This cosmic perspective refreshes our understanding of suffering, cautioning us to seek remedies that engage both prayer and practical care. Recognizing the biblical cosmology of conflict readies us to discern spiritual roots of illness without neglecting natural causes. It also grounds our confidence in the sovereign Christ who has already triumphed on the cross. With this foundation, we turn to how sickness often plays out amid the clash between two kingdoms.

3.0.2 Sickness in the Crossfire of Two Kingdoms

When illness strikes unexpectedly, it can feel like a random blow, yet Scripture invites us to see many afflictions as skirmishes in a larger war. The dragon of Revelation seeks every opportunity to devour those who bear the woman's offspring, suggesting that disease can be a weapon aimed at discouraging faith. In Luke's healing narratives, sickness is sometimes tied to demonic bondage, as in the bent woman who had been crippled for eighteen years by a spirit of infirmity (Lk 13:11–16). At the same time, God "permits" certain trials to test and strengthen believers, as He did with Job, crafting situations that reveal hearts and display divine glory. Thus sickness may arrive both as demonic aggression and as a permitted test from the sovereign Lord. The tension between spiritual attack and divine permission means that healing prayer engages both rebuking of darkness and submission to God's timing. Spiritual warfare ministries emphasize this dual reality, teaching intercessors to bind demonic assignments while pleading for God's mercy and purpose to prevail. Pastoral training increasingly integrates prayer for deliverance with instruction on medical intervention, acknowledging that God often employs physicians as agents of deliverance. Congregations learn to mount corporate worship gatherings as strategic resistance, flooding the spiritual atmosphere with praise that dispels fear and oppressive powers. Meanwhile, doctors and nurses, guided by compassion, bring relief through antibiotics, surgery, and palliative care, enacting God's common grace. This interplay between unseen forces and visible remedies highlights that no healing path is purely secular or purely spiritual. Believers discover that faith without works is incomplete, and that prayer without practical action may lack tangible results. As we move into Job's experience, we will see an archetype of this crossfire where Satan's accusations met God's sovereign permission, resulting in profound lessons for our own trials.

3.1 Job's Ordeal Revisited (Job 1–2)

3.1.1 Accusation in the Heavenly Court

Job's story opens on a stage where heavenly beings present themselves before the Lord, including a figure introduced as "the Satan," the accuser or adversary. This courtroom scene reveals a legal framework in which the adversary challenges Job's integrity, suggesting that his piety is merely a result of God's blessing. Satan contends that if those blessings are removed, Job will curse God to His face. The dialogue underscores that behind every believer stands an accuser ready to attribute impure motives or hidden sins for their devotion. God grants Satan limited access to Job's possessions and health, not because God approves of suffering, but to expose the depth of Job's faith. This divine permission establishes boundaries: Satan may accuse, but ultimate authority rests with the Lord. Job's innocence prior to the trials becomes the test's focal point, offering a template for understanding how suffering can serve both to unmask hidden motives and to demonstrate genuine loyalty. The narrative communicates that believers are not exempt from divine scrutiny, nor from satanic slander. Job's plight invites readers to consider how complaints about unexplained suffering often echo Satan's accusations rather than reflecting God's will. By portraying the adversary's limited role, the account reassures believers that God retains control even when Satan's accusations seem overwhelming. This heavenly courtroom motif challenges us to trust God's judgment over demonic insinuations, shaping a posture of humility and perseverance in affliction. As we move to the limits placed on the adversary, we see how God's sovereignty frames every trial.

3.1.2 The Limits Placed on the Adversary

After granting Satan leave to test Job, God delineates strict limits: his possessions and body may be touched, but his life must not be taken. This divine decree reveals God's ultimate authority over Satan's operations, preventing arbitrary or infinite harm. The text emphasizes that every stroke of affliction occurs within God's permissive will, not outside His sovereign oversight. While Job loses children, wealth, and health, the adversary cannot extinguish his life, signifying a protective boundary. This tension between suffering and protection informs Christian confidence: even when we endure great trials, God preserves us for His purposes. The narrative demonstrates that limits on demonic agency often precede redeeming interventions; God permits affliction but also plans restoration. Job's endurance under these constraints teaches that faithfulness does not guarantee exemption, but does ensure divine custody. The restraint on the adversary also invites theological reflection on prayer: when believers plead for relief, they appeal to the One who set the boundaries. Understanding these limits helps prevent spiritual despair, reminding sufferers that demonic forces cannot act independently of God's will. Ministry to the afflicted can therefore reassure individuals that their trials, however intense, serve within redemptive parameters. Pastors can point to Job's unbroken life as evidence that God's protective purposes prevail over every storm. With this assurance, Job's lament and eventual vindication gain deeper resonance, illustrating how faithful endurance under God's constraints leads into divine blessing.

3.1.3 Job's Lament, Faith, and Divine Vindication

As the calamities unfold, Job's initial response of worship—"Naked I came from my mother's womb, and naked shall I return; the Lord gave, and the Lord has taken away; blessed be the name of the Lord"—reveals extraordinary trust in God's character despite piercing loss. His lament evolves into raw, honest complaint, questioning the justice of his suffering and demanding an audience with God to plead his case. Job's dialogues with friends expose common misconceptions about suffering and retribution, as his counselors insist that sin must lie behind every wound. Yet Job refuses to accept their simplistic theology, insisting on an advocate who can vindicate him before the divine throne. His assertion that he would present his cause to God foreshadows Christ's intercession as our perfect advocate. When God finally answers from the whirlwind, He does not give a direct explanation but invites Job to consider divine wisdom displayed in creation's grandeur. This response reframes suffering within a cosmic context, shifting Job's perspective from legal demands to trust in God's inscrutable purposes. Job's humble response—"I had heard of You by the hearing of the ear, but now my eye sees You"—marks the beginning of his restoration. God rebukes the friends for their misguidance and instructs them to offer sacrifice with Job's intercession, symbolizing communal healing through prayer and sacrifice. The narrative concludes with God restoring Job's fortunes, doubling his previous possessions, granting him new children, and giving him long life. Job's journey from lament through faith to vindication exemplifies how deep suffering can lead to deeper knowledge of God and renewed blessing. This story sets the stage for Old Testament foreshadows of deliverance, where divine activity intersects with human struggle.

3.2 Old-Testament Foreshadows of Deliverance

3.2.1 David's Plague and Angelic Judgment (2 Sam 24)

King David's decision to conduct a census of Israel, motivated by pride and self-reliance, triggers divine displeasure that results in a deadly plague. The angel of the Lord moves through the land, slaying seventy thousand men, illustrating how sin at the national level can precipitate widespread bodily affliction. David's terror and intercession—offering himself in place of his people—mirror the role of the intercessor who stands between divine justice and communal penalty. When David builds an altar on the threshing floor of Araunah and offers sacrifices, the plague ceases, demonstrating that sacrifice and repentance can turn back divine wrath. This episode foreshadows the protective work of the Messiah, who intercedes for sinners, and anticipates the temple as a place of atonement and healing. The narrative teaches that plague can serve as both judgment for sin and catalyst for communal repentance leading to deliverance. It also highlights that leaders bear responsibility for corporate health, as David's folly brought widespread suffering. Modern parallels appear when national decisions—war, injustice, corruption—correlate with public health crises, reminding us to consider moral dimensions in policy. The interplay of angelic action, royal repentance, and sacrificial cessation of plague offers a model for intercessory ministry in times of epidemic. As we explore Daniel's account of spiritual conflict, we see complementary patterns of divine protection amid hostile realms.

3.2.2 Daniel's Protection in a Hostile Realm (Dan 10)

Daniel's vision of a heavenly messenger delayed by the "prince of the kingdom of Persia" reveals a layer of spiritual warfare over nations. The text describes Michael, one of the chief princes, coming to assist, illustrating that God dispatches angelic allies to carry out His purposes in the earthly realm. This divine intervention occurs after Daniel endures a period of mourning and fasting, signaling that personal spiritual discipline can unlock heavenly resources. The adversary's initial resistance parallels the assaults of demonic powers seeking to thwart God's plans for human flourishing. Yet limits on the prince's power demonstrate that God's sovereign agents can overcome hostile forces. Daniel emerges from this encounter not physically harmed but spiritually enlightened, equipped to deliver prophetic words that shape national destiny. The story underscores that believers in exile or persecution need not fear unseen oppressors when they cultivate prayerful perseverance. It further teaches that heavenly beings take interest in earthly affairs, responding to faithful petition through spiritual warfare. This Old Testament example complements Job by showing divine protection without affliction, reminding readers that not every spiritual conflict manifests physically. Daniel's experience encourages faith communities to develop robust prayer disciplines, trusting that corporate and individual devotion can tip the scales in spiritual battles that affect health and well-being.

3.2.3 Prophetic Symbols of Messianic Victory (Zech 3)

In Zechariah's vision, Joshua the high priest stands before the angel of the Lord with Satan accusing him, a scene echoing Job's heavenly court but within a priestly context. The angel rebukes Satan and commands Joshua's filthy garments to be replaced with clean vestments, symbolizing purification from sin. This act prefigures the Messiah's work, who cleanses His people and silences accusers through forgiveness. The removal of Joshua's sin-stained robes anticipates the imputed righteousness believers receive, a transformation that brings both spiritual and, by extension, physical renewal. The prophetic figure speaks of a coming Branch, a Messianic deliverer who will build the true temple and bring in peace. These symbols offer hope that heavenly courts will ultimately vindicate God's servants and confer garments of health and wholeness. The interplay of accusation, rebuke, and restoration in Zechariah's night vision mirrors themes in Job and Daniel, weaving a tapestry of deliverance that culminates in Christ. For pastoral care, this vision reassures that no charge against believers ultimately prevails, and that God actively cleanses and defends His servants. As communities face accusations—spiritual, moral, or medical—this prophetic tableau points them to the ultimate vindication and restoration found in the Messiah's completed work.

3.3 New-Testament Confrontations

3.3.1 "Whom Satan Has Bound" — A Case Study (Lk 13:11–16)

In Luke 13, Jesus encounters a woman who had been bent over for eighteen years by "a spirit of infirmity," demonstrating that some illnesses in the New Testament are explicitly attributed to demonic bondage rather than natural causes. When Jesus calls her to Himself and declares her set free, He touches her, immediately restoring her erect posture. This case reveals that demonic spirits can inflict physical disability as a means of subjugation, yet they remain subject to Christ's authority. The synagogue ruler objects to Jesus healing on the Sabbath, exposing the religious system's greater concern for ritual than for human liberation. Jesus responds by highlighting mercy over legalism, stressing that freeing a daughter of Abraham from Satan's bond is a higher act of covenantal love. This confrontation illustrates that spiritual warfare often unfolds in public, challenging both satanic oppression and religious hypocrisy simultaneously. The woman's immediate response—praising God—models the proper human reaction: gratitude and worship, not theological debate. The narrative reframes sickness as a condition with both spiritual and social dimensions, since her deformity likely marginalized her in community life. Jesus's healing dismantles the isolation that demonic-inflicted infirmity can impose, restoring the woman to full participation in family, worship, and work. Her freedom also anticipates the eschatological reality when Christ finally eradicates every form of bondage (Rom 8:21). Pastors and deliverance teams can learn from this model: identifying when spirit-induced illness demands confrontation of demonic power, and when it also calls for pastoral support to reintegrate the healed into community life. The balance of authority and compassion evidenced here informs contemporary deliverance ministry, grounding it in Christ's restorative agenda. As we see the kingdom break in through such miracles, we prepare to explore the broader dynamics of deliverance in the next subsection.

3.3.2 Deliverance and the Kingdom Break-In

The cumulative effect of Jesus's exorcisms and healings in the Gospels signals the inbreaking of God's kingdom into a world dominated by evil powers. Each deliverance event—from the Gerasene demoniac to the epileptic boy in Mark 9—serves as evidence that the age to come has dawned, marked by the defeat of demonic forces and restoration of human dignity. These episodes reveal that healing ministry is inherently eschatological, inviting sufferers into foretaste of final redemption. When Jesus commands unclean spirits to depart, He not only frees individuals but reclaims territory formerly held by darkness. Disciples are then sent out with authority to continue this work (Lk 9:1–2), indicating that deliverance is central to the church's mission. Early believers demonstrated this kingdom break-in in Acts, where Peter and John cast out a lame man and Paul confronted a spirit of divination in Philippi. These acts often sparked both faith and opposition, showing that spiritual warfare provokes resistance from entrenched powers. Deliverance thus becomes a communal enterprise, requiring bold proclamation, prayerful preparation, and reliance on the Spirit's power. The Gospels teach that liberty comes through word and deed: Jesus combines authoritative speech with tangible acts—touch, gesture, command. Modern ministry follows this integrative pattern, blending gospel proclamation with prayer for healing and deliverance. The goal is not sensationalism but clear evidence that Christ's reign over sin and sickness is both present reality and future hope. As the kingdom continues to advance, the church must remain alert to opportunities for spiritual confrontation, always anchored in Jesus's victorious example.

3.3.3 Apostolic Healings and Territorial Clash (Acts 19:11–20)

In Acts 19, the apostle Paul's shadow heals the sick and delivers the oppressed, demonstrating that the power which raised Christ from the dead now operates through His followers. Extraordinary signs accompany Paul's ministry, provoking both awe and alarm. When itinerant Jewish exorcists attempt to use Jesus's name without true faith, they are overpowered by a demoniac, illustrating that authority without relationship yields chaotic results. This misuse triggers a public clash: many who practiced magic bring their scrolls to be burned, signaling a mass renunciation of occult practices and a decisive shift in spiritual allegiance. The account highlights the territorial nature of spiritual warfare: demonic strongholds in Ephesus were dismantled, and Christian witness spread throughout the province. The economic impact—silversmiths losing business—confirms that spiritual victory often entails cultural and material consequences. The story underscores that deliverance ministry must include accountability, public confession, and systemic transformation, not merely private prayer. It also shows that God's power through the church can outmatch elaborate religious and magical systems. For contemporary communities, this means that reclaiming spiritual ground involves both personal repentance and corporate action: worship gatherings, teaching against false practices, and community justice efforts. The Ephesian example teaches that authentic spiritual breakthroughs compel lasting lifestyle change and cultural renewal, foreshadowing the comprehensive healing Christ will bring at His return.

3.4 Christological Center — The Cross as Cosmic Triumph

3.4.1 Disarming the Powers (Col 2:15)

Colossians 2 proclaims that on the cross Christ "disarmed the rulers and authorities and put them to open shame," presenting His triumph as a courtroom drama in which the principalities and powers are stripped of their weapons. This cosmic act secures believers' freedom from the legal charges the enemy brought against humanity—charges that once justified oppression, sickness, and death. By nailing the record of debt to His cross, Jesus canceled the authority Satan wielded through condemnation (Col 2:14). The cross thus functions as the definitive exposé of demonic pretensions, broadcast on Golgotha for all creation to witness. This victory does not simply remove charges against individuals but dismantles the structural domination of spiritual forces over creation. Believers participate in this triumph by faith, sharing in Christ's death to sin and resurrection to new life. When communities embrace the cross's cosmic scope, they approach deliverance ministry not as ad hoc spiritual warfare but as an integral outflow of redemption already secured. The proclamation of the cross becomes both a banner of victory and a weapon against ongoing oppression. As disciples, we live under the shadow of that victory, empowered to stand firm against every assignment of darkness. This theological center shapes all subsequent strategies for prayer, healing, and deliverance.

3.4.2 Healing in the Atoning Exchange (Mt 8:16–17)

Matthew interprets Jesus's healing ministry as fulfillment of Isaiah's prophecy that the Messiah would "take our infirmities and bear our diseases" (Mt 8:17). The atoning exchange concept posits that Christ's substitutionary suffering extends beyond sin-bearing to encompass physical maladies. His wounds inaugurate the holistic redemption of persons—spirit, soul, and body. This multi-dimensional atonement reframes healing not as a separate gift but as a facet of Christ's reconciliatory work. In every healing miracle, believers glimpse the comprehensive nature of salvation: forgiveness of sins intertwined with liberation from disease. The cross and the resurrection thus invite both spiritual and somatic restoration, pointing us to a future where every tear is wiped away (Rev 21:4). Understanding healing in the atoning exchange encourages ministers to pray in the name of Jesus with confidence that they stand within the scope of His redemptive work. This perspective also guards against dualistic tendencies that relegate bodily healing to the natural realm alone. When gospel proclamation includes petitions for physical health, it reflects the fullness of Christ's redeeming purposes.

3.4.3 Resurrection Authority and the Spirit's Power (Rom 8:11)

The resurrection of Christ empowers believers not only to face death but to battle the forces that afflict the living. Romans 8 affirms that the same Spirit who raised Jesus from the dead dwells in us, giving life to our mortal bodies (Rom 8:11). This indwelling Spirit is the guarantee of ultimate bodily redemption and the present source of power for deliverance and healing. Spiritual warfare, then, depends on the Spirit's action within us, shaping prayers and empowering ministry. When believers pray in the Spirit, they invoke the life-giving power that first broke the chains of death around Jesus Himself. This resurrection authority validates Christian healing prayer as more than sympathetic petition—it is a mandate executed in the Spirit's power. The church's confidence in prayer for the sick rests on this pneumatological foundation, ensuring that spiritual warfare is not human-centered but Spirit-led. As we transition to practical strategies, our understanding of resurrection authority will infuse every step of discernment and intercession with divine potency.

3.5 Discernment and Prayer Strategy

3.5.1 Distinguishing Warfare from Natural Causes

Effective ministry to the sick begins with careful discernment between afflictions arising from demonic attack, divine testing, or natural pathology. Observers note that demonic activity often presents with supernatural signs—violent behavior, knowledge beyond natural memory, or multiple symptoms that defy medical explanation. Divine testing, in contrast, may resemble natural illness but yields character refinement, deeper faith, and increased compassion in the sufferer. Natural causes manifest within known medical patterns and respond predictably to appropriate treatment. Discerning ministers ask questions about medical history, environmental exposure, and emotional stressors while also assessing spiritual indicators. Collaboration with medical professionals ensures that natural conditions are addressed, preventing misattribution of disease to spiritual causes. Pastors learn to listen for clues in sufferers' language—references to oppression or bondage that might signal demonic influence versus metaphors of trial and endurance that point toward testing. Prayer for wisdom, as James instructs, becomes an essential first step in discernment (Jas 1:5). Discernment teams—composed of pastors, deliverance ministers, and healthcare advisors—gather to review each case, ensuring balanced perspectives. Such process honors both scriptural patterns and scientific knowledge, fostering integrated care that meets the whole person.

3.5.2 Testing Spirits and Reading Providential Signs (1 Jn 4:1; Acts 16:16–18)

John's exhortation to "test the spirits" warns believers against receiving every manifestation as divine, urging them to measure experiences against the person and work of Christ (1 Jn 4:1–3). In Acts 16, Paul discerns that a fortune-telling spirit, though accurate in proclamation, is not from God and commands it to depart. This contrast shows that truth alone does not guarantee divine origin. Testing spirits involves evaluating worship outcomes—whether Christ is exalted—or the promotion of self, fear, or control. Providential signs, such as peace accompanying prayer or corroboration of scripture, guide discernment. Ministers learn to seek confirmation through multiple witnesses, scriptural alignment, and fruit of the Spirit—love, joy, peace—in the afflicted. Patterns of repeated oppression or temporary relief help distinguish persistent spiritual strongholds from episodic demonic assignments. Recording case notes and tracking prayers' outcomes provide data for ongoing discernment and strategic adjustment. This disciplined approach to testing spirits safeguards against deception and ensures that deliverance remains anchored in God's revealed truth.

3.5.3 Armor of God and Persistent Intercession (Eph 6:10–18)

Ephesians 6 outlines a comprehensive strategy for spiritual warfare: donning the belt of truth, breastplate of righteousness, shoes of peace, shield of faith, helmet of salvation, and sword of the Spirit. These elements equip believers to stand firm against the devil's schemes, including those that manifest in bodily trials. Truth dispels the enemy's lies about identity and destiny. Righteousness protects the heart from condemning accusations. Peace readies the feet to carry the gospel of comfort. Faith extinguishes fiery darts of fear and doubt. Salvation secures the mind against despair. The Spirit's word becomes an offensive weapon, carving paths through demonic strongholds. Persistent intercession undergirds this strategy; prayer must be continuous, fervent, and aligned with God's will. Communities organize prayer watches, rotating intercessors around the clock for those in critical conditions. Worship services incorporate prayer vigils, anointing services, and corporate declarations of Christ's lordship over sickness. Intercessors learn to pray Scriptures—confessing promises of health and freedom from bondage. Accountability partners uphold one another in perseverance, recognizing that fatigue can weaken spiritual defense. As believers engage in this armor-based prayer, they participate in Christ's ongoing conquest of darkness, bringing tangible relief to those besieged by both visible illness and invisible adversaries. This practical framework prepares us to move into pastoral protocols for deliverance ministry in the next chapter section.

3.6 Pastoral Protocols for Deliverance Ministry

3.6.1 Ethical Guidelines and Informed Consent

Deliverance ministry carries profound spiritual power and therefore demands rigorous ethical guardrails. Ministers should clearly explain the nature and purpose of deliverance prayers before beginning, ensuring those who seek help understand what to expect. Informed consent involves discussing potential emotional, spiritual, and even physical reactions so participants can choose freely without coercion. Confidentiality is paramount; what is shared in the context of deliverance must remain private, safeguarding vulnerable individuals from stigma or gossip. Pastors ought to establish consent forms or verbal agreements that outline participants' rights, including the option to pause or stop the session at any time. Training in trauma sensitivity helps deliverance ministers avoid retraumatizing those who have endured abuse or severe hardship. Ethical guidelines also call for cultural sensitivity, recognizing that spiritual beliefs and expressions vary widely across backgrounds. Ministries should prohibit any form of manipulation, fear tactics, or deceptive practices that pressure people into participation. Deliverance leaders must operate under accountability structures—supervisory teams or denominational oversight—to review challenging cases and receive constructive feedback. Regular debriefings and spiritual supervision help ministers maintain integrity, avoid burnout, and detect any inappropriate behaviors early. Scripture affirms that gifts of healing and discernment are to be exercised "decently and in order" (1 Cor 14:40), guiding ministers to maintain respectful, orderly procedures. Ensuring that deliverance remains voluntary, transparent, and compassionate reflects the heart of Christ, who never coerced but always invited people into freedom. By adhering to clear ethical standards, the church honors both the dignity of those seeking help and the holiness of God's work among us. As these guidelines are internalized, ministries can move forward with confidence, knowing that their practices align with biblical values and human rights.

3.6.2 Team-Based Models and Medical Collaboration

Deliverance often intersects with medical and psychological realities, making team-based approaches invaluable. A multidisciplinary team typically includes pastors trained in prayer ministry, mental-health professionals, and, where appropriate, medical practitioners. Collaboration begins by sharing confidential case details—always with consent—so that each expert understands the full picture. A mental-health counselor can assess whether symptoms stem primarily from trauma, mental illness, or spiritual oppression. Medical input clarifies whether there's a diagnosable condition requiring treatment, such as epilepsy or chronic fatigue syndrome. Pastoral members then shape prayer strategies that respect professional recommendations while inviting God's transformative power. Regular coordination meetings foster mutual respect and avoid conflicting messages to the person seeking help. Teams agree on referral protocols: when to pause deliverance prayers and encourage medical follow-up or psychiatric evaluation. Clear communication ensures that deliverance ministry does not undermine compliance with prescribed medications or therapies. Reciprocal education equips ministers to understand basic mental-health warning signs—suicidal ideation, self-harm, psychosis—while clinicians learn to appreciate spiritual dimensions of healing. Case conferences, with participant permission, allow the team to adjust approaches based on emerging needs. This integrated model prevents fragmentation of care and honors the holistic nature of the Imago Dei in each person. As trust grows between church and clinic, stigma around mental illness and spiritual oppression diminishes. The result is a unified front offering prayer, counseling, and medical treatment in concert, embodying Christ's compassion through both word and deed.

3.6.3 After-Care, Discipleship, and Relapse Prevention

The work of deliverance does not end when demonic oppression lifts; ongoing after-care is essential to consolidate freedom and prevent relapse. Discipleship groups provide supportive environments where former captives of strongholds learn to root their identity in Christ rather than in past afflictions. Mentors—spiritually mature believers—meet regularly with those delivered, offering encouragement, accountability, and prayer. This relational care helps sustain breakthroughs and addresses lingering doubts or temptations. Structured discipleship curricula often include Bible study on themes of victory, identity in Christ, and spiritual disciplines such as prayer and fasting. Worship gatherings dedicated to testimonies empower deliverance recipients to share their stories, reinforcing faith within the community. Practical life skills training—anger management, conflict resolution, emotional regulation—equips individuals to navigate stressors that formerly opened doors to oppression. Relapse prevention strategies might involve personalized action plans identifying triggers, early warning signs, and coping mechanisms anchored in Scripture. Churches may provide hotlines or on-call prayer teams for crises, ensuring that individuals never feel abandoned when shadows threaten to return. Regular health check-ins, whether spiritual or medical, monitor overall well-being, signaling when additional support is needed. Group retreats or conferences focused on renewal and refreshment replenish spiritual reserves. Integrating sacraments—communion, confession—into ongoing care reminds believers of God's continued grace. Through sustained community care, delivered individuals grow in resilience, discovering that ongoing transformation is a journey rather than a one-time event. This holistic after-care ushers participants toward lasting freedom and maturity in Christ.

3.7 Suffering, Sanctification, and Redemptive Mystery

3.7.1 When Deliverance Delays: Paul's Thorn (2 Cor 12)

Even the apostle Paul, endowed with visions and spiritual authority, experienced a "thorn in the flesh" that God would not remove, illustrating that not all afflictions yield to immediate deliverance (2 Cor 12:7–9). Paul's thorn, which may have been physical, emotional, or spiritual, served to keep him humble and dependent on divine strength. His three pleas for relief demonstrate that persistent prayer does not guarantee removal of suffering but can deepen intimacy with Christ. God's response—that His grace is sufficient and power perfected in weakness—reframes hardship as a context for experiencing divine sufficiency. Paul's subsequent boast in weaknesses marks a radical shift: affliction becomes a platform for Christ's power rather than Satan's triumph. This pattern invites ministers to recognize when deliverance delays may be instruments of sanctification. Pastoral care in such cases focuses on nurturing patience, perseverance, and a theology of God's hidden purposes. Sufferers learn to rejoice in weaknesses, finding that vulnerability often invites tangible expressions of God's grace from fellow believers. Communities affirm that delayed deliverance does not indicate spiritual failure but participation in Christ's own suffering and glory. Understanding this dynamic helps avoid discouragement when immediate freedom does not arrive, sustaining hope through divine companionship amid trials.

3.7.2 Sharing in Christ's Afflictions (Phil 3:10)

The call to "know Christ and the power of His resurrection, and may share His sufferings" (Phil 3:10) links Christian identity intrinsically with cruciform living. Believers are invited to walk the path of the cross, embracing trials that refine faith and produce Christlike character. This participation extends beyond moral imitation to experiential solidarity with Christ's own afflictions—rejection, betrayal, physical pain, and death. When illness strikes, sufferers are not abandoned but carried within the heart of the incarnate God, who understands every pang. The Spirit uses bodily trials to cultivate qualities such as compassion, perseverance, and spiritual insight. Churches that teach this theology prepare congregants to view suffering not as a detour from God's plan but as a corridor through which transformation occurs. Group studies on Christ's passion encourage members to contemplate how their own afflictions echo the Savior's journey. Worship songs and liturgies can integrate themes of suffering as participation in divine redemptive work. Pastors guide congregations in mapping their pain onto Christ's wounds, discovering that in sharing His sufferings, they also anticipate sharing His glory. This perspective balances the urgency of deliverance ministry with recognition that some suffering carries profound redemptive value.

3.7.3 Lament, Hope, and Eschatological Healing (Rev 21:4)

Biblical lament provides a structured way for communities to voice grief and anger before God, acknowledging the reality of pain without abandoning faith. The psalms of lament model how to bring raw emotions—tears, cries, questions—into the presence of the holy One who hears and heals. Worship services that incorporate corporate lament create safe spaces for expressing grief over sickness, loss, and injustice. These seasons of lament often transition into proclamations of hope, as congregants recall God's promises of restoration. Revelation 21:4 supplies the ultimate horizon: a future where God will wipe away every tear, and death, mourning, and pain will be no more. Preaching on this eschatological hope sustains believers amid prolonged or terminal illness, reminding them that present sufferings are temporary in light of the coming new creation. Creative liturgies—using symbols of tears, ashes, and then white robes—guide congregations through grief to expectation. Pastoral counseling employs visualization of the new heavens and earth to comfort those nearing end of life. Integrating lament and hope affirms that sorrow and joy coexist in the Christian journey, blending honest reflection with confident waiting for full healing. This redemptive mystery carries communities forward, anchoring them in sacramental and prophetic anticipation of God's final restoration.

3.8 Communal Warfare — Intercession for Cities and Nations

3.8.1 Spiritual Mapping and Corporate Repentance

Spiritual mapping involves identifying spiritual strongholds—patterns of sin, historical injustices, or entrenched evil influences—that hinder communal flourishing. Churches research local history, demography, and social issues to discern areas in need of spiritual intervention. Corporate repentance services address collective sins such as violence, racism, economic exploitation, or environmental neglect, acknowledging that these patterns correlate with regional health disparities. Scripture examples—such as Nineveh's fast and repentance in Jonah's day—demonstrate how national turning can avert judgment. Pastors lead prayer walks through neighborhoods, praying over institutions and landmarks while confessing communal failures. These acts symbolize reclaiming territory for the kingdom of God, serving as catalysts for social renewal. Worship nights devoted to corporate confession draw diverse congregations into unified mourning for societal sin. Intercessors study prophetic warnings in Amos and Jeremiah, applying them to current contexts and calling for structural change. As communities repent together, social cohesion often improves and public health outcomes can follow, reflecting God's blessing on societies that humble themselves.

3.8.2 Worship as Strategic Resistance (2 Chr 20)

In 2 Chronicles 20, King Jehoshaphat appoints singers to lead the army into battle, declaring, "Give thanks to the Lord, for His steadfast love endures forever." Their worship precedes military victory, illustrating that praise can disarm hostile forces. Modern churches replicate this model by organizing worship gatherings in city centers, parks, or hospitals, declaring God's lordship over illness and social ills. Strategic worship events target areas plagued by gang violence, addiction, or disease, believing that heartfelt praise dismantles spiritual barricades. These public declarations of God's sovereignty inspire hope and galvanize communities toward collective action. Hospitals have hosted worship services in chapels and atria, inviting patients, staff, and families to join in songs of trust. Such gatherings often foster unexpected partnerships between faith groups, civic leaders, and medical professionals. By shifting spiritual atmospheres, worship as resistance opens doors for social programs—recovery ministries, food banks, and clinics—to gain traction. This approach demonstrates that the worship of God is not a detached ritual but a frontline strategy in the battle for human well-being.

3.8.3 Public Health, Justice, and Spiritual Strongholds

Prophetic ministry calls the church to speak truth to power, advocating for policies that promote justice, equity, and health. Scriptural mandates—"Let justice roll down like waters" (Amos 5:24)—connect spiritual renewal with social reform. Churches engage in public health campaigns addressing issues like clean water, vaccination access, and pollution control, confronting systemic injustices that disproportionately affect the marginalized. Faith communities partner with NGOs to offer free clinics and legal aid, modeling holistic compassion that links spiritual intercession with practical outreach. Prayer vigils for healthcare workers and solidarity fasts highlight the spiritual dimension of public health. By challenging corrupt practices—such as profiteering from essential medicines—the church asserts moral authority in civic life. Advocacy efforts grounded in biblical justice principles can influence legislation on housing, nutrition, and environmental standards, reflecting God's concern for the whole person. As spiritual practitioners join hands with policy experts, they break down the false divide between sacred and secular, enacting God's kingdom through both prayer and protest. These combined efforts weaken spiritual strongholds rooted in greed, oppression, and neglect, leading toward healthier, more just societies.

3.9 Epilogue — Courageous Faith on Contested Ground

Chapter 3 has unveiled the multifaceted interplay of spiritual warfare and human trials, affirming that sickness can stem from natural, demonic, or testing origins. Believers learn that thorough discernment—grounded in Scripture and aided by medical insight—is essential before acting. Leaders glean that ethical deliverance requires informed consent, team-based collaboration, and structured after-care. The cross stands as the ultimate cosmic triumph, disarming hostile powers and empowering the church to proclaim healing. Christ's atoning exchange and resurrection authority frame every prayer for the sick, preventing dualistic separation of body and soul. Corporate intercession, strategic worship, and prophetic advocacy demonstrate that communal warfare against sickness extends beyond personal ministry into public life. Suffering, when embraced as participation in Christ's afflictions, yields sanctification and deeper hope. Lament and eschatological vision provide liturgical tools for communities to navigate grief toward renewal. Together, these insights equip both laypeople and leaders to minister with humility, courage, and wisdom on contested spiritual terrain.

Conclusion Our journey through spiritual warfare and bodily trials has shown that suffering never arrives unaccompanied by purpose—whether to expose false loyalties, deepen dependence on the Almighty, or herald the inbreaking of God's kingdom. We have seen that Satan's accusations operate within divine boundaries, that Christ's cross disarms hostile powers, and that the Spirit's resurrection life empowers persistent intercession. Deliverance ministry, when practiced with ethical care, team collaboration, and ongoing discipleship, becomes a conduit of God's compassion and justice. Even in thorny seasons where relief is delayed, participation in Christ's afflictions shapes us into vessels of His grace. As congregations unite in worship, lament, and prophetic advocacy, they reclaim contested ground for healing and wholeness. Armed with these insights, we are now prepared to turn toward the redemptive purposes of affliction itself—discovering how God uses illness to display His glory, form Christlike character, and equip us for service in a weary world.

Chapter 4 – God's Redemptive Purposes in Affliction

Affliction often feels like an unwelcome interruption to life's plans, yet Scripture reveals that God repurposes even our deepest trials to display His glory and to shape our souls. In this chapter, we follow the thread of redemptive suffering from the classroom of chronic pain to the bedside of miraculous healing, discovering how every tear, groan, and unanswered prayer serves God's higher purposes. We will witness how sickness becomes a living portrait of divine power, how persistent weakness forges compassion and humility, and how personal trials prepare servants for future ministry. As we navigate the tension between present struggle and promised restoration, we will learn to recognize providential design amid apparent randomness, to celebrate foretaste glimpses of resurrection life, and to integrate pastoral care that attends to body, mind, and spirit. In charting these pathways, we embrace the remarkable truth that none of our suffering is wasted but instead is woven into the tapestry of God's redemption.

4.0 Prelude — The Alchemy of Suffering

4.0.1 The Paradox of Weakness and Power (2 Cor 4:7–9)

Paul's metaphor of treasure in jars of clay captures the paradox that human frailty becomes the vessel for divine glory. Though our bodies crack under pressure—through illness, injury, and chronic pain—the very cracks permit the light of Christ to shine more brightly (2 Cor 4:7). Each blow that brings us low exposes the power sustaining us, revealing that strength is perfected in weakness, not in self-sufficiency. Paul lists persecutions, perplexities, and pressures, yet declares that we are not crushed, driven to despair, forsaken, or destroyed. These four negations paint a portrait of resilience grounded not in human resolve but in the resurrection life at work within us. Sickness, then, becomes an opportunity for the community to witness God's sustaining power amid trials. As believers gather around the afflicted, the jars of clay demonstrate both human vulnerability and divine treasure, modeling that our limitations invite God's unlimited resources to flow through us. This paradox reframes suffering from an obstacle to faith into a strategic vantage point for spiritual impact. Frontline ministries, hospitals, and home visits become stages where God's power outshines human weakness. Recognizing this truth prevents either toxic positivity that denies real pain or despair that dismisses divine presence. Instead, we learn to embrace both honesty about suffering and confidence in God's sustaining grace. With this alchemical perspective in place, we transition to consider how providence and randomness interplay in the experiences we call misfortune.

4.0.2 Providential Design versus Random Misfortune

Not every illness carries a divine message, yet Scripture affirms that nothing escapes God's sovereign oversight. Ecclesiastes observes that time and chance befall all, suggesting that randomness coexists with providence (Eccl 9:11). From thunderstorms that disrupt lives to pandemics that sweep the globe, we confront events that appear arbitrary. Yet faith invites us to trust that God weaves even these occurrences into His redemptive tapestry, working through both the intended and the unexpected. Joseph's journey from pit to palace, though his brothers meant it for harm, illustrates how suffering with no apparent purpose can advance divine plans (Gen 50:20). Jesus's own parable of the unjust judge and the persistent widow uses the metaphor of persistent pleading to show that providence sometimes requires our engagement, even amid seeming indifference (Lk 18:1–8). In pastoral practice, we resist spiritualizing every ailment while also refusing to compartmentalize medicine and prayer into separate spheres. A holistic approach holds that antibiotics and miracles both flow from God's common and special grace. Congregations learn to pray for scientists and policymakers as partners in God's care for humanity, recognizing that public health measures reflect God's mercy extended through human wisdom. Simultaneously, believers maintain alertness to the Spirit's promptings, discerning when affliction speaks of deeper spiritual realities. This balanced posture—neither fatalistic nor prescriptive—prepares us to see how, within both design and randomness, God can transform affliction into occasions for manifesting His glory. We now move from broad principles into the first specific way God displays His works through sickness.

4.1 Sickness as a Canvas for Glory (Jn 9:3)

4.1.1 Manifesting Divine Works

When Jesus healed the man born blind, He declared that the man's condition existed so that the works of God might be displayed (Jn 9:3). In similar fashion today, each story of healing or endurance becomes a living testimony to God's character—His mercy, power, and faithfulness. In clinics and hospitals, when a patient experiences unexpected remission, those present glimpse a force beyond human skill. Such moments invite questions: What caused this turnaround? Who intervened in the natural order? Pastors encourage congregations to gather around medical wards, praying aloud for healing and bearing witness to God's intervention. Missionaries in hostile regions report that miraculous healings often grant them access to otherwise closed communities, as people seek answers beyond secular medicine. When faith communities share these testimonies through social media, they create digital "canvases" where God's works are visible to a global audience. Yet care is taken to frame these stories accurately, avoiding sensationalism or exaggerated claims. Ethical storytelling honors the individual's experience while pointing consistently to God's action. In worship, song lyrics frequently reference divine healing—"He makes all things new"—reminding believers that each recovered function of the body reflects God's creative and restorative artistry. Over time, a collection of such accounts builds a portrait of God as the Great Physician, compelling skeptics to confront spiritual realities. Recognizing sickness as a canvas for divine works therefore reshapes pastoral and evangelistic strategies, integrating personal testimonies into preaching, teaching, and communal prayer. From the bedside to the broadcast, God's works displayed through affliction open hearts to the gospel's life-transforming power. As testimonies multiply, they prepare the way for exploring the evangelistic impact of these narratives.

4.1.2 Testimony and Evangelistic Impact

Testimonies of healing and endurance carry significant persuasive power, especially when shared by those who authentically lived through the trial. As the blind man after his healing became a bold proclaimer of Jesus, modern believers are called to testify to leads others to Christ (Jn 9:25). In many unreached people groups, local stories of miraculous health interventions provide openings for gospel conversations where theological arguments might fail. Evangelistic teams train members to listen for "openings" created when sickness resolves unexpectedly—neighbors ask, "What happened to you?"—and to answer with compassion and clarity about Christ's work. Radio and television programs featuring authentic testimonies reach millions weekly, transcending cultural and geographical barriers. Pastors equip congregants to frame their stories biblically, focusing on God's grace rather than personal achievement or health rituals. This biblical framing prevents syncretism, ensuring that salvific credit rests with Christ alone. Universities that host medical mission conferences highlight case studies where spiritual and medical interventions combined to heal both body and soul. These academic presentations underscore that the evangelistic impact of healing testimonies depends on theological integrity and clinical credibility. As churches incorporate testimonies into their outreach—through open-air events, health clinics, and social media—they amplify the gospel's reach. Over time, communities become known for their care, and the name of God is lifted up through both word and deed. Having seen how divine works manifest through sickness and how testimonies advance the kingdom, we now turn to the communal dimension: public worship as a celebration of healing.

4.1.3 Public Worship and the Celebration of Healing

In the early church, believers gathered daily in the temple courts, where signs, wonders, and healings accompanied apostolic teaching (Acts 5:12). Public worship served as both spiritual formation and communal testimony of God's healing presence. Contemporary worship services can similarly incorporate moments dedicated to healing—anointing at altars, corporate laying on of hands, and times of testimony. These corporate celebrations reinforce the message that healing belongs to the community, not only to individuals. Thereafter, worship elements—songs, Scripture readings, prayers—focus on themes of restoration and life, creating an atmosphere saturated with expectancy. Annual healing services or revival meetings draw crowds not only for dynamic worship but also for tangible encounters with divine power. Music teams carefully select songs that reflect both God's sovereignty over sickness and His tender care for sufferers. Liturgical calendars may include "World Healing Sundays," emphasizing global intercession and solidarity with afflicted populations. These gatherings often partner with medical professionals who offer free screenings, embodying the integration of spiritual and physical care. As attendees leave with stories of encouragement, they become ambassadors of hope in their neighborhoods and workplaces. By embedding healing celebrations into public worship, churches declare that God's redemptive purposes actively include the restoration of bodies, thereby strengthening the faith of both the afflicted and onlookers. Having seen the manifold ways that sickness becomes a canvas for glory—through divine works, evangelistic testimony, and public worship—we now examine how affliction shapes personal formation.

4.2 Formation through Pain (2 Cor 12:7–10)

4.2.1 Humility and Dependence

Paul's admission that his "thorn in the flesh" kept him from exalting beyond measure unveils a profound truth: pain humbles the proud and dismantles self-reliance (2 Cor 12:7). When chronic illness or recurring pain resists cure, sufferers confront their limitations and dependency on God's sustaining grace. This realization shatters illusions of control, driving individuals to their knees in genuine prayer and vulnerability. In pastoral counseling, leaders guide the afflicted through exercises of confession, acknowledging pride and cultivating humility before the Lord. Spiritual retreats for those with chronic conditions often incorporate solitude, reflection, and guided prayer to help participants release self-sufficiency. As humility grows, reliance on God's wisdom and provision deepens, leading to spiritual maturity. Families and communities witness this transformation firsthand, as formerly hard-headed individuals begin to lean on God and others for support. Humility also opens the door for authentic community, as people no longer feel compelled to hide weakness, but embrace interdependence. As together they navigate daily challenges—choosing treatments, adjusting to new limitations—they learn to trust God moment by moment. This posture of dependence honors God's sustaining power and aligns the heart with the truth that "apart from me you can do nothing" (Jn 15:5). With humility and dependence established through pain, we now turn to how affliction deepens compassion toward others.

4.2.2 Deepening Compassion for Others

Encountering personal suffering cultivates empathy for those who share similar struggles, a compassion that cannot be taught but only learned through experience. When a person knows the sting of rejection due to visible disability or invisible chronic illness, they become advocates for others in vulnerable positions. Pastoral training programs include modules led by those who have endured, teaching future ministers to accompany the suffering rather than simply instruct them. Hospitals host volunteer programs where survivors of serious conditions—cancer, neurological disorders—visit newly diagnosed patients, offering firsthand encouragement. These "compassion teams" model Christ's tender presence, showing that empathy arises from shared pain. In congregational life, support groups for caregivers and the bereaved become contexts where compassion is both given and received. Testimonies of compassion encourage broader communities to remove barriers—physical and attitudinal—that isolate the vulnerable. Churches that integrate accessibility measures and mental-health ministries demonstrate how personal formation through pain expands into systemic compassion. Compassion also fuels social action: sufferers often champion healthcare reform, disability rights, and poverty alleviation, propelled by an intimate understanding of need. As this compassion ripples outward, communities reflect the character of Christ, who "had compassion on the crowds" (Mt 9:36). The compassionate posture forged in the crucible of personal affliction thus becomes a powerful tool for ministry in broken contexts. Having explored the inward formation of humility and empathy, we now consider how persistent prayer amid pain refines faith.

4.2.3 Refining Faith through Persistent Prayer

Chronic or recurring affliction provides a context for deepening prayer life, moving believers beyond casual requests into sustained dialogue with God. As Paul's three pleas for removal of his thorn illustrate, persistent prayer can become an arena for intimate engagement with the divine (2 Cor 12:8). Sufferers discover that prayer transforms not only circumstances but hearts, aligning their desires with God's will as they learn to say, "Nevertheless, not my will, but yours, be done." Prayer rhythms take on new depth: long vigils, early-morning intercession, and Scripture-soaked meditations become the lifeblood of those walking through pain. Prayer groups specifically for the chronically ill provide mutual encouragement, as members pray for each other's specific needs and share evidences of God's faithfulness. Digital prayer chains, leveraging technology, keep sufferers connected to worldwide intercession networks, reminding them that their struggles matter in the global body of Christ. As prayers are answered—sometimes through unexpected healing, sometimes through peace in suffering—faith is refined, producing perseverance and spiritual fruit. This persistent prayer also impacts the broader community; as churches unite in long-term intercession for those afflicted, collective faith matures, and the congregation witnesses God's sustaining power over extended seasons. Through refining fire of ongoing prayer, believers emerge with fortified faith capable of withstanding future storms. With this understanding of formation through pain, Chapter 4 moves next into preparation for future ministry forged by affliction.

4.3 Preparation for Future Ministry

4.3.1 Priestly Empathy (Heb 4:15)

Jesus, our great High Priest, understands every dimension of human suffering, having been "tempted in every way, just as we are—yet did not sin" (Heb 4:15). This empathetic model shapes Christian ministry, calling pastors and caregivers to enter the inner world of those who suffer. When ministers have themselves walked through seasons of illness, they carry a credibility and compassion that textbooks cannot provide. Their stories validate the pain of others, signaling that God's presence does not exempt us from trials but sustains us through them. In seminary settings, modules led by faculty who have navigated chronic conditions help students appreciate the pastoral power of shared experience. Worship services that include testimonies of personal trials cultivate a culture where vulnerability is honored and pastoral empathy flourishes. Empathy shaped by affliction enables ministers to ask better questions, listen more deeply, and respond with both Scripture and sensitivity. It prevents platitudes that minimize pain and replaces them with prayers that acknowledge suffering while pointing to God's sustaining grace. Congregations led by empathetic shepherds often develop robust care networks—hospital visitation teams, meal rotas, and prayer chains—because their leaders model genuine compassion. This priestly empathy also equips clergy to advocate for those marginalized by illness, ensuring equitable church policies on accessibility and pastoral care. As empathy builds bridges between pastor and parishioner, it sets the stage for authentic witness in weakness and for the development of trial-tested spiritual authority.

4.3.2 Authentic Witness in Weakness

When leaders disclose their own struggles, they shatter illusions of pastoral perfection and invite congregants into a shared journey of faith. Authentic witness arises when ministers do not merely preach about suffering but live through it, modeling reliance on God in real time. This transparency counters toxic "health and wealth" messages, replacing them with the biblical rhythm of brokenness and restoration. Churches that expect vulnerability from their leaders cultivate environments where members also feel safe to admit struggles—be they physical, emotional, or spiritual. Authentic witnesses draw upon personal diaries, sermons, and small-group talks that chronicle the ebb and flow of health, prayer, and healing. These narratives teach that faith is not a one-time assent but a daily surrender amid uncertainty. As ministers recount moments of despair followed by glimpses of God's goodness, they equip congregants to persevere in their own trials. This genuine testimony becomes a powerful apologetic, demonstrating that the gospel speaks to all facets of human experience. It also forges deep relational bonds within the church, as people rally around leaders in prayer and practical support. Authentic witness in weakness thus becomes a conduit for communal growth, reinforcing the truth that God's power is most visible in human frailty.

4.3.3 Shaping Spiritual Authority through Trial-Tested Character

Spiritual authority in the New Testament often emanates from suffering endured with faithfulness. Paul claimed that his hardships validated his apostleship, as signs of authenticity rather than mere rhetoric. Similarly, contemporary leaders who bear the marks of affliction carry a credibility grounded in character formed through trials. Congregations recognize that those who have faced suffering without turning away from Christ possess insights and resilience that inspire trust. In leadership training, emphasis on "character under pressure" highlights how affliction refines integrity, humility, and compassion—qualities essential for guiding others. Trial-tested character resists the temptations of pride and burnout, as leaders remain dependent on God's grace rather than their own strength. Churches that affirm the growth of leaders through suffering foster succession models where emerging pastors are mentored in both theological skill and perseverance. This form of authority avoids authoritarianism, instead inviting people to follow a shepherd who knows the way through the valley. As leaders shape their leadership style around lessons learned in pain—listening, serving, and empowering—the entire congregation benefits from a culture of grace and resilience. Trial-tested character thus transforms personal affliction into a foundational credential for effective, enduring ministry.

4.4 The Mystery of Delayed or Partial Healing

4.4.1 Learning Endurance in the "Already–Not Yet" Tension

Christian hope lives in the tension between the present reality of suffering and the future promise of complete restoration. The "already–not yet" framework teaches that while Christ inaugurated the kingdom of healing, its fullness awaits His return. Believers with chronic or incurable conditions learn endurance as they reconcile answered prayers of peace with unanswered prayers for cure. This spiritual maturity emerges when sufferers acknowledge God's sovereign timing and rejoice in small mercies—relief from pain flares, stabilization of symptoms, or unexpected moments of strength. Community support groups offer spaces for sharing strategies of endurance, from pacing daily activities to weaving prayer throughout the day. Pastors preach that endurance yields character and hope (Rom 5:4), encouraging congregants to view prolonged affliction as a pilgrimage toward final glory. Liturgical rhythms—festivals of thanksgiving, seasons of lament—equip the church to hold both joy and sorrow, reinforcing that neither define the totality of Christian identity. As sufferers cultivate endurance, they bear witness to a hope that transcends circumstance, attracting others to the faith's resilience. This endurance also guards against disillusionment when cures do not arrive, fostering a trust that God's purposes are deeper than immediate relief.

4.4.2 Discernment between Discipline, Warfare, and Providence

Not all delays in healing bear the same meaning; affliction may serve as divine discipline, spiritual warfare, or a facet of providential design. Discipline arises when suffering responds to personal or corporate sin, inviting repentance and restoration (Heb 12:6). Warfare manifests when demonic forces resist kingdom advance, requiring spiritual confrontation and deliverance prayer. Providence encompasses illnesses that test character or emerge as part of God's broader plans, neither punitive nor demonic. Discerning these categories demands prayerful reflection, biblical knowledge, and often counsel from trusted spiritual mentors. Journaling prayers and tracking correlations between confession, deliverance efforts, and health changes can reveal patterns. Worship leaders guide congregations through confession songs, intercession chants, and meditative Scripture readings to aid discernment. Christian medical ethics seminars encourage doctors and pastors to consider spiritual dimensions while honoring professional standards. Discernment prevents mislabeling providential trials as demonic, which can lead to spiritual abuse, or viewing discipline as random, which can breed fatalism. As congregants learn to differentiate these divine dynamics, they approach suffering with appropriate responses: repentance where needed, deliverance prayer where welcomed, and patient trust where providence calls. This discerning posture readies people for wholeness that integrates every dimension of God's redemptive work.

4.5 Communal Edification and Mutual Care

4.5.1 Bearing One Another's Burdens (Gal 6:2)

The command to "bear one another's burdens" creates a communal network of support where the weight of sickness is shared collectively. When individuals disclose their struggles, small groups, prayer chains, and care ministries mobilize to provide practical aid—meals, transportation to appointments, financial assistance—while also offering spiritual encouragement. Churches equip members with training in active listening, empathy, and confidentiality, ensuring that care efforts honor dignity and privacy. Deacons coordinate meal schedules and home visits, creating predictable rhythms of support that alleviate anxiety and isolation. Congregations post prayer requests on secure platforms, inviting intercession that binds hearts across physical distances. Shared testimonies in worship of how burdens have been lightened strengthen communal identity and inspire others to participate in care ministries. This reciprocal bearing of burdens goes beyond sporadic acts of kindness, cultivating a culture where mutual care is woven into every aspect of church life. As members experience being carried in their times of need, they in turn learn to care for others, perpetuating a cycle of compassion that reflects the body of Christ in action.

4.5.2 Spiritual Gifts Activated amid Affliction

Suffering often surfaces hidden spiritual gifts—of mercy, helps, and encouragement—as members step forward to meet unmet needs. Romans 12 encourages believers to exercise gifts in proportion to their faith, and affliction provides many occasions to deploy those gifts. The gift of mercy comforts the grieving; the gift of helps coordinates logistics; the gift of faith sustains hope in the face of uncertainty; the gift of discernment guides appropriate responses. Congregational leaders identify and affirm these gift-bearers, integrating them into formal care teams and commissioning them in worship services. Training workshops refine their skills: hospitality seminars for home caregivers, listening labs for pastoral visitors, and prayer ministry intensives for intercessors. As gifts activate, the church body functions more effectively, reflecting Paul's image of interconnected parts each contributing to the whole. Testimonies of gift-driven care encourage others to discover their own gifts in the crucible of need. This activation of spiritual gifts during times of affliction underscores that God intends suffering not only for individual growth but for the flourishing of the entire community.

4.5.3 Corporate Lament as Pathway to Revival

Corporate lament provides a structured, communal outlet for expressing grief over personal and systemic afflictions, uniting sorrow with hope. Gatherings designed for lament involve scripture readings that voice communal pain—psalms of lament, prophetic lament texts—and spaces where participants write laments on cards or ribbons to be symbolically buried or burned. These rituals validate collective grief—over disease epidemics, natural disasters, or community trauma—while inviting God's intervention. The act of lamenting together fosters empathy, as individuals discover shared experiences and break down walls of isolation. Pastors lead prayers that transition from lament to proclamation of God's promises, reminding the community that sorrow does not have the final word. Stories of revival often follow seasons of corporate lament, as renewed unity and clarity of vision spur social action, church planting, and evangelistic outreach. Historical revivals, from Asbury College to Azusa Street, frequently trace roots to communal cries for mercy, illustrating that lament precedes revival. Incorporating corporate lament into the church calendar—during Lent, anniversaries of tragedies, or days of national mourning—establishes a rhythm of confession and renewal. As communities lament together, they open pathways for God's restorative work, moving from brokenness to revival, from tears to testimonies of joy.

4.6 Eschatological Horizon of Wholeness

4.6.1 The Firstfruits of Resurrection Power (Rom 8:23)

Believers are described as eagerly awaiting adoption as children of God, the redemption of their bodies being the "firstfruits" of that future transformation (Rom 8:23). This firstfruits imagery speaks of an initial harvest that guarantees the fullness to come, assuring suffering Christians that the same power animating Christ's resurrection will one day renew every wounded cell. In the present, Spirit-briefed hearts experience glimpses of that power in moments of unexpected strength, peace, or joy amid pain. Small mercies—an afternoon without pain, a wave of spiritual consolation, a deep night's sleep—function as down payments on the greater reality awaiting us. Pastors teach congregations that these "firstfruits" are not random gifts but strategic previews of ultimate restoration, inviting gratitude even in trial. When praying for healing, communities remember that full bodily redemption has already been procured by Christ; prayer petitions then become expressions of faith in God's promised completion. Spiritual disciplines—worship, Scripture meditation, and communal celebration of small breakthroughs—help sustain hope that the firstfruits will give way to the final harvest. Those who endure chronic illness often testify that these foretaste experiences reshape perspectives: suffering no longer defines identity, and anticipation of resurrection life reframes present hardship. The "firstfruits" concept also informs evangelism, as testimonies of Spirit-empowered endurance become tangible invitations to new life in Christ. As congregations cultivate awareness of firstfruits, they press on with confidence that every moment of suffering participates in God's unfolding redemption plan, bridging us toward the new creation.

4.6.2 New-Creation Bodies and Cosmic Healing (Rev 21:4)

John's vision of the new heavens and new earth culminates in the promise that God will wipe away every tear and banish death, mourning, crying, and pain forever (Rev 21:4). This eschatological decree assures believers that the brokenness of bodies and environments will give way to complete wholeness. The cosmic scope of this promise extends healing to lands, seas, and every creature, indicating that God's redemptive purposes encompass more than individual salvation—they reclaim all creation. In practical ministry, churches portray this vision through art, preaching, and liturgy, helping congregants fix their eyes on the coming reality. Environmental justice efforts thus become prophetic enactments of cosmic healing, as faith communities work to restore polluted rivers and devastated forests. Medical missions that bring clean water, vaccines, and surgeries model the inauguration of a renewed world. As children receive medical care alongside gospel proclamation, they glimpse both present and future restoration. Liturgical seasons like Advent and Easter emphasize these themes: Advent waits for the approach of the healer-King, Easter celebrates the firstfruits of resurrection, and Pentecost inaugurates the new covenant power. Incorporating Revelation's promise into worship aligns hearts with the hope that every affliction is transient. The knowledge of an ultimate end to pain reorders priorities, spurring both personal holiness and social engagement. As communities embody this vision, they testify to skeptical onlookers that gospel hope extends beyond spiritual platitudes into real, future transformation of bodies and planet alike.

4.6.3 Living Today in Light of Ultimate Restoration

Awareness of the coming new creation shapes daily living, prompting believers to invest energy into what endures. Sufferers who anticipate a world without pain approach treatment decisions with eternal perspective, balancing efforts for health with readiness to glorify God regardless of outcome. Medical ethics discussions within churches draw on eschatological hope to inform debates on end-of-life care, disability inclusion, and resource allocation. Congregations establish ministries that support families caring for chronically ill members, recognizing that true discipleship cares for the most vulnerable in anticipation of a world healed of all suffering. Sunday school curricula teach children about the new creation, reinforcing that the world God will make is free from the ills they already face, such as bullying or chronic allergies. Prayer meetings include declarations of Revelation's promises, strengthening intercessors to persist amid global crises like pandemics and climate disasters. This forward focus also revitalizes faith in present-day healing: knowing that God's power is not limited by current limitations encourages bold prayer for breakthroughs. Pastors remind congregations that every act of compassion, justice, and environmental stewardship participates in the divine narrative that culminates in cosmic restoration. As believers integrate this eschatological vision into daily rhythms—work, leisure, service—they become agents of the kingdom now, living testimonies of heaven's coming reality.

4.7 Pastoral and Practical Frameworks

4.7.1 Theological Counseling for Sufferers

Theological counseling combines solid doctrinal grounding with clinical awareness to address the spiritual, emotional, and cognitive dimensions of suffering. Counselors initiate sessions by exploring sufferers' theological convictions about God's character, allowing misbeliefs—such as "God is punishing me"—to surface and be reshaped by Scripture. Narrative therapy techniques are adapted to help clients reframe their life stories within the grand biblical narrative of redemption, finding purpose even amid affliction. Counselors draw upon passages like Psalm 34, which promises deliverance to those who seek God in their distress, and 2 Timothy 1:7, affirming that God has not given a spirit of fear but of power and love. An emphasis on the Trinity's involvement in suffering—Father's sovereignty, Son's solidarity, Spirit's comfort—provides a robust theological framework that avoids reductionist explanations of pain. Ethical standards require counselors to refer clients to medical or psychiatric professionals when signs of serious mental illness or suicidal ideation emerge, ensuring holistic care. Supervision groups led by experienced theological counselors maintain accountability and prevent burnout. Training includes understanding attachment theory and trauma-informed practices, so that theological insights translate into compassionate responses that avoid re-traumatization. Churches offering theological counseling integrate these services into existing pastoral care structures, promoting accessibility and reducing stigma. As believers encounter care that addresses both soul and mind, they experience wholeness that reflects God's comprehensive healing design.

4.7.2 Liturgies of Hope: Sacrament, Anointing, and Blessing

Rituals and sacraments anchor hope in tangible actions that convey God's promises amid uncertainty. The Lord's Supper, understood as a foretaste of the heavenly banquet, reminds participants that Christ's body was broken and His blood shed for their healing (1 Cor 11:24–26). Churches designate portions of worship services for anointing the sick with oil while praying for restoration, drawing on James's instruction to call the elders for prayer and anointing (Jas 5:14). These liturgies are accompanied by Scripture readings—Isaiah 61 for comfort and Ezekiel 47 for flowing life—linking ritual action to biblical imagery. Blessing ceremonies for newly diagnosed congregants involve laying on of hands, words of benediction, and the presentation of prayer shawls or oil vials, providing enduring symbols of God's presence. Seasonal liturgies—such as a Healing Service during Lent or Easter—gather testimonies of healing and lament songs, weaving hope and honesty. Training worship leaders to facilitate these services ensures theological integrity and pastoral sensitivity. Post-service follow-up by care teams connects ritual experience to ongoing support, preventing liturgy from becoming a one-off event. Through these sacramental and ritual practices, worshipers receive visible tokens of invisible grace, reinforcing faith that God works through both word and action to bring wholeness.

4.7.3 Integrating Medical, Psychological, and Spiritual Care

Holistic ministry to the afflicted demands collaboration across medical, psychological, and spiritual arenas. Churches forge partnerships with local clinics and counseling centers, hosting joint health fairs where congregants access blood pressure checks, mental-health screenings, and pastoral prayer stations. Prayer chapels within hospitals staffed by chaplains and trained lay ministers offer spiritual support alongside clinical care. Community health workers recruited from church membership receive training in trauma-informed care and basic psychological first aid, bridging gaps between pulpit and practice. Interdisciplinary case conferences convene weekly, reviewing complex cases to coordinate care plans that honor medical prescriptions, therapeutic interventions, and prayer strategies. A shared database—maintaining confidentiality—logs patient progress, allowing minister and clinician to track responses to treatments and prayers. Bioethics committees within the church guide decision-making on emerging medical technologies, ensuring that spiritual convictions inform choices like genetic screening and end-of-life care. Such integrative frameworks turn isolated efforts into cohesive ministry, reflecting the unity of body, mind, and spirit that God intends. As boundaries between sacred and secular blur in service of the whole person, churches become beacons of comprehensive healing, embodying the gospel in every dimension of care.

4.8 Epilogue — From Wounds to Wellsprings

Chapter 4 has traced how God transforms affliction into a platform for displaying divine power, shaping character, and equipping ministry. Disciples learn that sickness can become a canvas for glory, not through mere symptom removal, but through testimonies that galvanize faith and invite unbelievers to behold God's works. Formation through pain cultivates humility, compassion, and persistent prayer, producing leaders with trial-tested character and authentic empathy. The mystery of delayed or partial healing teaches endurance within the already–not yet tension, refining discernment between discipline, warfare, and providence. Communal practices—from bearing one another's burdens to activating spiritual gifts and corporate lament—build resilient networks of mutual care. Eschatological hope anchors every effort, reminding believers that present struggles are temporary preludes to cosmic restoration. Pastoral frameworks integrate theological counseling, sacramental liturgies, and interdisciplinary care, ensuring that ministry addresses body, mind, and soul. These insights call both laypeople and clergy to embrace affliction as a formative gift and a missional opportunity, transforming wounds into wellsprings of spiritual vitality.

Conclusion Our exploration has shown that affliction is far more than a medical problem—it is a divine canvas, a training ground, and a missional frontier. We have seen how God displays His power through stories of healing, how pain cultivates dependence on Him and shapes compassionate ministers, and how trials refine character for service. We have embraced the paradox that delayed or partial cures can deepen endurance and sharpen discernment, and we have envisioned the eschatological promise that all wounds will one day be healed in the new creation. Practical frameworks—from theological counseling and sacramental liturgies to interdisciplinary care—equip the church to embody these truths. As we move into Chapter 5's focus on newborn suffering and divine compassion, let us carry forward the confidence that God's redemptive purposes penetrate the most fragile stages of life, assuring families that even the tiniest cries matter deeply to the heart of the Great Physician.

Chapter 5 – The Innocent Sufferer: Newborn Illness and Divine Compassion

Few moments pierce the human heart like seeing a newborn tethered to machines meant to keep fragile life pulsing. The innocence of the sufferer magnifies every question about God's goodness, justice, and presence. In this chapter we linger at those incubators, weaving Scripture, neonatal science, pastoral practice, and family testimony into a tapestry of tender theology. Rather than rushing to easy answers, we will trace how divine compassion meets infant pain—through the mystery of original sin without personal culpability, through Jesus' fierce advocacy for little ones, and through the surprising ways common–grace medicine becomes an instrument of providence. Along the way, we will explore rituals and ethical frameworks that help parents, clinicians, and congregations shoulder the weight of unanswered "why?" while still daring to hope.

5.0 Prelude — When the Cradle Becomes a Cross

5.0.1 The Shock of Fragility at Life's Dawn (Job 3:11)

The day parents first behold their child is meant to brim with joy, yet the sudden discovery of a life-threatening condition transforms that anticipation into disorienting grief. Job's ancient cry—"Why was I not stillborn, why did I not perish as I came from the womb?"—echoes eerily through neonatal intensive-care units, capturing the raw bewilderment of families who never imagined that swaddling blankets could be replaced by tangle of tubes (Job 3:11). Modern monitors beep with clinical precision, yet every tone reminds caregivers that fragile breaths hang in the balance. Nurses whisper statistics, physicians outline protocols, chaplains murmur prayers, but a parent's heart translates it all as a single plea: please let my child live. In those first hours, time slows to the rhythm of pulse oximeters, and parents learn an unfamiliar vocabulary of Apgar scores, surfactant doses, and bilirubin levels. Grief and hope intermingle; one moment the father feels devastated by a report of brain hemorrhage, the next he marvels at the rhythmic rise of a tiny chest. Scriptures once read casually now sting with urgency—Psalms of lament become lifelines, and every story of Jesus lifting children into His arms feels intensely personal. Extended family gather in waiting rooms, clutching coffee cups and silent prayers; friends send meals that sit untouched because appetite disappears when anxiety rules. Pastors arrive, not with theological lectures, but with tear-filled eyes and hands that squeeze shoulders in shared helplessness. In the hush of nighttime alarms, mothers pump milk while humming lullabies that mingle with ventilator hisses, trying to imprint maternal presence on a child separated by incubator walls. This cruciform cradle exposes human limits, dismantles illusions of control, and thrusts ordinary believers into extraordinary dependence on God's mercy. Incarnation theology takes on flesh again: if God once entrusted Himself to the vulnerability of a manger, perhaps He is still cradling this fragile life. The Spirit whispers comfort too gentle for clinical charts, reminding grieving hearts that divine compassion encompasses every neonatal isolette. Out of this immediate shock grows a humble readiness to search for God's footprints in sterile hallways. That shift—from panic to tentative trust—alters the atmosphere, inviting caregivers and clergy to collaborate as midwives of hope. With the shock named and tears acknowledged, the next question surfaces: where is God in the NICU?

5.0.2 God's Presence in the NICU: A Theology of Tender Vigil

Hospitals can feel like secular spaces, yet Psalm 139 insists that God knits each life together in the secret place, even when that secret place becomes a plexiglass incubator rather than a mother's womb. Staff narrate vital signs, but believers perceive a more mysterious vigil: the Shepherd who neither slumbers nor sleeps hovers over every bassinet (Ps 121:4). Chaplains witness this presence in the tender rituals of exhausted parents tracing crosses on foreheads before stepping away for naps. Nurses, whether confessing faith or not, participate in sacramental moments when they whisper "good morning" to infants who cannot yet respond. Medical rounds become liturgies of intercession as clinicians discuss ventilator settings with humility, knowing that the tiniest fluctuation can tip the balance between life and death. Some nights a spontaneous hymn rises from a night-shift nurse humming "Great Is Thy Faithfulness" while checking IV lines, transforming fluorescent glare into temple light. Physicians speak of "micro-miracles": kidneys beginning to function, infection markers dropping after a prayer circle, oxygen needs decreasing hours after anointing oil touched fragile skin. Families often place scripture cards or baby shoes near incubators, silent testimonies that science and faith need not compete; both serve the Author of life. The NICU thus becomes a liminal space where heaven and earth intersect, and the presence of God is mediated through stethoscopes, tears, and whispered blessings. That persistent presence stabilizes souls rattled by alarms, grounding them for the deeper theological wrestling that follows. Having glimpsed God beside the cradle-cross, parents next confront the puzzle of infant pain, where doctrines of sin and accountability strain under the weight of an untouched innocence.

5.1 Theological Tension of Infant Pain

5.1.1 Original Sin versus Personal Accountability

Christian theology affirms that all humanity inherits the consequences of Adam's fall, yet newborns have neither spoken a deceitful word nor committed a deliberate act of rebellion (Rom 5:12). This reality presses believers to distinguish inherited corruption from personal culpability. Augustine argued that original sin stains every conception, explaining why even infants need grace, yet he also recognized the tenderness of their moral ignorance. Contemporary theologians revisit this paradox, noting that while babies share in a broken creation, they do so without volitional guilt. Neonatal intensive-care chaplains wrestle with parents who wonder if God is punishing them through their child's condition; pastoral guidance clarifies that the cross already absorbed punitive judgment. Psalm 51 speaks of being "brought forth in iniquity," but the same psalmist celebrates God's desire for truth in the inward being, hinting at future moral agency rather than present culpability. In counseling sessions, ministers describe how sickness arises from a world still groaning, rather than discrete misdeeds of a two-hour-old child. The orthodox doctrine of prevenient grace comforts worried hearts: before infants can reach for God, divine mercy reaches for them. Baptismal traditions—whether infant or child-dedication—publicly declare that covenant love covers the powerless, offering visible assurance that guilt is not theirs to carry. When ventilators obscure soft cries, families cling to Christ's words that the kingdom belongs to such as these, undermining accusations of hidden fault. This theological clarity relieves parental shame and orients prayer toward intercession rather than apology. Understanding inherited brokenness without personal blame lays a foundation for seeing Christ's unique compassion for children.

5.1.2 Christ's Special Regard for Children (Mk 10:14)

In Mark's Gospel, Jesus rebukes disciples who view children as interruptions, insisting, "Let the little children come to me…for the kingdom of God belongs to such as these" (Mk 10:14). His arms become safe haven, signaling divine esteem for those without social status or cognitive sophistication. In hospital corridors, these words grant parents permission to imagine Jesus stooping over incubators, blessing tiny foreheads beneath oxygen caps. The narrative also subverts cultural hierarchies: whereas the ancient world often considered sickly infants dispensable, Jesus ascribes them kingdom priority. Pastoral teams read this passage aloud during bedside vigils, situating fragile newborns not at the margins but at the very center of God's redemptive story. Visual artists within congregations paint murals of Christ cradling premature infants, reinforcing the message that divine tenderness envelops NICU realities. The story shapes ethics as well; clinicians influenced by Christian worldview advocate fiercely for pain management protocols and developmental care, reflecting Jesus's protecting stance. Prayer groups adopt the posture of those ancient parents, "bringing" children to Jesus through intercession when physical touch is impossible. Mark's account also informs liturgical language: blessings for newborns reference Jesus's hands laid upon infants, creating continuity between Galilee's village roads and modern neonatal units. Because Christ dignified children regardless of health, pastors discourage language that labels babies "defective" or "damaged," choosing instead descriptors like "beloved" and "treasured." Acknowledging Jesus's special regard paves the way for eschatological assurance, anchoring hope in reunion if earthly healing does not come.

5.1.3 Eschatological Assurance for Little Ones (Isa 11:6; Rev 7:17)

Prophetic visions depict a restored world where children play safely near once-dangerous creatures and the Lamb shepherds every tear-stained face (Isa 11:6; Rev 7:17). For grieving parents, these images promise that infant lives, however brief, are not extinguished but hidden with Christ until the new creation. Early church fathers comforted bereaved families by envisioning toddlers skipping in fields of peace, free from the limitations earth imposed. Funeral liturgies for infants weave Revelation's language of "springs of living water" with Jesus's promise that not even a sparrow falls outside the Father's care, thereby situating tiny graves within cosmic resurrection hope. Theologians debate the exact mechanism of infant salvation, yet all streams of orthodox Christianity affirm God's righteous mercy toward those without conscious rebellion. Parents who release their child into God's hands find solace imagining a reunion at a banquet where developmental delays, ventilator scars, and genetic anomalies are forever eclipsed by resurrection wholeness. Pastoral letters often encourage families to plant a tree or establish a scholarship in their child's memory, symbolizing life that will flourish fully in the age to come. Catechism classes teach older siblings that heaven will include their lost brother or sister, fostering anticipatory hope rather than unresolved sorrow. This eschatological vision also reshapes NICU prayers: intercessors petition boldly for present healing, yet rest ultimately in God's promise of eternal restoration. With theological tensions addressed and hope articulated, attention turns to tangible expressions of divine compassion through medical science.

5.2 Medical Advances as Providential Care

5.2.1 Neonatal Science and Common Grace

The doctrine of common grace asserts that God disperses wisdom broadly, enabling even secular researchers to develop life-saving technologies. Incubators, first introduced in the late nineteenth century, now mimic womb environments and are calibrated with predictive algorithms that adjust humidity and temperature. Surfactant therapy, derived from pulmonary research, has slashed mortality rates in premature infants with respiratory distress syndrome. Each breakthrough exemplifies James 1:17's truth that every good and perfect gift comes from above, even when delivered through the hands of scientists unaware of the Giver. Christian neonatologists often testify that their research feels like worship, an exploration of God's intricately woven physiology. Parents touring NICU equipment frequently express awe, realizing that behind each ventilator lies decades of collaborative innovation fueled by grants, late-night experiments, and global knowledge sharing. Churches celebrate these advancements on Sanctity of Life Sundays, featuring testimonies from families whose babies survived at twenty-three weeks due to cutting-edge care. Biomedical engineers in congregations host seminars explaining how modern monitors detect apnea spells and prompt nurses before oxygen levels plummet, demonstrating providence via circuitry. Meanwhile, missions hospitals partner with Western institutions to install low-cost warmers and train staff, extending common grace to low-resource areas. Recognizing medical advances as expressions of God's kindness encourages believers to fund research, volunteer for clinical trials, and pray for scientific insight. Understanding technology as providential does not negate prayer; it harmonizes intercession with innovation, inviting churches to pray for breakthroughs in neonatal brain injury or infection control. This synergy grounds discussions about ethical boundaries, where faith communities must navigate marvels and moral limits.

5.2.2 Ethical Boundaries in Treatment Decisions

Rapid advances raise complex questions: when does aggressive intervention honor life, and when might it prolong suffering? Bioethical principles—beneficence, non-maleficence, autonomy, and justice—intersect with theological convictions about the sanctity of life and the reality of eternal hope. Multidisciplinary ethics committees comprising neonatologists, chaplains, ethicists, and parent representatives review cases such as extremely premature infants with low survival prospects. Pastors accompanying families translate medical jargon into moral categories, helping them weigh feeding tubes, ventilator settings, and quality-of-life projections in prayerful discernment. Scripture does not dictate oxygen saturation thresholds, but it does counsel love, wisdom, and stewardship, guiding parents to act in the child's best interest without fear or guilt. Situations of potential futility—where interventions cannot achieve intended goals—require courage to shift from curative to palliative care. Ecclesiastes reminds us there is a time to heal and a time to refrain, urging honest acknowledgment of medicine's limits (Eccl 3:3). Ethical boundaries demand transparency; clinicians respectfully present data and prognoses, while families voice values and hopes. Churches develop resources—booklets, support groups, companion volunteers—to assist members navigating these heart-rending choices. Acceptance of palliative paths never diminishes divine sovereignty; it entrusts the child into God's ultimate healing. Recognition of ethical limits ensures that faith-driven zeal does not eclipse compassion, preserving the dignity of the innocent sufferer. As boundaries clarify, believers maintain expectancy that God can still intervene miraculously, respecting that providential care includes both technological capacities and Spirit-initiated surprises.

5.2.3 Palliative Care, Miraculous Healing, and the "Already–Not Yet"

When medical teams conclude that curative options are exhausted, palliative care teams step in to maximize comfort, manage symptoms, and nurture family bonds. Psalm 23's image of God leading beside still waters guides chaplains as they create soothing atmospheres— soft lighting, gentle music, kangaroo care sessions where parents hold their child skin-to-skin. Even in palliative mode, vigilant prayer continues, trusting that God's kingdom sometimes breaks in with unexpected reversals. Documented cases exist where infants deemed incurable recover after communities fast and intercede, illustrating the "already" dimension of kingdom power. At the same time, many families walk the "not yet," holding their child as breathing slows, believing that immediate release into Christ's arms is itself a form of healing. Nurses trained in spiritual sensitivity note that even brief lives can transform entire units, forging camaraderie among staff and awakening dormant faith among observers. As monitors silence and tiny hearts cease, parents who have invited both medical excellence and fervent prayer experience peace that transcends understanding (Phil 4:7). Funerals become celebrations of a life that, though short, radiated divine love, prompting donations to NICU charities and renewed commitment to advocacy for vulnerable children. Integrating palliative care with openness to miracles prevents false dichotomies, fostering holistic trust in God's multidimensional compassion. This integration completes the medical discussion and transitions naturally to the liturgical responses that surround grieving families, where lament and hope intertwine in communal worship.

5.3 Liturgy of Lament and Hope for Families

5.3.1 Biblical Lament Models (Ps 13)

Psalm 13 moves from anguished questions—"How long, O Lord?"— to a final stanza of trust, and its structure has become a pastoral template for parents pacing NICU corridors. Chaplains invite mothers and fathers to read the psalm aloud, pausing after every line of complaint so they can voice their own "how long" in language that names monitors, transfusions, and sleepless nights. The lament's pivot—"But I trust in your unfailing love"—gives caregivers permission to hold anxiety and faith in the same breath rather than waiting for perfect composure. Prayer teams adapt the psalm into responsive readings, allowing congregations to shoulder the family's questions collectively instead of leaving them to grieve in private corners. During bedside vigils, the psalm's cadence regulates breathing for parents caught in shallow panic, functioning almost like contemplative prayer. Neonatal nurses have reported that when a parent whispers lament psalms, infants' heart rates sometimes stabilize, suggesting that Scripture spoken in love alters the bedside environment. Pastors preach from the lament genre to normalize tears, reminding churches that even Jesus wept at a friend's tomb and later cried out on the cross with the words of another lament psalm. Biblical lament thus becomes a divinely sanctioned language for NICU realities, freeing believers from the pressure to protect God's reputation with premature praise. Once families find their voice in lament, they can receive hope not as forced optimism but as a gift that rises naturally from honestly expressed pain, setting the stage for tangible rituals that embody that hope.

5.3.2 Rituals, Blessings, and Community Support

Practical liturgies translate theology into gestures that families can touch, smell, and see when exhaustion erodes abstract belief. Churches assemble "NICU blessing boxes" containing scented candles, soft prayer quilts, tiny hats crocheted by seniors, and handwritten notes quoting Moses's blessing: "The Lord bless you and keep you" (Num 6:24–26). At weekly services, congregations stand in proxy, extending hands toward photos of hospitalized infants and speaking a communal benediction that echoes through hospital walls via livestream. Meal trains morph into sacramental acts as volunteers slip Psalm-inscribed cards beneath casseroles, reminding weary parents that manna still arrives daily. Some congregations schedule midnight prayer rotations that coincide with the NICU's darkest hours, ensuring spiritual covering when anxiety peaks. Pediatric chaplains craft short blessing liturgies using sterile water and a single drop of lavender oil on the incubator, symbolizing the fragrance of Christ (2 Cor 2:14) permeating antiseptic spaces. When a baby reaches a milestone—breathing unassisted, digesting a first feed—the family rings a small bell and sings the Doxology right in the unit, embedding gratitude into clinical progress notes. Such rituals bind the church's worship rhythm to the family's fluctuating timeline, reinforcing that no medical chart is outside God's liturgical calendar. As these embodied blessings accumulate, parents discover reservoirs of resilience, and the wider community learns to see caregiving as a shared vocation rather than a private ordeal. Extending the circle of care naturally draws in siblings and grandparents, whose grief is often overlooked yet whose presence profoundly shapes the family system.

5.3.3 Siblings, Grandparents, and the Wider Circle of Grief

Older children watch their parents vanish for long hospital shifts and begin to wonder whether the tiny sibling has displaced them in family affections. Pastoral counselors use storytelling play—building incubators with blocks and placing dolls inside—to explain medical realities in age-appropriate ways, preventing imagination from conjuring fears worse than truth. Family devotionals incorporate Luke 12:6-7, reminding siblings that every hair on their heads is counted alongside their sister's heartbeats. Grandparents face a double sorrow: worry for the infant and helplessness as they watch their own children suffer, so churches form "legacy prayer groups" where seniors intercede together, drawing consolation from Psalm 145's promise that one generation will commend God's works to another. Community care teams schedule respite moments—ice-cream runs, homework help, park outings—so siblings experience tangible love unmatched by hospital gift-shop trinkets. Grandfathers often find purpose assembling cribs or painting murals at home, transforming waiting into active hope. When medical updates arrive, a designated family liaison relays information to extended relatives, reducing rumor-driven anxiety. Congregations host multi-age lament services where toddlers scribble prayers on paper butterflies that are later hung over the NICU chapel altar, visually declaring that every family member's voice counts. As the wider circle discovers roles in prayer, logistics, and symbolic acts, collective sorrow becomes shared discipleship, preparing hearts for sacramental encounters that convey Christ's nearness in crisis.

5.4 Covenant Signs and Sacramental Consolation

5.4.1 Emergency Baptism and Dedication in Critical Care

When neonatologists warn that hours or minutes might be all a child has, chaplains stand ready with sterile water in a plastic ampoule, recalling early-church midwives who baptized in secret catacombs. Parents often hesitate, fearing baptism equates to giving up; pastoral sensitivity reframes the rite as welcome into covenant love rather than concession to death. Water streams over a forehead scarcely larger than a thumbprint, and Psalm 23 is whispered so softly that only heaven and the heart monitor bear witness. In traditions that practice child dedication, ministers invite parents to lay a gentle hand on the isolette and pledge trust in God's sovereignty, echoing Hannah's offering of Samuel (1 Sam 1:27–28). Medical staff pause, some crossing themselves or bowing heads, acknowledging a sacred moment in an otherwise clinical shift. Photographs of these ceremonies later provide families with tangible proof that their child's story was marked by grace, not solely by machines. Even if the infant survives and thrives, the emergency sacrament stands as a milestone of God's presence in extremis. Follow-up pastoral visits revisit the baptismal promise, reminding parents that the covenant ink has not faded with improving vitals. The rite's brevity does not diminish its depth; instead, it compresses centuries of ecclesial hope into a hospital room, foreshadowing other sacramental acts that convey healing oil and sustaining bread.

5.4.2 Anointing with Oil: Scriptural Roots and Clinical Sensitivity

James 5:14 commands the elders to anoint the sick with oil, yet NICU protocols forbid introducing contaminants. Chaplains work with infection-control nurses to select sterile, single-use vials of pharmaceutical-grade olive oil. A cotton swab dipped lightly carries the sign of the cross onto the child's shoulder or the exterior of the incubator, respecting skin fragility while honoring biblical mandate. Parents often join, dipping their finger in the same oil to anoint one another, symbolizing family solidarity under God's healing authority. The aromatic trace lingers, blending with antiseptic smells and testifying that sacred and scientific domains coexist in God's world. Nurses note that parents appear calmer after anointing rites, correlating spiritual reassurance with stabilized blood pressure in the caregivers themselves. The practice is paired with short readings—perhaps Isaiah 61:1, proclaiming good news to the broken-hearted—linking prophetic hope to present need. Documentation in the chart records "spiritual care provided," ensuring continuity among the care team and reminding clinicians that holistic healing is multi-dimensional. Training sessions for medical staff outline why anointing matters, fostering respect even among non-religious personnel and preventing misunderstandings. Such sensitivity paves the way for Eucharistic moments that nourish weary parents whose mealtimes revolve around hospital cafeterias.

5.4.3 Eucharistic Hope for Parents at the Bedside

Amid relentless beeps and feeding schedules, the Lord's Table becomes an oasis of sustenance for parents who feel spiritually starved. Chaplains wheel a compact communion cart—chalice, paten, pre-sealed elements—between isolettes during quiet hours, whispering liturgy that reminds parents of Christ's broken body healing theirs. The bread's texture contrasts hospital fare, and the cup's sweetness interrupts the metallic taste of anxiety. Parents report sensing solidarity with Mary at the foot of the cross, understanding that divine compassion flows most freely where human vulnerability peaks. Communion also provides theological orientation: if God can redeem the brutal crucifixion into resurrection glory, He can work through an IV-pierced infant. Some couples choose to renew wedding vows right after Eucharist, pledging anew to walk together "in sickness and health," their covenant deepened by NICU fires. Pastors caution against triumphalist interpretations, emphasizing that communion does not guarantee a specific medical outcome but does guarantee God's unwavering presence. Clinical staff appreciate that post-communion parents often approach care discussions with calmer demeanors, demonstrating sacrament's psychosomatic benefit. Sharing the Table at the bedside lays groundwork for the next aspect of care: the ongoing presence of pastoral companions who translate sacramental grace into daily support.

5.5 Pastoral Presence in the NICU

5.5.1 Ministry of Quiet Companionship and Guided Prayer

A NICU's soundtrack is incessant; thus, pastors practice a ministry of strategic silence, sitting beside parents without filling the air with platitudes. Eye contact, a hand resting briefly on a shoulder, and measured breathing synchronize with the infant's ventilatory rhythm, signaling solidarity. Guided prayers use breath phrases—inhale "Lord Jesus," exhale "have mercy"—providing anxious parents with a portable liturgy that steadies racing thoughts. When words fail, chaplains open a Book of Psalms and simply read; Scripture's cadences do heavy lifting that conversation cannot. During crises, pastors shift from passive presence to assertive intercession, praying aloud for medical staff, wisdom, and supernatural peace. They also model healthy boundaries, encouraging parents to rest or step outside while assuring them that spiritual vigilance continues. Overnight chaplaincy programs guarantee that at any hour, a trained listener can hold space for grief. Written prayers slipped into chart holders remind rotating nurses that spiritual care accompanies clinical notes. Over time, quiet presence cultivates trust, enabling deeper pastoral conversations about fear, guilt, or theological confusion. This foundation equips pastors to translate complex medical jargon into faith-framed narratives, building bridges between hospital teams and weary families.

5.5.2 Navigating Medical Language with Theological Clarity

Medical rounds can feel like foreign-language conferences to stressed parents. Pastors attend rounds when invited, jotting notes, then meet parents to unpack jargon—apnea spells, patent ductus arteriosus, intraventricular hemorrhage—into understandable terms. Using biblical metaphors—"the doctors are pruning branches so new life can flourish, much like John 15"—clarifies difficult procedures without trivializing them. When prognosis shifts, chaplains help families process implications in light of Romans 8: nothing separates them from God's love. They caution against prophetic shortcuts, acknowledging uncertainty while affirming God's sovereignty. During ethics consults, pastors translate theological convictions into concise statements clinicians respect, bridging belief and bioethics. Their clarity prevents medical fatigue from mutating into spiritual despair. By framing treatment paths within redemptive arcs, pastors empower parents to participate in decisions with informed faith rather than passive acquiescence. This interpretive role dovetails with interdisciplinary collaboration, ensuring theological insights enrich—not hinder—team dynamics.

5.5.3 Interdisciplinary Teamwork with Doctors, Nurses, and Social Workers

Effective NICU ministry functions best when chaplains integrate seamlessly with healthcare teams. Weekly huddles include spiritual-care updates alongside nutritional plans and medication adjustments, signaling institutional commitment to whole-person healing. Social workers share psychosocial histories, enabling pastors to tailor prayers that address financial stress or immigration anxieties impinging on parental stamina. Nurses cue chaplains when a family faces a difficult procedure, prompting timely pastoral visits. Physicians welcome spiritual input, knowing families often process prognosis through theological lenses. Joint debriefings after infant death allow staff to grieve collectively, reducing burnout and fostering team resilience. Chaplains offer blessing prayers over new machines or renovated units, acknowledging that technological spaces can be consecrated. Shared continuing-education workshops on cultural humility teach staff to respect diverse spiritual practices—Muslim, Hindu, secular humanist—present within NICUs. Such collaboration models Ephesians 4's picture of diverse gifts building one body, each role distinct yet interdependent. Interdisciplinary synergy ensures that divine compassion and clinical excellence converge, closing this chapter's exploration of neonatal suffering and opening pathways toward broader discussions of bodily ailments in the next chapter on acute and chronic conditions.

5.6 Compassion-Driven Ethics and Advocacy

5.6.1 Justice for Preterm and Low-Resource Infants Worldwide

Across the globe, 15 million babies are born too soon every year, and the survival gap between high-income and low-income settings remains staggering. Proverbs 31:8–9 urges believers to speak for those who cannot speak for themselves, a mandate that fits squarely over the fragile lungs of premature infants on makeshift ventilators. Christian NGOs collaborate with ministries of health to supply cost-effective bubble CPAP machines that cut respiratory mortality by half in rural hospitals. Advocacy teams lobby pharmaceutical companies to reduce surfactant prices, framing access to lifesaving medicine as a modern Good-Samaritan imperative. Seminaries host conferences where theologians, neonatologists, and economists strategize ways to channel global church funds toward equipment grants, staff training, and kangaroo-care campaigns. Mission trips replace outdated narratives of "rescuing" children with partnership models that center local expertise and cultural humility. International prayer networks circulate monthly lists of under-resourced NICUs, linking intercession to concrete fundraising goals. Psalm 72's vision of a king who delivers "the needy who cry out" becomes a rally cry, reminding advocates that the Great Physician cares about ventilator shortages in Sahelian clinics as much as suburban wards. Stories of villages celebrating their first surviving 28-week infant inspire further activism, showing that justice is measurable in birth-weight grams and oxygen percentages. These global engagements feed back into domestic congregations, broadening their understanding of neighbor love and preparing them to navigate ethical complexities at home.

5.6.2 Parental Autonomy, Medical Counsel, and Church Support

When complex diagnoses arise, parents stand at a crossroads where professional recommendations, personal convictions, and ecclesial voices converge. Romans 14 affirms that believers must be "fully convinced in their own mind," an ethic that translates into respecting parental autonomy while offering robust pastoral guidance. Medical teams provide statistical outcomes, yet parents weigh these numbers alongside prayer, prophetic impressions, and the community's counsel. Churches form ethics-support circles—small groups trained to facilitate decision-making without coercion—ensuring that couples hear themselves think aloud before God. Pastors remind physicians that informed consent must include time for reflection and spiritual consultation, not just hurried signatures. At the same time, ministers caution parents against rejecting standard treatments out of misplaced fear, emphasizing Proverbs 11:14's wisdom in many counselors. Workshops equip elders to parse medical terminology so that their advice rests on accurate understanding, not rumor. When disagreements erupt—one parent favoring surgery, the other palliative care—mediators trained in peacemaking step in, preserving marital unity under stress. Case studies explored in adult-education classes highlight pitfalls of spiritual triumphalism that shames families who choose hospice. As congregations mature in navigating autonomy and counsel, they embody Galatians 6:2, bearing one another's burdens without seizing control. This balanced ethic protects vulnerable infants from both overtreatment born of panic and undertreatment born of despair.

5.6.3 Pro-Life Theology Beyond Birth: Long-Term Disability Care

Jeremiah 1:5 declares that God knew each person in the womb, a cornerstone text for pro-life advocacy. Yet fidelity to that conviction requires sustained commitment after delivery-room crises fade. Infants who survive extreme prematurity may face cerebral palsy, vision loss, or learning challenges that demand years of specialized care. Churches partner with disability ministries to retrofit buildings, ensuring wheelchairs can approach the baptismal font without obstacle. Financial-aid committees allocate benevolence funds for adaptive equipment, therapy co-pays, and respite breaks for exhausted parents. Youth groups buddy with differently-abled peers, modeling inclusion that dismantles stigma one friendship at a time. Sermons incorporate testimonies from adults with disabilities who contribute richly to congregational life, reframing "quality of life" debates around Imago Dei rather than productivity. Policy advocacy extends to securing equitable insurance coverage and educational accommodations, fulfilling Isaiah 1:17's call to defend the cause of the fatherless. Long-term discipleship curricula teach families to cultivate vocational hope for children with disabilities—artists who paint with adaptive brushes, tech enthusiasts who code with eye-tracking software. By accompanying these children into adolescence and adulthood, churches prove that pro-life theology is not a nine-month project but a lifelong covenant reflecting God's steadfast love.

5.7 Testimonies and Missional Impact

5.7.1 Stories of Survival, Loss, and Transformative Faith

Revelation 12:11 proclaims that believers overcome "by the blood of the Lamb and the word of their testimony," a pattern vividly displayed in NICU narratives. Parents of micro-preemies recount nights when oxygen saturation dipped to single digits yet prayer chains ignited across time zones, coinciding with miraculous stabilization. Others speak of holding their baby's lifeless body, yet experiencing an unexplainable peace that redirected their grief into hospice volunteering. Documentary teams collect these testimonies, weaving them into short films shown at medical conferences, where clinicians confess renewed motivation after seeing spiritual dimensions of their labor. Survivors themselves—now toddlers with hearing aids or teens advocating for disability rights—stand before congregations to declare God's faithfulness in every therapy session and surgery. Testimonies avoid triumphalism by including setbacks: feeding-tube failures, insurance appeals, and lingering PTSD, thereby honoring the full arc of redemption. Small-group leaders employ these stories as case studies in resilience, prompting members to reflect on their own trials through a gospel lens. Each narrative becomes a micro-parable illustrating 2 Corinthians 1:4—comfort received, comfort shared—catalyzing fresh prayer and generosity.

5.7.2 How Infant Suffering Catalyzes Community Service and Adoption Ministries

Witnessing a fragile life fight for breath awakens congregations to broader needs of vulnerable children. Families who navigated NICU complexities often discern a call to foster or adopt infants with medical challenges, translating personal empathy into long-term hospitality. Churches establish medical-care grants for adoptive parents facing costly equipment, echoing James 1:27's pure religion caring for orphans. Women's ministries sew adaptive swaddles for trach-tube babies, while men's groups build wheelchair ramps for newly discharged children. Hospital social workers refer overwhelmed parents to church-run support networks that coordinate meal deliveries, sibling playdates, and overnight lodging near urban hospitals. Collaboration with local pregnancy-resource centers expands to include prenatal classes addressing high-risk pregnancies, forging a continuum of care from womb to home. Mission committees redirect funds toward international orphanages specializing in neonatal HIV treatment, inspired by local testimonies of God's compassion. As service multiplies, communities experience what Acts 20:35 promises—greater blessing in giving than receiving—and the ripple reaches civic authorities who invite faith groups into health-equity task forces.

5.7.3 Evangelistic Doors Opened through Compassionate Outreach

Compassion ministry softens skeptical hearts more effectively than argument alone. When church volunteers sit nightly with single mothers in neonatal wards, hospital staff notice the relentless kindness and inquire about its source. Parents from secular or other-faith backgrounds attend follow-up grief workshops hosted by the church, where they encounter the gospel spoken through shared tears rather than aggressive debate. Chaplains invited to memorial services present the hope of resurrection to audiences who might never darken a sanctuary door. Language-specific care teams—Spanish, Arabic, Mandarin—translate medical updates and simultaneously translate the story of Jesus, contextualizing it within each culture's honor-shame framework. Short-term missioners trained in neonatal care teach village health workers, opening relational bridges for local pastors. As compassion evangelism gains credibility, new believers often trace their conversion not to a sermon but to a casserole, a midnight prayer, or a volunteer's gentle rocking of a crying infant. Thus, the innocent sufferer becomes an unlikely evangelist, drawing many to the Healer who said, "Whoever welcomes one such child in my name welcomes me" (Mt 18:5).

5.8 Eschatological Comfort and the Hope of Reunion

5.8.1 The "Little Ones" in the New Creation (Mt 18:10)

Jesus declares that the angels of children "always see the face of my Father in heaven," granting them privileged status in the celestial court (Mt 18:10). The image assures grieving parents that their baby is not lost in cosmic vastness but escorted by angels into divine presence. Christian art depicts infants cradled by seraphim, visual sermons preached to eyes that can no longer read for tears. Theologians point to David's confidence that he would go to his deceased child (2 Sam 12:23) as a faint Old-Testament echo of reunion. Eschatology classes in seminaries engage this promise, exploring how resurrected bodies may mature to ideal flourishing while retaining personal identity known to parents. Pastors integrate these themes into All Saints' celebrations, lighting candles for babies who now belong to the cloud of witnesses (Heb 12:1). Lullabies once sung beside incubators are reintroduced in worship services as laments that anticipate heavenly fulfillment. Every reminder of angelic guardianship reframes earthly absence as heavenly presence, tilting sorrow toward hope.

5.8.2 Memorial Practices that Anticipate Resurrection

From planting community gardens with plaques bearing children's names to releasing biodegradable lanterns over rivers at dusk, memorial rituals weave resurrection hope into grief's fabric. Churches host "Day of Hope" services each October, aligning with Pregnancy and Infant Loss Remembrance Day, where parents place tactile symbols—booties, ultrasound photos—on the altar before receiving communion. Some families craft memory boxes including hospital bracelets, a lock of hair, and letters of blessing, stored in church columbaria niches awaiting the great reunion. Gravestones inscribed with butterflies or budding acorns remind visitors that dormancy preludes blooming. Digital memorial walls invite global friends to post prayers and verses, forming an enduring litany of remembrance that testifies to Revelation 21's promise of no more pain. Liturgical calendars schedule a "White Balloon" release the first spring after a loss, echoing 1 Corinthians 15's imagery of seeds sown in weakness raised in power. These practices foster communal participation in grief, guarding against isolated mourning while keeping the resurrection horizon in clear view.

5.8.3 Living Families' Ongoing Witness of Hope

Years after leaving the NICU empty-handed, many parents lead support groups, embodying 2 Corinthians 1:4 by comforting others with comfort they received. They speak at nursing-school graduations, thanking future caregivers and sharing how compassionate touch etched eternal memories onto brief lives. Some establish charities funding pulse oximeters for clinics, transforming loss into lifesaving legacy. Annual birthday-heaven parties gather relatives to bake cupcakes, take family photos holding stuffed animals, and donate gifts to pediatric wards, signaling that remembrance coexists with forward movement. Social-media pages dedicated to a child's memory morph into prayer hubs where followers request intercession, turning personal grief into global ministry. Parents participate in church baptism classes, testifying that anticipated reunion fuels their celebration of others' covenant milestones. Their witness disrupts secular assumptions that tragic loss inevitably ends faith, demonstrating instead that hope anchored in Christ's resurrection endures storms. As these living testimonies circulate, they knit the bereaved into the broader narrative of redemption, preparing congregations to extend holistic compassion in future crises.

5.9 Epilogue — Cradling Mystery in the Arms of Mercy

Chapter 5 has charted a journey from the shock of NICU alarms to the horizon of new-creation reunion, revealing that divine compassion surrounds newborn suffering at every turn. Parents can lament honestly, knowing Christ treasures their child and records every tear (Ps 56:8). Pastors are equipped with rituals—anointing, emergency baptism, bedside Eucharist—that translate theology into touchable grace. Healthcare professionals witness common grace in every ventilator and learn to welcome chaplains as allies, not intruders. Congregations discover that justice for vulnerable infants extends from local meal trains to global equipment grants. Ethical discernment balances aggressive treatment with palliative wisdom, guided by love, truth, and hope. Testimonies of survival and loss become seeds of mission, catalyzing adoption, advocacy, and evangelism. Memorial practices prevent grief from ossifying, instead directing it toward resurrection anticipation. Together these insights call the church to cradle mystery—the unanswered "why?"—within the larger embrace of divine mercy that never fails.

Conclusion Our journey through neonatal suffering has revealed a God who stoops lower than any isolette, cradling powerless children and the anguished adults who love them. We have seen lament become a bridge to trust, medical skill serve as an expression of grace, and fragile lives ignite ministries of justice, adoption, and evangelism. Even when healing is partial or postponed to eternity, the gospel speaks a word of worth over every heartbeat and a promise of reunion beyond every grave. Equipped with liturgies, ethical wisdom, and a vision of resurrection, the church can stand faithfully in NICU corridors and family living rooms alike, bearing witness that no life is too brief to display the mercy of Christ. With this conviction, we now widen our gaze in the next chapter to embrace the broader landscape of bodily ailments—acute, chronic, curable, and incurable—carrying forward the lessons learned beside the tiniest sufferers.

Chapter 6 – Bodily Ailments: Acute, Chronic, Curable, Incurable

Our bodies bear the imprint of a world both majestic and marred, where fevers flare, joints stiffen, and wounds heal—or sometimes do not. In this chapter, we chart the terrain of physical illness, from sudden infections that demand immediate intervention to lifelong conditions that call for sustained care. We'll wrestle with how medical classifications—acute versus chronic, curable versus incurable—intersect with covenantal theology and the promise of resurrection. As we navigate prognoses, treatment options, and ethical complexities, we'll discover how embodied spiritual practices and integrative partnerships between church and clinic foster hope and resilience. Preparing hearts and hands for the many ways our fragile bodies can falter, we equip the believer to minister faithfully to every form of broken flesh.

6.0 Prelude — Our Common Frailty, God's Persistent Care

6.0.1 Dust and Glory: The Human Body in Biblical Perspective (Gen 2:7; Ps 103:14)

The Bible begins with God forming the first human from the dust of the ground, imparting life by breathing into lifeless clay, linking our physical origin to divine breath (Gen 2:7). This humble origin reminds us that our strength is never merely self-generated but sustained by God's ongoing life-giving presence. David in the Psalms reflects on humanity's frailty, recognizing that God remembers we are dust and extends compassion accordingly (Ps 103:14). Every heartbeat, every cell division, attests to God's faithful oversight, even as mortality looms over each moment. The biblical trajectory moves from dust to glory: Adam's fall brings corruption, but Christ's resurrection promises transformation from mortal bodies to imperishable ones (1 Cor 15:53). Pastoral reflection on our dust-to-glory journey fosters humility, gratitude, and hope. In clinical settings, reminders of dust and breath encourage medical teams to approach patients with reverence for the divine image in each wounded body. Liturgies often incorporate ashes or water to symbolize our dust and God's cleansing power, inviting worshipers to live in dependence on divine breath. The knowledge that our bodies will one day share in Christ's resurrected glory reframes present ailments as temporary stages in a grand narrative. This tension between our fragile dust and promised glory undergirds every discussion of acute, chronic, curable, and incurable conditions, reminding us that physical decline is not the final word but a chapter in God's redemptive story. Having contemplated our origin and destiny, we turn to the stark reality of illness statistics and personal stories that animate these doctrines.

6.0.2 Statistics, Stories, and the Ubiquity of Illness

Globally, noncommunicable diseases account for 71% of deaths, illustrating how degenerative conditions now overshadow infectious outbreaks. Yet in low-income regions, infectious illnesses remain pervasive, underscoring a dual burden. Personal narratives—of a teenager's acute appendicitis, a grandmother's chronic arthritis, a toddler's congenital heart defect—bring these dry statistics to life. Hospitals display walls of photographs featuring survivors of polio eradication campaigns, each face a testament to God's common grace in medical triumphs. Pastors cite Acts 4:23–31, where believers pray for boldness after a threat, as an example of community response that parallels modern support groups facing widespread illness. In small-group gatherings, members share medical updates alongside prayer requests, knitting personal stories into communal ministry. Statistical dashboards in public health remind churches to engage with their neighbors' needs, mobilizing health fairs and vaccine clinics. Social-media platforms amplify testimonies, enabling distant communities to pray and support families across borders. The ubiquity of illness challenges any illusion of invulnerability, pressing congregations to develop sustainable care ministries rather than episodic responses. Recognizing that sickness spares no age, race, or station fosters empathy and collective responsibility. With the scope of human frailty laid bare, we next categorize the ailments that afflict us, establishing a taxonomy that will guide both medical stewardship and faith-filled response.

6.1 Taxonomy of Physical Diseases

6.1.1 Infectious vs. Degenerative Conditions

Infectious diseases arise when pathogens—viruses, bacteria, fungi, or parasites—invade and multiply within host bodies, provoking immune responses that range from mild fever to systemic shock. Degenerative conditions, by contrast, stem from deterioration of tissues or organs over time, as seen in osteoarthritis, Alzheimer's, and chronic obstructive pulmonary disease. The Bible itself recounts outbreaks—Levitical laws on leprosy and quarantine anticipate modern infection control (Lev 13). Early church hospitals cared for plague victims, modeling mercy in the face of contagion. Degenerative illnesses, invisible at first, reveal themselves slowly through cognitive decline or loss of mobility, calling for long-term care strategies. Both categories demand distinct medical interventions: antibiotics, antivirals, or immunizations counter infections, while rehabilitative therapies, dietary changes, and gene-targeted treatments address degeneration. Pastors working in each domain learn to pray for swift relief from acute infections and enduring patience amid chronic decay. Pentecostal healers sometimes report instantaneous clearing of infections, while compassionate communities ensure sewage sanitation and public education as preventative measures. For degenerative diseases, faith communities sponsor support groups emphasizing daily rhythms of worship, exercise, and medication adherence. Epidemiologists and theologians collaborate to examine how social determinants—poverty, nutrition, stress—modulate both infection risk and degenerative progression. The taxonomy reminds believers that while cures for infections may come quickly, degenerative healing often unfolds over years, calling for sustained spiritual and practical care. This distinction informs pastoral hope: praying for immediate deliverance in one sphere and long-term companionship in the other, both reflecting God's multifaceted healing.

6.1.2 Autoimmune, Genetic, and Trauma-Related Disorders

Autoimmune diseases occur when the immune system mistakenly attacks healthy tissues, producing illnesses such as rheumatoid arthritis, lupus, and multiple sclerosis. These conditions straddle the line between degenerative and inflammatory pathologies, requiring immunomodulatory drugs alongside lifestyle interventions. Genetic disorders—cystic fibrosis, sickle-cell disease, Huntington's chorea—result from inherited mutations affecting cellular functions; recent gene-therapy trials offer new hope by editing faulty DNA sequences, demonstrating human ingenuity and divine providence intersecting. Trauma-related disorders include physical injuries—spinal cord damage, traumatic brain injury—and psychosomatic responses to severe stress. Rehabilitation centers pair physiotherapy with pastoral care, fostering both bodily recovery and spiritual resilience. Biblical narratives, like Jacob's healing at Bethel, remind us that transformation can follow bodily brokenness, while Psalm 73's journey from envy to worship illustrates how cognitive distortions parallel physical ones. Churches host DNA-testing ethics workshops, debating CRISPR applications through theological lenses that honor the Imago Dei. Pastors guide families through grief when genetic diagnoses portend life-shortening conditions, leaning on Jeremiah 29:11's promise of hope and future. Trauma survivors find solace in support groups where worship songs become anthems of liberation. Understanding the varied origins of disease—immune, genetic, or traumatic—prevents simplistic attributions of blame and equips believers to tailor prayers, interventions, and advocacy. From gene labs to trauma wards, recognizing these subcategories deepens faith-informed compassion.

6.1.3 Operable, Non-Operable, and Palliative Paths

Some conditions invite surgical cure: appendectomies eliminate inflammation before rupture, joint replacements restore mobility, and tumor resections prevent metastasis. Operating rooms become arenas of redemption, where skillful surgeons enact God's common grace. Other diseases, like advanced heart failure or inoperable glioblastoma, resist curative surgery; specialists focus on symptom management, quality of life, and extending vitality as long as possible. Palliative care teams—nurses, chaplains, social workers—coordinate pain control, psychosocial support, and spiritual comfort, embodying Jesus's promise to bind up the brokenhearted (Isa 61:1). Families making decisions about candor versus hope navigate complex emotions; pastoral discernment aids in balancing realism with expectancy. Churches organize "Homebound Calls" to include those under palliative regimes in communal prayers and sacramental visits. Hospice volunteers draw on 2 Corinthians 1:3–4, offering consolation shaped by the hope of resurrection even at life's thresholds. Case conferences address when to shift from curative to comfort focus, ensuring that faith does not impose undue burdens of endless interventions. Ethical guidelines prohibit abandonment: even when cure is impossible, believers commit to continuous presence. Training modules in seminaries include rotations with palliative teams, exposing future pastors to the art of accompanying patients toward dignified ends. Understanding operable, non-operable, and palliative options equips communities to serve with both surgical precision of compassion and the soft touch of hospice grace.

6.1.4 Psychosomatic Interplay: When Mind and Body Collide

Psychosomatic illnesses demonstrate the profound connection between emotional states and physical health, as stress, anxiety, and depression can manifest as stomach ulcers, chronic pain syndromes, or heart palpitations. Jesus's healing ministry often addressed psychosomatic dimensions—restoring peace to anxious hearts and healthy bodies (Mk 4:39). Contemporary research on the gut-brain axis reveals that neurotransmitters produced in the intestines influence mood, exemplifying biblical insight that mind and body form a unity God intends to flourish (1 Thess 5:23). Prayerful counseling that includes cognitive behavioral techniques integrates faith and psychology, helping sufferers reframe negative thought patterns that exacerbate symptoms. Churches host mindfulness retreats rooted in biblical meditation—chewing on God's promises rather than worrying thoughts—to calm physiological stress responses. Support groups for those with psychosomatic disorders combine Scripture readings with relaxation exercises, fostering wholeness across mind and body. Pastoral care teams collaborate with mental-health professionals to design crisis plans for panic-attack scenarios, ensuring that spiritual and clinical interventions align. Viewing the psychosomatic interplay as a gospel field invites holistic ministry that neither stigmatizes mental-health issues nor ignores physical symptoms. As this taxonomy concludes, we are equipped to navigate prognoses in faith, translating medical categories into discipleship and decision-making frameworks.

6.2 Navigating Prognosis in Faith

6.2.1 Stewardship of Medical Options

Every diagnosis unveils a menu of choices: immediate surgery versus watchful waiting, aggressive chemotherapy versus targeted biologics, lifestyle modifications versus technological interventions. Believers approach these options as stewards before God, called to manage bodily "vessels" entrusted to them (2 Cor 4:7). Ethical stewardship means balancing risks and benefits, consulting medical experts while seeking wisdom through prayer and Scripture. The parable of the talents inspires proactive engagement: neglecting medical opportunities can reflect poor stewardship, yet pursuing every experimental trial may display distrust in divine provision. Pastoral counselors guide families to establish priorities—extending life, preserving quality, or minimizing pain—by discerning values rooted in God's sovereignty and the sanctity of life. Congregational elders might organize "Medical Wisdom Workshops" where Christian physicians present standard-of-care options alongside spiritual perspectives. Faithful stewardship also includes prudent resource allocation: generous yet responsible use of insurance, medical savings accounts, and church benevolence funds. When multiple viable treatments exist, teams encourage families to pray for clarity and to seek counsel from mature believers. Documented care plans entered into advance directives honor the body as temple (1 Cor 6:19) while preparing for unforeseen crises. Recognizing medicine as a gift, Christians steward options with gratitude, discernment, and obedience to God's call on each life.

6.2.2 Shared Decision-Making and Advance Directives

Medicine today emphasizes shared decision-making, a process perfectly compatible with Christian community. Patients, families, and clinicians convene care conferences where prognosis is explained, hopes are voiced, and values articulated. Scripture counsels seeking multiple counselors for wise plans (Prov 15:22), reinforcing that medical decisions flourish under communal discernment. Advance directives—living wills, power of attorney for healthcare—embody proactive discipleship, ensuring that one's desires for life-sustaining treatments align with faith commitments even if incapacitated. Pastors facilitate workshops on crafting such documents, framing them as acts of love that relieve family burden and honor God's sovereignty over life and death. Discussing Do-Not-Resuscitate orders, palliative extubation, or feeding-tube removal in advance prevents hasty choices driven by crisis. Churches may offer legal clinics to assist with directive preparation, bridging spiritual guidance with practical support. In multicultural congregations, translators and culturally sensitive counselors ensure that families from diverse backgrounds understand implications, preventing confusion and conflict. Shared decision-making rooted in advance planning cultivates trust, reduces moral distress among clinicians, and upholds patient autonomy as a reflection of created dignity. As these processes mature, believers demonstrate that medical agency and divine sovereignty coexist under the banner of the gospel.

6.2.3 Accepting Limitations without Despair

Even the most fervent prayers and skilled interventions cannot guarantee cure, teaching Christians to face bodily limitations without succumbing to despair. The story of Paul's "thorn in the flesh" illustrates that unanswered pleas for relief can become conduits of sufficiency and grace (2 Cor 12:9). Pastors preach that finitude does not negate God's love; rather, it magnifies reliance on His strength. Support groups for the incurably ill gather around themes of lament and thanksgiving, acknowledging sorrow while celebrating small joys. Spiritual directors employ Ignatian exercises that invite sufferers to find God's presence in weakness, recognizing that divine power often shows itself in human limitation. Congregations install "Quiet Rooms" with soft lighting, Scripture art, and cushions for those needing respite, embodying care for bodies that cannot meet communal performance standards. Celebrating milestones of endurance—birthdays, years of living with chronic disease—reframes longevity as blessing despite ongoing limitations. Moreover, telling stories of biblical figures like Job and Jeremiah helps congregants see that faith and lament coexist. Accepting limitations as part of the Christian pilgrimage fosters resilience, prevents bitterness, and prepares hearts for the final healing when mortality gives way to eternity.

6.2.4 Hope-Filled Language in Clinical Conversations

Words wield power, especially when spoken in medical contexts where hope can wither under clinical jargon. Pastors train families and chaplains to translate phrases like "poor prognosis" into honest yet hopeful language—"challenges ahead, but God remains with you." Drawing on Colossians 3:16, caregivers teach that Scripture should dwell richly in patient-family dialogues, countering fear with promises such as Isaiah 41:10. Medical students attend workshops featuring role-plays where actors simulate delivering bad news alongside a pastor offering spiritual accompaniment. Language checklists help clinicians replace "there's nothing more we can do" with "while we've used all available measures, we'll continue supporting comfort and dignity." Chaplains coach providers in offering spiritual referrals: "Would it be helpful to pray with a chaplain after rounds?" When preparing for surgery, anesthesiologists and chaplains co-lead briefings that blend technical explanations with Psalm 23 assurances. Training in empathetic communication improves patient satisfaction and can even influence objective outcomes like pain tolerance and recovery times. As congregations learn these hope-filled modes of speech, they become advocates for language policies in hospitals that honor both clinical accuracy and pastoral sensitivity. This combined approach to prognosis conversations preserves realism while nurturing faith, setting the stage for the embodied spiritual practices explored in the next section.

6.3 Embodied Spiritual Practices

6.3.1 Anointing with Oil (Jas 5:14)

The practice of anointing the sick with oil is rooted in James's instruction to the elders of the church, signifying God's healing presence mediated through visible substance (Jas 5:14). Chaplains train to use sterile, fragrance-free oil to avoid allergic reactions while honoring the ancient symbol of consecration. When a pastor dips a finger into the vial and traces a cross on a patient's forehead or chest, the simple gesture becomes a profound reminder of Christ's wounds that bore our infirmities. Family members often join in the anointing, their touch reinforcing communal participation in divine compassion. In Parkinson's support groups, participants report that having a loved one anoint their hands before workshops imparts unexpected steadiness, illustrating psychosomatic synergy. In pediatric wards, nurses place tiny drops of oil on infant cards, creating a tactile connection between spiritual care and fragile new lives. Medical staff, observing calmer vital signs post-anointing, recognize that the ritual can reduce anxiety and pain perception. Seminarians learn that anointing must be accompanied by prayer and Scripture reading for full sacramental effect. Communities provide lightweight "anointing kits" to homebound members, ensuring that no one is beyond the reach of this embodied ministry. Anointing services often conclude with communal singing of the "Shepherd Psalm," linking physical touch to liturgical song. As congregations integrate anointing into regular ministry, they reclaim a biblical practice that powerfully unites body, mind, and spirit under God's healing hand. Having anointed the body, the church invites the soul to feast at the Lord's Table.

6.3.2 Eucharist as Medicine of Immortality

The early church revered communion as the "medicine of immortality," believing that partaking of Christ's body and blood imparted life and strength (Ignatius of Antioch, Letter to the Smyrnaeans). In modern hospitals, chaplains offer compact communion kits—unleavened bread wafers and pre-sealed juice cups—to patients and families during mealtimes that often become moments of despair. The Eucharistic prayer emphasizes that Christ bore our sicknesses on the cross, merging atonement and healing into one act of grace (Mt 8:17; 1 Pet 2:24). Spiritual directors report that patients who receive communion experience reduced perceptions of loneliness and pain, correlating with studies on sacramental participation and lowered stress hormones. In hospice settings, last communions become treasured memories, bringing peace to both recipients and families. Liturgical catechesis teaches that the Table is a foretaste of the banquet in God's kingdom, where no eyes will cry and no bodies will fail (Rev 21:4). Shared Eucharist fosters solidarity: immunocompromised patients, unable to attend church, receive home-based ministry that declares them full members of the body of Christ. Music therapists accompany communion with simple refrains of "Be Still My Soul," linking sacrament and song to holistic restoration. Seminary courses on liturgical theology now include modules on hospital-based communion, training future pastors to navigate medical protocols without compromising sacramental integrity. As congregations reclaim eucharistic ministry in healthcare contexts, they embody the unity of spiritual and physical nourishment ordained by Christ.

6.3.3 Fasting, Rest, and Rhythms of Healing

Fasting has been a spiritual discipline since Moses, who fasted forty days before receiving the tablets (Ex 34:28), and it remains a practice that recalibrates body and soul in anticipation of God's intervention. In pastoral care, clinicians and ministers collaborate to recommend medically safe fasts—such as dawn-to-dusk water fasts—tailored to individual health conditions, ensuring fasting does not compromise nutritional needs. Worship guides encourage congregants undergoing treatment to observe gentle fasts, replacing physical sustenance with extended prayer and Scripture meditation. Rest rhythms, modeled on the Sabbath command, become crucial for those with chronic illness, preventing burnout and promoting cellular repair. Hospitals incorporate "rest times" in treatment schedules, echoing monastic rhythms that intersperse work with periods of quiet reflection. Support groups practice communal fasts during months of high infection rates, coupling spiritual solidarity with public health measures. Pastors preach on "holy rhythm" from Jesus's example of withdrawing to solitary places to pray (Mk 1:35), linking spiritual replenishment to bodily recuperation. Retreat centers offer "fast and retreat" weekends for caregivers, combining instruction on stress biology with contemplative silence. Studies show that intermittent fasting can reduce inflammation, a medical benefit that underscores the wisdom God embedded in fasting practices. As churches integrate fasting and rest into congregational life, they rediscover God's design for bodily healing through balanced rhythms of self-denial and renewal.

6.3.4 Breath Prayer, Movement, and Holy Touch

Breath prayer—simple two-part invocations synchronized with inhalation and exhalation—offers a portable spiritual practice that also calms the nervous system. For example, breathing in "Jesus" and out "have mercy" can slow heart rate and promote vagal tone, demonstrating mind-body unity. Pastoral health workshops teach techniques drawn from ancient hesychasm, adapting them to Christian prayers rather than Eastern mantras. Gentle movement practices—liturgical dance, Tai Chi informed by prayerful meditation—help patients recovering from stroke rebuild proprioception while praising God. Hospitals with "healing gardens" provide outdoor spaces for walking prayers, linking movement with creation care and spiritual reflection. Holy touch ministries train volunteers in therapeutic touch—laying hands with mindful intention—to channel compassion and reduce anxiety, echoing Jesus's many healing touches. Physical therapists collaborate with chaplains to incorporate prayer and music into rehabilitation exercises, boosting patient motivation and perceived outcomes. Care instruction leaflets include diagrams of prayerful hand placements for spastic limbs, blending kinesiology with sacramental theology. As participants engage breath, movement, and touch, they experience holistic practices that honor the body as God's temple (1 Cor 6:19). These embodied spiritual practices serve as a bridge between contemplative tradition and modern therapies, enriching care with ancient wisdom.

6.4 Integrative Medicine and Faith

6.4.1 Complementary Therapies: Evidence and Discernment

Complementary therapies—such as acupuncture, massage, aromatherapy, and herbal supplements—have gained traction alongside conventional medicine. Psalm 104 celebrates God's provision through both visible plants and unseen processes, framing botanical remedies as gifts of common grace. Pastors consult with naturopathic practitioners to vet safety and efficacy, ensuring no harmful interactions with prescription drugs. Hospitals set up integrative clinics where licensed acupuncturists work in tandem with oncologists, providing nausea relief for chemotherapy patients. Research shows that massage can lower cortisol levels and improve immune response, reinforcing the biblical principle that anointing oil soothes the soul and body (Ps 23). Faith communities host educational seminars that distinguish evidence-based complementary treatments from unverified claims, equipping congregants to make informed choices. Ethical discernment warns against substituting unproven modalities for life-saving interventions; rather, complementary therapies are presented as adjuncts enhancing quality of life. Local herbalists partner with church gardens to grow Beneficial plants—like echinacea and chamomile—for educational workshops. Church health ministries develop resource guides listing vetted complementary practitioners who share Christian faith, establishing referral networks that integrate body, mind, and spirit care. As the church embraces evidence-based complementary therapies, it participates more fully in God's healing work by combining diverse gifts and disciplines.

6.4.2 Mental-Health Interventions alongside Prayer

The prevalence of anxiety, depression, and trauma-related disorders has drawn churches into mental-health advocacy and care. Scripture urges believers to "cast all your anxiety on him" (1 Pet 5:7), yet pastoral care alone cannot address severe clinical conditions. Integrative models pair cognitive-behavioral therapy with devotional practices—journaling prayers, gratitude lists based on Philippians 4:8, and group Scripture memory—that bolster therapeutic progress. Churches host support groups for PTSD survivors, incorporating guided art therapy sessions where participants create visual prayers. Clinical psychologists collaborate with pastors to deliver trauma-informed sermons, preventing retraumatization in preaching on violent biblical texts. Retreat centers offer weekend mental-health intensives combining professional counseling, prayer walks, and worship, fostering environments where emotional healing parallels spiritual renewal. Mental-health professionals teach congregations to recognize signs of crisis—suicidal ideation, self-harm—and navigate emergency protocols while maintaining spiritual accompaniment. Local clinics invite chaplains to participate in case conferences, ensuring spiritual dimensions inform treatment planning. The integration of mental-health interventions with prayer prevents stigmatization of psychological care, highlighting that emotional and spiritual well-being are inseparable. As faith communities become adept in this integrated approach, they create safe spaces for the whole person to find healing and hope.

6.4.3 Ethical Boundaries in Alternative Treatments

While integrative medicine offers promise, churches must guard against exploitation and pseudoscience. Principles of non-maleficence and justice guide discernment: treatments must have a reasonable evidence base and be accessible without undue financial burden. Workshops on "red flags" teach congregants to spot promises of guaranteed cures or "secret" protocols lacking transparency. Pastors caution that "faith healing" events must never dissuade individuals from seeking necessary medical care, emphasizing that "serving the Lord with fear" includes fear of harming one's body (Rom 12:1). Denominational ethics committees review emerging wellness trends—like stem-cell tourism and unregulated supplements—issuing pastoral advisories grounded in both biblical stewardship and clinical data. When members decline proven therapies in favor of unverified alternatives, pastors engage in compassionate dialogue, affirming the value of faith while presenting medical facts. Churches establish "health covenant" statements outlining balanced commitments to both prayer and medicine, ensuring respect for individual conscience and communal well-being. Institutional policies prohibit financial or spiritual coercion in promoting treatments, safeguarding vulnerable members from undue pressure. By setting clear ethical boundaries, the church affirms both the goodness of God's gifts and the importance of wise stewardship, modeling gospel-centered discernment in the ever-evolving landscape of alternative care.

6.5 Communities of Care and Accountability

6.5.1 Small-Group Support for the Chronically Ill

Chronic illness often isolates sufferers as they navigate unpredictable symptoms and fluctuating capacities. Small groups dedicated to chronic-condition support—arthritis, diabetes, multiple sclerosis—gather weekly for Bible study, prayer, and sharing of coping strategies. These groups often include brief teaching segments on nutrition, exercise modifications, and symptom management drawn from both medical and spiritual wisdom. Lay facilitators receive training in "active listening" and confidentiality, ensuring that personal stories remain within the circle. Peer mentoring pairs newer members with veterans who model resilience, providing practical tips on medication schedules and energy conservation. Virtual breakout rooms extend support to homebound individuals, while in-person gatherings in accessible venues emphasize hospitality and inclusion. Groups celebrate individual milestones—first pain-free day in months, successful transition to new insulin regimens—with prayer and testimonies, reinforcing communal joy. Pastoral oversight ensures that group dynamics remain healthy, intervening if unhealthy dependency or unhelpful spiritual shaming arises. Over time, participants witness that bearing one another's burdens in small groups mirrors the early church in Acts, strengthening faith and reducing isolation. From these grassroots communities, whole-church health ministries often develop, extending care to broader membership.

6.5.2 Deacons, Meal Trains, and Accessible Architecture

The New Testament model of deacon ministry in Acts 6—serving tables to ensure equitable care—finds modern expression in deacons coordinating meal trains for families wrestling with acute or chronic conditions. Deacon teams use digital platforms to schedule deliveries, accommodating dietary restrictions and medical recommendations. Congregations retrofit buildings with ramps, automatic doors, and reserved seating for those with mobility aids, reflecting Jesus's welcome to all (Mt 11:28). Nursing mothers and those with service animals find designated spaces, signaling pastoral attention to diverse needs. Periodic "accessibility audits" engage volunteers with disabilities to identify barriers in worship spaces, restrooms, and fellowship halls. Deacons also organize transportation networks, ferrying patients to appointments and ensuring the body of Christ goes beyond Sunday fellowship to real-world solidarity. Training in safe meal preparation—avoiding allergens, respecting texture-modified diets—prevents harm and honors recipients' dignity. Celebratory meals marking remission, transplant anniversaries, or successful rehabilitation become communal pilgrimages where the whole church shares in individual victories. Through deacon-led logistical care, physical structures and social systems conspire to uphold the sanctity of every body, completing the bridge from small-group intimacy to congregational hospitality.

6.5.3 Digital Pastoral Care for Home-Bound Members

Technology extends pastoral presence beyond physical walls, critical for those bound at home by severe chronic or acute illness. Video-call visits, using secure platforms, allow pastors to administer communion, pray audibly, and read Scripture in real time with homebound members. Dedicated phone prayer lines operate around the clock, staffed by trained volunteers who pray through anxieties and match callers with Scripture passages. Congregations host virtual worship services captioned and described for those with sensory impairments, ensuring full participation. Digital bulletin boards share meal-train sign-ups, prayer requests, and visitor rotation schedules, giving community members clear ways to serve. Online support forums moderated by clergy and counselors provide safe spaces for sharing emotional struggles and receiving peer encouragement. Pastoral newsletters include health tips, spiritual reflections, and resource links for telemedicine, mental-health hotlines, and disability benefits. Churches offer Zoom-based small groups for various conditions—Lyme disease, chronic fatigue, rare genetic disorders—ensuring specialized peer connection. As technology evolves, virtual-reality prayer rooms simulate presence in shared sacred space, countering isolation in profound ways. These digital ministries recognize that God's care transcends walls, media, and distance, embodying the promise that "where two or three gather in my name, there am I with them" (Mt 18:20) even online.

6.6 Eschatological Vision and Present Resilience

6.6.1 The Resurrection Body as Motivator of Perseverance (1 Cor 15)

Paul's reflection on the resurrection body in 1 Corinthians 15 offers a powerful incentive for persevering through bodily trials. He describes our mortal bodies as perishable seeds sown into the earth that will rise as imperishable, spiritual bodies, reflecting Christ's glorious transformation (1 Cor 15:42–44). This promise encourages the chronically ill to view each infusion, dialysis session, or physical therapy appointment as an act of faith in a future redemption of their bodies. Believers learn to frame pain-management benchmarks not only as medical victories but as echoes of the greater victory of resurrection. Congregations celebrate "resurrection anniversaries," marking the day a friend began chemotherapy or completed a significant surgery, linking present healing with future hope. Worship songs that recount "This mortal shall put on immortality" become personal anthems for those whose ailments remind them of fragility. In prayer, survivors petition for endurance, invoking the Spirit's promise to "give life to your mortal bodies" (Rom 8:11), trusting that the same power raising Jesus animates their cells. Sunday school classes unpack Paul's agricultural metaphor—dying seed becoming abundant crop—to help youth understand perseverance as preparation for abundance. Pastoral counselors encourage journaling reflectively: noting small improvements today as foretastes of wholeness yet to come. Hospice caregivers use resurrection imagery to comfort families, conveying that even as earthly decline completes its course, a new form of life awaits beyond human sight. Artistic ministries craft visual narratives of seed-to-tree transitions, exhibited in hospital corridors to inspire patients' resolve. The resurrection body motif also undergirds ethical debates: when considering discontinuing life support, families anchor decisions in the promise that no earthly body is final, reducing fear of earthly demise. As this vision saturates church teaching and medical chaplaincy, it supplies resilient hope that bridges the gap between present suffering and promised restoration.

6.6.2 Lament, Gratitude, and the "Already–Not Yet" Tension

Christian experience inhabits a space between lamenting present brokenness and rejoicing in future consummation. The Psalms of lament—like Psalm 42's cry, "Why, my soul, are you downcast?"—invite believers to articulate grief honestly (Ps 42:11). Congregations designate "Lament Sundays," where pews fill with spoken sorrow over pain and loss, and worship leaders guide transitions into thanksgiving by quoting Paul's exhortation to give thanks in all circumstances (1 Thess 5:18). Support groups practice gratitude journaling, listing daily mercies—pain relief, supportive caregivers, moments of laughter—reminding participants that joy can coexist with ongoing symptoms. Retreat centers offer "lament-to-gratitude" workshops, teaching art therapy that moves from dark sketches of suffering to vibrant paintings of hope. The "already–not yet" tension becomes a theological framework: we possess the Spirit as down payment of future redemption (2 Cor 5:5), yet await full healing at Christ's return. Healthcare chapels display dual imagery—crucifixion and resurrection—prompting patients to reflect on both present pain and promised life. Pastoral letters encourage families enduring chronic illness to host "practice feasts," celebrating small victories as foretaste of eternal banquet. Hospital rooms feature Scripture art contrasting Lifetime and Eternity scales, aiding patients in orienting priorities. Sermon series titled "Between Cross and Crown" explore biblical characters like David and Habakkuk who balance lament with declarations of trust. As sufferers learn to hold sorrow and hope in tandem, they cultivate resilience that transcends circumstances. This theological posture alleviates guilt over feeling joy amid pain and empowers believers to bear others' burdens while awaiting the ultimate end of sickness. From lament and gratitude we proceed to practical pastoral tools that embody these truths.

6.7 Pastoral Tools for Diverse Diagnoses

6.7.1 Hospital Visitation Guides and Bedside Liturgies

Effective hospital visitation requires more than presence; it needs structured guides that help pastors navigate clinical settings sensitively. Visitation guides include checklists: introduce oneself by name and role, ask permission before touching, inquire about spiritual needs, offer a brief prayer, and coordinate follow-up visits. These guidelines ensure consistency across pastoral staff and volunteers, preventing intrusive or off-the-cuff approaches that may overwhelm vulnerable patients. Bedside liturgies are curated to fit various diagnoses: a liturgy for acute trauma focuses on immediate comfort prayers and psalms of deliverance, while a liturgy for chronic illness incorporates confession of fatigue and petitions for perseverance. Chaplains carry pocket-sized booklets containing short liturgical scripts keyed to common medical events—start of chemotherapy, pre-op anxiety, hospice transition—enabling immediate, context-appropriate ministry. Training workshops simulate hospital environments, with role-plays that challenge pastors to respond to code blue scenarios with calm presence and brief, powerful prayers. Spiritual care cards—printed prayers and Scripture verses—are given to patients to keep at their bedside, inviting moments of personal devotion when clergy cannot visit. Visitation logs document spiritual needs and promised prayers, communicated to the broader care team to foster integrated support. Family chapels adjacent to ICU units host rotating visitation hours, where pastors lead mini-services featuring candle lighting for each patient. These chapel services bridge private bedside liturgy with communal worship, reinforcing that each individual diagnosis matters to the entire church. By providing these structured tools, congregations ensure that ministry to the hospitalized is both theologically rich and practically effective.

6.7.2 Pre- and Post-Surgical Blessings

Surgery, whether minor or major, can evoke anxiety about bodily integrity and postoperative pain. Pre-surgical blessings serve as rituals commissioning patients into divine care before anesthesia disconnects conscious awareness. Pastors anoint foreheads and palms, pray for skilled hands of surgeons, and read scriptures such as Isaiah 41:10 to comfort fears of the unknown. Families participate by laying hands on the patient or presenting symbolic objects—a small cross, a favorite hymn sheet—embedding relational support into the rite. In recovery rooms, post-surgical blessings acknowledge successful procedures while praying for swift healing, guiding patients to see their recovery as a cooperative venture between medical expertise and divine sovereignty. Chaplains coordinate with nursing staff to schedule these blessings at optimal times, ensuring medical protocols—sterile fields and vital signs—are respected. Educational pamphlets explain the purpose of these blessings to non-religious or interfaith patients, framing them as expressions of pastoral empathy rather than proselytism. When complications arise, repeated blessings offer reassurance that God's presence is not contingent on immediate medical outcomes. Nursing students who observe these rituals report increased appreciation for spiritual dimensions of care, influencing their own professional attitudes. Pastoral offices track surgical rounds and send follow-up notes, reminding patients that prayer continues beyond the operating room. As blessing practices become integrated into surgical pathways, patients develop a sense that their spiritual needs matter at every stage of medical intervention.

6.7.3 Funeral and Memorial Templates for Prolonged Illness

When patients endure long-term illnesses, preparation for potential memorials can be a sensitive pastoral task. Funeral and memorial templates offer customizable liturgies that families can adapt, reflecting the individual's journey of faith and the community's shared grief. Templates include suggested readings—Romans 8:18–25 on future glory or 2 Timothy 4:7–8 on finishing the race—for choices that resonate with the deceased's testimony. Hymn suggestions align moods—from somber reflection to triumphant hope—helping families navigate emotional transitions. Sections for personal stories allow space to commemorate milestones: the patient's first remission, participation in support groups, or acts of advocacy. Inclusion of a "Celebration of Milestones" segment honors the life before death, reminding mourners that each year of perseverance mattered. Pastors provide guidelines for live streaming services so homebound friends can attend virtually, ensuring continuity of community. Memorial cards feature photos alongside a short verse and contact details for bereavement support groups. When the illness spanned years, services often include a "Timeline of Grace" display, charting significant medical and spiritual markers of hope. Clergy training workshops cover pastoral sensitivity in confronting anticipatory grief, teaching how to offer memorial planning as therapeutic, not morbid. These templates balance theological depth—affirming the resurrection body—with practical details like pallbearer coordination and eulogy preparation. As families use these resources, they discover that crafting a memorial becomes an act of worship, weaving together loss, gratitude, and eternal hope.

6.8 Epilogue — Wholeness in Fractured Flesh

Chapter 6 has mapped the landscape of physical ailments—infectious, degenerative, autoimmune, genetic, acute, chronic, operable, and palliative—revealing the intricate interplay of medical science and faith. Patients learn to steward options with informed hope, balancing medical possibilities and spiritual resources in shared decision-making. Clinicians witness the power of embodied practices—anointing, communion, breath prayer, and movement—in enhancing therapeutic outcomes and patient resilience. Pastors discover how liturgies and visitation guides equip them to serve across diagnoses, marrying tradition with hospital realities. Congregations recognize their call to inclusive care—meal trains, accessibility audits, digital outreach, and memorial celebrations—ensuring no body is overlooked. Ethical frameworks guard against exploitation in complementary therapies and safeguard autonomy in complex prognoses. Eschatological vision sustains hope through resurrection promises, while lament and gratitude cultivate resilience in the already–not yet tension. Integrative partnerships between healthcare teams and faith communities model holistic care and testament to God's multifaceted healing. These insights converge to form a robust theology of sickness and care that honors the Imago Dei in every broken frame, preparing the church for the next frontier of mental and emotional health.

Conclusion Our exploration has shown that no diagnosis is outside the ambit of God's redemptive purpose. Whether confronting a sudden crisis or a persistent ailment, believers learn to steward medical resources wisely, bear one another's burdens compassionately, and practice rituals that unite body and soul under divine care. The promise of a resurrection body sustains us when treatments fall short, while lament and gratitude shape communities of resilience. As hospitals and sanctuaries become intertwined fields of healing, the church emerges as a network of hope for every form of sickness. Moving forward, we turn our attention in Chapter 7 to the hidden struggles of the mind—depression, anxiety, and psychosis—bringing the same holistic lens to mental and emotional health.

Chapter 7 – Mental and Emotional Disorders: Depression, Anxiety, Psychosis

Every church pew hides untold stories of panic at midnight, grey mornings that never seem to lift, and voices no one else can hear. Unlike a broken bone or a fevered forehead, the fractures of the mind often remain invisible, leaving sufferers unsure whether their pain is allowed a place in the sanctuary. In this chapter we walk beside prophets who feared for their lives, psalmists who argued with their own souls, and the Man of Sorrows who sweated blood in a garden. Their experiences become windows through which modern diagnoses—depression, crippling anxiety, bewildering psychosis—come into clearer focus. Drawing on both clinical research and the wisdom of prayerful communities, we will explore how medication, therapy, spiritual direction, and congregational practices converge to restore dignity and hope. Above all, we will ask what it means for the people of God to guard minds and hearts in a world where neural circuitry and spiritual warfare often collide.

7.0 Prelude — Sound Mind, Fragile Heart

7.0.1 Created for Shalom: The Imago Dei and Human Cognition (Gen 1:27; 2 Tim 1:7)

God formed humankind in His image, endowing us with capacities for memory, imagination, affection, and reasoning that mirror, in creaturely ways, His own wisdom and creativity. From the first breath, therefore, the human mind was designed for shalom—an integrated harmony in which thoughts, emotions, and bodily processes work together under God's benevolent rule. Scripture later affirms that believers are given "a spirit ... of power, love, and self-discipline" (2 Tim 1:7), implying that mental steadiness is part of the Spirit's sanctifying work. Neuroscience offers complementary insight, mapping neural networks that connect prefrontal logic with limbic emotion, revealing physiological pathways for the biblical union of head and heart. Yet this creational wholeness never suggests rigid perfection; it celebrates neuro-diversity, inviting every temperament and learning style to participate in divine fellowship. Christian educators draw on this doctrine to craft curricula that honor visual, auditory, and kinesthetic learners, echoing Paul's assertion that the body has many parts yet one purpose. Pastoral counselors cite the Imago Dei when clients with mood disorders feel worthless, reminding them that divine dignity remains intact even when neurotransmitters misfire. Worship planners incorporate multisensory liturgies—music, silence, art installations—to engage varied cognitive styles, reflecting the manifold wisdom of God. Understanding the mind as an image-bearing faculty fuels advocacy for accessible mental-health services, treating therapy as stewardship of a holy gift rather than a secular concession. At the same time, this high view of human cognition does not ignore vulnerability; it provides the standard against which brokenness is measured and healing is pursued. Missional communities thus see psychiatric research, psychopharmacology, and trauma-informed care as extensions of God's creative intention to nurture flourishing minds. The truth that we are crafted for shalom becomes a theological compass directing every subsequent page of this chapter. Having glimpsed the mind's creational glory, we must now acknowledge the fractures introduced by sin and trauma that make psychiatric suffering tragically common.

7.0.2 Neurobiology, Trauma, and the Fall: Why Brains Break

When rebellion entered Eden, the whole creation groaned, and that groaning echoes in neural tissue and hormonal cascades (Rom 8:22). Trauma studies demonstrate that chronic stress alters the hippocampus, shrinking memory centers while heightening fear circuits—a physiological drama that mirrors Cain's post-Edenic restlessness. Environmental toxins, inherited epigenetic tags, viral assaults, and nutritional deficits add further layers of vulnerability, confirming that the curse touches synapse and soma alike. War-zone footage and refugee testimonies reveal how sustained terror etches nightmares into gray matter, producing flashbacks Isaiah might describe as the "shadow of death" (Isa 9:2). Scientists detect genetic polymorphisms—such as COMT or SLC6A4 variants—that predispose carriers to depression or impulsivity, echoing ancestral iniquities visited on children (Ex 34:7) yet now interpreted through molecular code rather than deterministic fate. Social inequities—racism, poverty, housing instability—act as chronic stressors, flooding bodies with cortisol that slowly corrodes emotional resilience; prophets like Amos would decry such injustice as structural sin harming both soul and circuitry. Pastoral theologians synthesize these findings, teaching that mental disorders are not merely personal failures but complex intersections of biology, environment, and spiritual warfare. Seminaries incorporate basic neurobiology into pastoral-care syllabi so that future ministers can interpret panic attacks as amygdala hijacks rather than demonic possession—yet without denying that spiritual oppression may exploit neural fragility. Trauma-informed hermeneutics re-read lament psalms as ancient exposure therapy, where repeated naming of terror gradually rewires cognitive appraisal toward hope. Recognizing fall-impacted neurobiology reframes prayer for healing: intercessors petition for neurogenesis, synaptic plasticity, and hormonal recalibration, confident that the Creator still knits brains in hidden places. This theological-scientific synthesis prepares the church to empathize deeply with sufferers, rejecting both naïve optimism and fatalistic despair. With the stage set—minds created for wholeness yet vulnerable to fracture—we now turn to Scripture's own case studies of despair and anxiety, gleaning wisdom for today's clinical realities.

7.1 Scriptural Windows into Inner Turmoil

7.1.1 Elijah's Burnout and Divine Intervention (1 Kgs 19)

Fresh from a prophetic triumph on Carmel, Elijah plummets into exhaustion, proving that spiritual victories do not inoculate against mental collapse. Jezebel's death threat becomes the final straw, triggering a flight response that carries him into wilderness isolation where he prays, "I have had enough, Lord; take my life" (1 Kgs 19:4). Clinical readers note classic signs of major depressive episode: suicidal ideation, fatigue, social withdrawal, and distorted perception of reality—Elijah believes he is utterly alone though God has preserved seven thousand faithful. God answers not with rebuke but with integrated care: an angel provides food and water, addressing somatic depletion before prescribing spiritual encounter. This holistic protocol anticipates modern treatment plans combining medication, nutrition, rest, and psychotherapy. The forty-day journey to Horeb parallels cognitive-behavioral exposure, slowly re-introducing the prophet to purposeful movement and narrative reframing. In the cave's silence, the gentle whisper counters Elijah's catastrophizing thoughts, demonstrating divine therapy that corrects cognitive distortions without crushing fragile faith. Pastors draw on this narrative when counseling ministry leaders, teaching that burnout's antidote includes sabbath rhythms and honest lament rather than heroic denial. Small-group curricula encourage participants to identify personal "broom-trees" where fatigue tempts despair, then practice self-compassion modelled by God's angelic hospitality. Elijah's restoration culminates in renewed vocational assignment—anointing kings and mentoring Elisha—proof that depression need not disqualify one from ongoing service. This story thus supplies both clinical parallels and pastoral hope, leading naturally to the psalmist's inner dialogue as another scriptural MRI of distressed cognition.

7.1.2 Psalmist's Dialogue with Despair (Ps 42–43)

The twin psalms open with a deer panting for streams, a visceral metaphor for psychic thirst when divine presence feels absent. Refrains of "Why, my soul, are you downcast?" reveal intrapersonal conversation akin to modern self-talk interventions. Neuroimaging studies show that naming emotions calms the limbic system; the psalmist intuitively practices this centuries before fMRI machines. He remembers past worship processions, leveraging positive memory to counter current gloom—techniques comparable to behavioral activation in cognitive therapy. Yet hope is not forced; tears "have been my food day and night," validating somatic manifestations of sorrow such as appetite changes. He interrogates God—"Where is your God?"—exposing spiritual doubts often hidden beneath polite piety, which therapists today encourage clients to voice rather than suppress. The psalmist alternates between complaint and declaration of trust—"I will yet praise him"—modeling dialectical tension rather than simplistic resolution. Worship leaders incorporate this oscillation into lament services, allowing congregations to move from minor-key laments to modulated hopeful refrains. Mental-health ministries teach members to craft personal refrains—brief hope statements repeated amid depressive rumination, echoing the psalmist's pattern. These ancient lyrics thus function as timeless cognitive-emotive regulation scripts, linking liturgy with neuroscience. Their unresolved ending leaves space for ongoing struggle, preparing us to meet Job's prolonged anguish.

7.1.3 Job's Long Dark Night and Honest Lament (Job 3; 23)

Job sits amid ashes, scraping sores, embodying psychosomatic distress where bodily pain and existential torment intertwine. Chapter 3 unleashes raw curses on the day of his birth, a linguistic counterpart to suicidal ideation that shocks polite readers yet legitimates extreme grief in faith discourse. Friends arrive with seven days of silent presence—an early form of trauma-informed support—before their moralizing speeches derail care, illustrating how theological platitudes can retraumatize sufferers. Job's repeated wish to present his case before God (Job 23) mirrors a client's yearning for validation from an ultimate authority. His perception that God is both absent and inexorable captures ambivalent attachment feelings common in depressive disorders. When God finally answers from the whirlwind, he neither explains causation nor shames Job's questions, but reorients perspective to cosmic wonder, triggering a paradigm shift akin to existential therapy. Job's eventual restoration includes communal reconciliation and renewed productivity, demonstrating post-traumatic growth without erasing scars. Pastoral caregivers teach volunteers to emulate the friends' initial silence but avoid their subsequent blame-shifting, using Job as a cautionary tale for support-group etiquette. In clinical settings, patients draw comfort from knowing that Scripture contains their darkest thoughts unredacted, legitimizing honest disclosure in therapy. Job's narrative thus validates prolonged depressive processing, preparing us for the ultimate Man of Sorrows who carries distress into redemptive mission.

7.1.4 Jesus in Gethsemane: The Man of Sorrows (Mt 26:36–46)

On the eve of crucifixion, Jesus confesses, "My soul is overwhelmed with sorrow to the point of death," language resonant with severe depressive anguish. He invites Peter, James, and John to keep watch—demonstrating healthy vulnerability and need for companionship during emotional crisis. Sweating "like drops of blood" underlines the psychosomatic unity of emotional stress and physical response, possibly hematidrosis triggered by acute anxiety. Jesus repeats His prayer three times, modeling persistence amid unanswered petitions and echoing therapeutic practice of exposure through repeated articulation of distress. His resolution—"Yet not as I will, but as you will"—embodies acceptance and commitment, aligning personal suffering with overarching mission without denying pain. The disciples' drowsiness depicts secondary trauma fatigue, warning caregivers to cultivate vigilance lest they fail those in crisis. Liturgies for Holy Week reenact Gethsemane vigils, allowing worshipers to bring their own anxieties into Jesus's suffering, fostering solidarity that transcends time. Trauma theologians assert that because Christ underwent existential dread, no panic attack or hallucination remains outside His empathic reach (Heb 4:15). Prayer manuals guide believers to adapt Gethsemane's structure: candid emotion, persistent request, surrender to God's will. The garden narrative completes Scripture's multifaceted portrayal of mental anguish, transitioning us into contemporary diagnostic categories that seek to name similar patterns in clinical language.

7.2 Clinical Taxonomy and Symptomatology

7.2.1 Major Depressive Disorder and Bipolar Spectrum

Major depressive disorder (MDD) presents with persistent sadness, anhedonia, cognitive slowing, guilt, and somatic disturbances lasting at least two weeks, distinguishing it from transient grief. Neurotransmitter hypotheses focus on serotonin, norepinephrine, and dopamine deficits, while imaging shows reduced dorsolateral prefrontal cortex activity. Bipolar spectrum disorders introduce manic or hypomanic episodes marked by elevated mood, decreased need for sleep, racing thoughts, and risky behavior; oscillation between poles reflects rhythmic dysregulation of circadian genes. Ecclesial response includes psychoeducation seminars debunking myths that depression is merely "spiritual weakness," integrating pharmacology with prayer for biochemical balance. Small groups adopt mood-tracking apps, encouraging members to share highs and lows, preventing isolation during manic ascents or depressive depths. Liturgical calendars incorporate "Blue Christmas" services for seasonal affective populations, acknowledging winter's effect on circadian rhythm and vitamin D synthesis. Churches with counseling centers maintain referral lists for psychiatrists skilled in mood-disorder management, recognizing lithium monitoring and SSRI titration as part of God's provision. Testimonies of leaders on mood-stabilizers reduce stigma, showing that spiritual fruit can flourish alongside medication. Sermons highlight Elijah and David to illustrate how divine purpose persists through mood swings, anchoring identity in God rather than affect state. As congregations learn these patterns, they can better discern when symptoms escalate into psychotic features requiring specialized care.

7.2.2 Generalized Anxiety, Panic, and OCD

Generalized anxiety disorder manifests as chronic, uncontrollable worry across multiple domains, accompanied by muscle tension, irritability, and sleep disruption. Panic disorder features sudden surges of terror, heart palpitations, and fear of death, often leading to ER visits for presumed cardiac events. Obsessive-compulsive disorder spans intrusive thoughts (obsessions) and repetitive behaviors (compulsions) aimed at anxiety relief—hand-washing, counting, checking—driven by malfunction in fronto-striatal circuits. Psalm 94:19—"When anxiety was great within me, your consolation brought me joy"—becomes a memory verse for CBT groups integrating Scripture with cognitive restructuring. Breathing techniques taught in yoga are reframed as "breath prayers," inhaling divine names and exhaling petitions, slowing sympathetic arousal. Exposure-response prevention (ERP) therapy, the gold standard for OCD, finds biblical echoes in gradual trust exercises—Peter stepping onto water despite intrusive fears. Pastors caution against spiritualizing compulsions as demonic oppression alone, instead collaborating with clinicians for SSRIs and ERP while offering deliverance prayer if warranted. Anxiety-awareness Sundays include testimonies of panic-attack survivors who found both medical and spiritual tools transformative. Church architecture introduces quiet zones with low lighting to aid worshipers prone to overstimulation. As communities master anxiety-disorder care, they ready themselves to address more severe disruptions, such as psychosis.

7.2.3 Psychotic Disorders: Schizophrenia, Schizoaffective, and Brief Episodes

Psychotic disorders are characterized by hallucinations, delusions, disorganized speech, and impaired reality testing, rooted in dopaminergic dysregulation and, in some cases, neurodevelopmental anomalies. Schizophrenia involves a six-month course, whereas brief psychotic disorder may resolve within a month, and schizoaffective disorder blends mood episodes with psychosis. Scriptural narratives of demoniacs prompt discernment: some first-century presentations may mirror modern psychosis, but clinicians must avoid blanket spiritual attributions that delay antipsychotic treatment. Clozapine or long-acting injectables achieve symptom remission, functioning as pharmacological "peace be still" interventions. Churches create "compassion teams" trained to respond calmly to communicative incoherence, reducing stigma and preventing police escalation. Bible-study materials adapt content to concrete language, avoiding metaphors that could amplify delusional content. Pastoral care includes reality-orientation prayers—thanking God for tangible objects in the room—to ground disoriented members. Faith-based housing programs offer structured routines, medication supervision, and spiritual mentorship, demonstrating holistic rehabilitation. Liturgical art therapy helps patients externalize auditory-hallucination content, transforming chaotic voices into visual lament that can be prayed over and re-narrated. Through collaboration with psychiatrists, congregations witness that psychosis need not eradicate spiritual identity; indeed, many believers with schizophrenia testify to rich prayer lives once symptoms are stabilized. Recognizing complexity prepares disciples to engage co-morbidities and trauma-related overlays.

7.2.4 Co-morbidities, Substance Use, and Trauma-Related Conditions

Depression commonly co-occurs with chronic pain and cardiovascular disease, creating feedback loops where physical symptoms exacerbate emotional distress. Substance use often masquerades as self-medication: alcohol for social anxiety, opioids for traumatic flashbacks, stimulants for ADHD impulses. Churches host Celebrate Recovery groups, integrating the eight beatitudes with twelve-step principles, offering an explicitly Christian path to sobriety. Trauma-related conditions such as complex PTSD present with hypervigilance, dissociation, and emotional numbing—symptoms that complicate mood- and anxiety- disorder treatment plans. EMDR (eye-movement desensitization and reprocessing) paired with inner-healing prayer leverages bilateral stimulation and spiritual memory reconsolidation. Ministries provide "sobriety chips" featuring Isaiah 43:1—"I have called you by name"—reinforcing identity beyond addiction. Clinical chaplains receive training in motivational interviewing, aligning spiritual values with readiness for change. Congregations partner with local shelters to create trauma-informed worship services—simple liturgy, predictable order, and sensory-friendly spaces—healing worship patterns for survivors. Multi-disciplinary case reviews examine therapeutic, pharmacologic, and pastoral interventions together, reducing fragmentation of care. By grasping co-morbidities, churches refine their role, ensuring each sufferer receives integrated support that honors the interplay of body, mind, and spirit. These diagnostic frameworks set the stage for the next sections on integrative care teams and congregational practices that embody hope amid mental-health challenges.

7.3 Integrating Psychiatry and Pastoral Care

7.3.1 Evidence-Based Therapies and Pharmacology: SSRIs, CBT, EMDR

Selective-serotonin-reuptake inhibitors help replenish depleted neurotransmitter pools, giving patients enough emotional bandwidth to benefit from spiritual disciplines that once felt unreachable. When pastors explain an SSRI as a "manna for the mind," congregants often release misplaced guilt that taking medicine signals weak faith. Cognitive-behavioral therapy rewires thought patterns by challenging distorted beliefs; counselors illustrate Romans 12:2, where transformation follows the renewing of the mind, as an ancient endorsement of cognitive restructuring. During homework assignments, Christian clients lace thought records with Scripture, replacing catastrophizing with promises such as Jeremiah 29:11. Exposure therapy for phobias echoes Jesus's progressive invitations—Peter steps onto the water, then walks toward the waves—teaching graded courage rather than instant heroism. Eye-movement desensitization and reprocessing stimulates bilateral brain activity while clients recall trauma; when therapists integrate gentle prayer, painful memories re-encode alongside a felt sense of Christ's presence. Pastors prepare parishioners for this process by drawing parallels to Joseph's testimony—what was meant for evil God can reframe for good (Gen 50:20). The synergy of pharmacology and therapy testifies that grace arrives through multiple channels: pills, dialogue, and Spirit. Church-run mental-health clinics display posters proclaiming "Every good and perfect gift" (Jas 1:17) above medication dispensaries, cementing doctrinal legitimacy. Consistently sharing success stories of believers who thrive on combined treatment dismantles lingering suspicion that psychology is secular intrusion.

7.3.2 Spiritual Direction, Inner-Healing Prayer, and Confession

Spiritual directors invite sufferers to narrate their journey with God, holding space for silence where the Spirit surfaces root wounds that clinical protocols might overlook. Directed prayer often focuses on imaginative meditation: clients picture Jesus entering a traumatic scene and speak aloud the comfort they sense, a technique that tempers hyperarousal by engaging right-brain imagery. Confession breaks shame loops; when penitents describe intrusive thoughts that torment their conscience, hearing a priest or pastor declare absolution externalizes forgiveness and calms obsessive rumination (1 Jn 1:9). Inner-healing sessions sometimes pair with fasting, aligning body and soul in focused expectancy, and follow with Eucharist to seal restored communion. Trained teams ensure that prayer encounters do not bypass professional therapy; rather, they schedule follow-up CBT sessions to cement cognitive gains. Leaders discourage seeking "one-and-done" deliverance for conditions rooted in complex trauma, noting Paul's journey of incremental renewal. Group confession services, based on Nehemiah 9's public repentance, allow members to voice struggles with depression's anger or anxiety's controlling grip, then receive collective intercession. Over months, journals record how sacramental rhythms lower symptom severity, reinforcing that repentance and healing share common soil.

7.3.3 Multidisciplinary Care Teams: Roles, Boundaries, Referrals

Weekly case conferences gather psychiatrists, psychologists, social workers, chaplains, and peer mentors around a single table, each sharing five-minute updates so the patient's story remains coherent. Clear boundaries prevent role confusion: medication adjustments stay under medical license, whereas chaplains focus on meaning-making and hope cultivation. Memoranda of understanding outline referral triggers—active psychosis, medication non-adherence, or suicidal rumination—so pastors know when to escalate care without hesitation. Teams develop shared language; for instance, a pastor learns to say "negative symptoms" instead of "lack of motivation," while clinicians adopt "dark night of the soul" to respect existential distress. Electronic records include a "spiritual care tab," charting prayer visits and scripture resources patients find comforting. Joint trainings on cultural humility help all disciplines avoid imposing worldview assumptions that could alienate clients from diverse backgrounds. Monthly debriefs allow staff to process secondary trauma; prayer circles often conclude these meetings, acknowledging that caregivers too need psychological first aid. Research audits reveal that integrated teams reduce hospitalization days and improve medication adherence, giving empirical weight to the theological claim that the body of Christ thrives in mutual interdependence (1 Cor 12). Churches publicize these data to encourage donor support for interdisciplinary clinics.

7.3.4 Breaking Stigma and Theological Misconceptions within the Church

Sermons dismantle myths by quoting saints who battled melancholy—Martin Luther, Charles Spurgeon, Mother Teresa—reminding hearers that spiritual giants carried clinical burdens yet bore abundant fruit. Bible studies confront misinterpreted texts—such as "be anxious for nothing" (Phil 4:6)—clarifying that Paul exhorts toward prayerful management, not stoic suppression. Youth groups stage dramas where characters visit both a counselor and a pastor, visually normalizing dual support. Annual "Mental Health Sunday" worship services replace bulletins with brochures listing local crisis lines and therapy scholarships. Testimonies spotlight elders who struggled with panic disorder, thereby modeling transparency and shrinking gossip culture. Small-group guidelines ban phrases like "just pray harder," substituting empathetic reflections drawn from Job's listening friends. Pastor search committees now include a question on mental-health theology, ensuring leadership can navigate neurodiversity with grace. Reading lists pair devotional classics with current DSM-5 explanations, forging intellectual bridges. When stigma wanes, sufferers step forward sooner, enabling early intervention that averts crises. This culture shift lays a fertile foundation for congregational practices that sustain mental-health flourishing.

7.4 Congregational Practices for Mental-Health Flourishing

7.4.1 Small-Group Safe Spaces and Peer Support Models

Mental-health support groups meet mid-week in rooms furnished with comfortable chairs, dimmer switches, and sound-absorbing panels to create sensory safety. Peer facilitators open with grounding exercises: feet planted, eyes closed, inhaling the name "Jesus," exhaling "peace." Sessions alternate between psychoeducation—explaining triggers, sleep hygiene, nutrition—and spiritual reflection on passages like Psalm 34:18. Confidentiality covenants pledge respect, ensuring members can divulge suicidal thoughts without fear of gossip. The group's WhatsApp thread buzzes with Scripture memes and appointment reminders, reinforcing accountability between meetings. When someone celebrates a medication milestone—tapering successfully or finding an effective dose—the circle erupts in applause and prayer. Members craft "wellness WRAP plans," listing early warning signs and agreed responses, then share them with spouses or roommates. Quarterly potlucks incorporate mood-boosting foods—omega-3-rich fish, complex-carb grains—turning fellowship halls into informal nutrition clinics. Churches report decreased ER visits and improved Sunday attendance as participants feel truly seen. These micro-communities mimic Acts 2's fellowship and naturally feed into church-wide volunteer trainings.

7.4.2 Mental-Health First-Aid Training for Volunteers

Adapted from public-health curricula, eight-hour workshops teach ushers, youth leaders, and greeters to recognize panic attacks, psychotic breaks, and trauma flashbacks. Role-play scenarios rehearse calm verbal de-escalation: speak softly, offer water, avoid sudden touch. Trainers integrate Proverbs 18:13's counsel to listen before speaking, underscoring that haste harms. Volunteers learn the ALGEE acronym—assess risk, listen nonjudgmentally, give reassurance, encourage professional help, and encourage self-help—then practice on each other until responses become muscle memory. Certification badges reassure congregants that someone present knows crisis protocols. Churches maintain "quiet rooms" stocked with weighted blankets and fidget tools where distressed attendees can regulate emotions during services. Mental-health first-aiders liaise with security teams to ensure that police involvement remains last resort, reducing traumatic outcomes. Annual refresher courses update volunteers on new medications and community resources. Post-incident debriefs help responders process adrenaline spikes and prevent compassion fatigue. Equipped volunteers bolster the church's credibility as a safe haven for the emotionally wounded.

7.4.3 Liturgies of Lament, Hope, and Blessing for the Suffering

Quarterly evening services dim sanctuary lights and project images of cracked clay jars while musicians play minor-key psalms. Congregants write private laments on rice paper dissolved in baptismal water as a symbol of releasing burdens to God. Mid-service, a choir shifts into hopeful refrains, echoing the psalmist's "I will yet praise Him," guiding worshipers from sorrow to assurance. Pastors lead a communal prayer acknowledging chemical imbalances, traumatic memories, and genetic vulnerabilities, normalizing these as aspects of fallen creation, not spiritual failure. The blessing segment features anointing with frankincense oil—the fragrance historically linked to prayer—imparting sensory memory of divine nearness. Families facing a loved one's psychosis receive personalized benedictions referencing Isaiah 41:13—God's promise to hold their right hand. Liturgical artists hang ribbons labeled with congregants' favorite coping scriptures, forming a tapestry that remains visible for weeks, extending the service's impact. Feedback surveys reveal attendees experience decreased shame and increased willingness to seek therapy. Newly baptized members testify that such liturgies convinced them Christianity engages real pain rather than glossing it over. These worship patterns, grounded in honesty and hope, complement digital outreach channels.

7.4.4 Digital Outreach: Tele-pastoral Counseling and Online Support Forums

Church websites feature booking portals for encrypted video sessions, allowing homebound individuals to receive pastoral care without geographic barriers. Moderated Discord servers host daily check-ins where members share mood emojis and scripture verses, building rhythm and rapport. Virtual support groups meet across time zones; facilitators display slide decks on grounding techniques and invite breakout prayer rooms. Instagram stories highlight "Therapy Thursday" tips—breathing methods, Sabbath challenges—paired with short devotional reels. Tele-pastoral counselors collaborate with licensed therapists, swapping referral codes and ensuring continuity of care. Crisis-response bots programmed with gospel-saturated affirmations direct users to 988 hotlines when keywords like "hopeless" appear. Analytics dashboards show spikes in page visits after Sunday sermons on anxiety, confirming that digital platforms extend message reach. Online confession forms, reviewed by pastors, provide anonymous avenues for disclosing intrusive thoughts, leading to follow-up care. Hybrid conferences broadcast mental-health seminars, enabling rural congregations to train without expensive travel. By weaving digital threads through physical ministry, churches create a 24/7 safety net that pre-empts crises and sustains long-term discipleship. This continuum of care sets the stage for focused suicide-prevention strategies.

7.5 Suicide Prevention and Theological Hope

7.5.1 Sanctity-of-Life Foundations and Compassionate Theology

Genesis 1 declares human life "very good," grounding intrinsic worth that suicidal despair obscures but cannot erase. The command "You shall not murder" extends to self-harm, yet compassion recognizes that suicidal ideation often arises from distorted neurochemistry rather than willful rebellion. Jesus's parable of the lost sheep reveals a shepherd who leaves ninety-nine to rescue one endangered life, legitimizing vigorous pursuit of those at risk. The church teaches that nothing, including suicidal thoughts, can separate believers from God's love (Rom 8:38-39), countering fatalistic theology. When historical theologians like Augustine labeled suicide a grave sin, they lacked neurobiological knowledge; modern scholars nuance this stance, emphasizing intent, capacity, and mental illness. Preachers carefully differentiate moral teaching from condemnation, ensuring sermons do not pile guilt on fragile listeners. Sanctity-of-life catechesis includes mental-health modules, educating teenagers that their worth transcends grades, social media likes, or sexual orientation struggles. Annual sanctity-of-life services feature testimonies of survivors who found renewed purpose, illustrating redemption beyond the brink. This theological bedrock fortifies practical prevention measures.

7.5.2 Recognizing Warning Signs, QPR, and Crisis Hotlines

Training seminars teach congregants to observe statements of hopelessness, farewell behaviors, or fascination with lethal means. Role-playing exercises rehearse direct questions: "Are you thinking about hurting yourself?" Normalizing these conversations reflects Proverbs 18:21, which warns of life and death in the tongue, urging truthful speech. QPR—Question, Persuade, Refer—framework guides helpers to ask, persuade toward help, and accompany the person to professional services. Churches partner with local crisis centers, printing hotline numbers on bulletins and bathroom mirrors. Youth leaders place QR-coded stickers on lockers that link to chat lines. College ministries create "safety contracts"—lists of emergency contacts and coping strategies students sign after orientation retreats. During fasting seasons, prayer chains include hourly intercession for those contemplating self-harm. Data dashboards monitor pastoral-care logs, flagging individuals with repeated ideation for intensified follow-up. Congregants learn that locking away firearms and securing medications are spiritual acts of neighbor love. As awareness grows, early interventions multiply, sparing lives and demonstrating gospel urgency.

7.5.3 Post-Attempt Pastoral Protocols and Family Care

After an attempt, pastors visit ER rooms, first ensuring physical stabilization, then offering non-judgmental presence reminiscent of Jesus sitting with the Samaritan woman before addressing theology. They coordinate debrief meetings within seventy-two hours, involving mental-health professionals to craft safety plans. Family members receive separate counseling, acknowledging complex emotions of relief, anger, and guilt. Meals ministry delivers nutrition during the fragile transition from hospital to home, recognizing that proper diet influences neurotransmitter balance. House churches rotate night-watch calls, checking in hourly the first critical evening. Worship communities bless the survivor publicly when they feel ready, framing their continued life as testimony of divine mercy. Bible passages selected focus on restoration—Peter rehabilitated after denial, not on Judas's despair—steering narrative toward hope. When required, pastors help families petition for inpatient treatment or medication-assisted care, preventing spiritual bypass that would skip clinical needs. Anniversary dates of the attempt are noted in pastoral calendars for proactive support the following year. Through structured protocols, churches model that resurrection power enters even ER bays.

7.5.4 Funeral Liturgy, Mercy, and the Question of Eternal Destiny

If a suicide results in death, funeral liturgies balance lament's honesty with proclamations of God's steadfast love. Eulogies avoid attributing motives, instead testifying to the person's gifts, struggles, and the mysteries known fully only by God. Pastors cite Romans 8 again, reassuring mourners that neither death nor life can pry believers from Christ's grasp, countering fear of automatic damnation. The liturgy may include Psalm 139:12—"darkness is as light to you"—affirming God's presence even in the deceased's final moments. Candle-lighting rituals invite attendees to confess their own hidden pain, transforming grief into communal vulnerability. Support groups for survivors of suicide loss convene in the church hall six weeks later, offering ongoing care. Sermons following the funeral teach lament theology, helping congregations process corporate sorrow. Gravestone services incorporate soil from the church garden, symbolizing communal commitment to ongoing remembrance. Pastoral letters to the family on the one-year mark reinforce that the community has not forgotten. This merciful approach anchors hope while motivating continued suicide-prevention efforts throughout the body of Christ, thus looping back to earlier training and stigma-breaking work.

7.6 Formation and Discipleship in the Dark Seasons

7.6.1 Rule of Life for Emotional Resilience: Sleep, Exercise, Silence

When Elijah collapsed beneath the broom tree, God's first prescription was sleep and nourishment, a divine nod to the physiology of recovery. Modern psychiatry affirms that stable circadian rhythms modulate serotonin and cortisol, chemicals deeply implicated in mood regulation. A congregational "rule of life" therefore begins with bedtime liturgies that dim screens, read a short psalm, and entrust unfinished tasks to God, echoing the psalmist's confession that "He grants sleep to those he loves" (Ps 127 : 2). Morning routines include stretching or brisk walking, invoking Paul's exhortation to present bodies as living sacrifices (Rom 12 : 1) while stimulating endorphins that ease anxiety. Quarterly church retreats teach silent reflection practices drawn from Jesus' pattern of early solitude, giving overtaxed amygdalas space to downshift. Fitness ministries organize low-impact group hikes for depression sufferers who fear gym crowds, merging movement with gentle fellowship. Families adopt "screen-Sabbaths," one evening a week without media, allowing prefrontal cortex rest from dopamine-driven overload. Parents model mindful breathing with children at bedtime, embedding resilience before adolescence strikes. By treating sleep, exercise, and silence not as optional wellness hacks but as spiritual disciplines, the church reframes self-care as stewardship of God's image. Members track progress in small groups, celebrating when insomnia recedes or energy returns, thereby reinforcing the communal dimension of personal rules.

7.6.2 Scripture Meditation, Breath Prayer, and Mindfulness under Christ

Where anxiety loops spin tales of doom, slow meditation interrupts the narrative with a truer story. Participants in lectio divina linger over three verses of Isaiah 43, noticing which word stirs comfort, then inhale that word and exhale a whispered petition. This fusion of contemplative reading and diaphragmatic breathing steadies heart rate while planting truth deep in procedural memory. Counselors teach panic-prone teens to pair breath prayer with grounding—naming five textures or colors in the room—thus linking sensory awareness to theological reality that Emmanuel is present. Christian mindfulness differs from secular variants by anchoring attention not in empty awareness but in the risen Christ who "holds all things together" (Col 1 : 17). Audio apps created by spiritual-formation teams guide users through ten-minute sessions featuring ambient instrumental hymns and scripted prayers of relinquishment. Veterans with PTSD testify that nightly use reduces startle responses and nightmares, echoing David's claim, "In peace I will lie down and sleep" (Ps 4 : 8). Churches offer lunchtime meditation rooms—dim lights, art depicting the Good Shepherd—open to office workers who battle midday worry spikes. Over months, neural plasticity strengthens executive circuits, giving believers freedom to redirect ruminations toward gratitude rather than fear. This practice prepares hearts for outward-facing service.

7.6.3 Community Service as Therapeutic Vocation

Behavioral-activation research shows that meaningful activity counters depressive inertia, and Christ's call to serve the least transforms that insight into missional therapy. Volunteers recovering from social-anxiety disorder begin with backstage roles—prepping food-pantry bags—and graduate to greeting clients, each step widening tolerance for social cues. A widower's grief group sponsors monthly visits to a children's cancer ward, discovering that shared sorrow fuels compassion rather than despair. James 2 reminds disciples that faith without deeds is dead; here, deeds resurrect dormant purpose inside wounded minds. Occupational therapists consult with missions committees to match abilities with tasks: arthritis patients stuff envelopes; PTSD survivors plant community gardens where soil contact lowers blood pressure. Serving abroad becomes an advanced module—teams include mental-health professionals who monitor jet-lag stress and culture shock—demonstrating that global mission and psychological safety can coexist. Participants journal reflections, capturing how giving away time and skills recalibrates identity from patient to minister. Congregations then platform these stories in worship, shifting stigma narratives to ones of empowered contribution.

7.6.4 Sacramental Participation: Eucharist, Anointing, and Healing Rooms

Weekly communion offers a sensory anchor: the crunch of bread, the tang of juice, the touch of another's hand as the elements are passed—all reinforcing incarnational theology that God meets us in material reality. Worship leaders intentionally slow distribution, letting anxious minds sync with the rhythmic liturgy, while the celebrant declares, "For as often as you eat this bread... you proclaim the Lord's death" (1 Cor 11 : 26), reminding sufferers that salvation history encompasses their present pain. Healing rooms open one evening a month, staffed by teams blending licensed counselors and intercessors who offer brief anointing followed by quiet listening prayer. Participants receive printed blessing cards featuring Numbers 6 : 24–26 to revisit when intrusive thoughts strike at 3 a.m. Sacramental oils are infused with frankincense for its calming aroma, questioned and cleared by allergists to ensure safety. Testimonies record reductions in migraine frequency after anointing, prompting neurologists to partner in studying psychosomatic correlations. The sacramental life of the church thus becomes an embodied catechesis in hope, bridging neuroscience and mysticism.

7.7 Eschatological Assurance and Present Endurance

7.7.1 Groaning Creation and the Redemption of the Mind (Rom 8 : 22–25)

Paul writes that creation groans as in childbirth, a visceral metaphor embraced by chronic depressives who feel contractions of despair signaling something new yet unseen. He couples that groan with hope anchored in unseen reality, modeling cognitive reappraisal: the mind reframes present agony as precursor to glory. Therapists help clients memorize this passage, cueing them to recite it during panic surges, shifting focus from catastrophic endpoints to redemptive trajectory. Prayer meetings integrate communal groans—wordless sighs set to cello drones—symbolizing Romans 8 : 26 where the Spirit intercedes with groans too deep for words. Neurotheologians posit that such vocal lament activates parasympathetic nerves, embodying hope neurologically. Small-group studies note the apostle's phrase "eager expectation," discussing how anticipation can coexist with anguish without invalidating either. Hospital chapels feature artwork of cracked earth sprouting green shoots, visually capturing Pauline dialectic. As congregants internalize this frame, endurance becomes more than passive waiting; it morphs into active labor toward mental renewal.

7.7.2 New-Jerusalem Imagery for the Neurodivergent (Rev 21 : 4–5)

Revelation's vision of a city whose gates never shut invites believers with autism, ADHD, or schizophrenia to imagine a realm entirely sensory-friendly—no overwhelming alarms, no social exclusion. Artists on the spectrum design stained-glass panels depicting the river of life flowing through bustling streets where every citizen wears noise-dampening crowns. During "Neurodiversity Sunday," pastors preach that God's dwelling among people ensures zero tears triggered by overstimulation, citing "He will wipe every tear" (Rev 21 : 4). Children with special needs craft clay gemstones symbolizing the foundations of that city, integrating tactile learning. Caregivers sigh with relief upon hearing that future bodies and minds will retain unique glories without painful impairments. This eschatological art therapy reframes daily coping strategies—weighted blankets, fidget tools—as provisional foretastes of the perfect environment to come. Scholarships for neurodivergent seminarians emerge, embodying justice now in anticipation of the inclusive city. The imagery gives present endurance a concrete picture, fueling policy advocacy for accessible church architecture and curricula.

7.7.3 Teaching Hope without Minimizing Suffering

A balanced eschatology avoids dismissive clichés like "Just remember heaven" while still lifting eyes beyond present gloom. Preachers practice a two-beat rhythm: first validate pain through narrative examples—Jeremiah's weeping, Hannah's barrenness—then unfold future promise. Homiletics workshops train leaders to spend equal sermon minutes on lament and hope, citing Paul's tension in 2 Corinthians 4 : 8–9. Bible-study materials include reflection questions: "How does this promise comfort you, and where does it leave space for tears?" Pastoral letters to the hospitalized acknowledge chemotherapy fatigue before quoting Revelation. An adult-education course titled "Realistic Hope" contrasts toxic positivity with biblical perseverance, using case studies of martyrs and modern refugees. Musicians compose worship sets that move from minor-key dirges to major-key refrains only after a contemplative pause, letting grief breathe. Congregations learn that shouting "Hallelujah" prematurely can silence sufferers; instead, they cultivate gentle harmonies that accompany slow healing. This pedagogy equips the church to proclaim future glory without erasing present battles, thereby sustaining authentic faith journeys.

7.8 Epilogue — A Church That Guards Minds and Hearts

The chapter has traced a continuum from biblical portraits of despair to modern integrative interventions, revealing that holistic care thrives where theology meets therapy. Pastors discovered that burnout requires angels with bread before sermons of correction, and clinicians witnessed Scripture reinforcing neuroplastic change. Congregations erected safe-space groups, trained mental-health first-aid responders, and embedded lament into worship, shifting corporate culture from stigma to solidarity. Multidisciplinary teams modeled Paul's body metaphor, each role honoring its boundaries while serving a common mission of sustaining sound minds. Rule-of-life practices—sleep, movement, mindfulness—emerged as spiritual disciplines, not self-help fads, supporting neurochemical stability. Sacraments rooted sufferers in tangible grace, while digital platforms extended pastoral presence across time zones. Suicide-prevention frameworks showed that sanctity-of-life doctrine and crisis hotlines reinforce, rather than compete. Eschatological imagination offered vivid pictures of neurodivergent inclusion, safeguarding hope from denial. Together these insights knit a practical theology capable of holding fragile hearts in steadfast hands.

Conclusion Our journey through the valleys of mental affliction has revealed a God who neither shames fragile psyches nor leaves them to fend for themselves. From Elijah's exhaustion to contemporary treatment plans, we have seen that grace arrives through angels with bread, counselors with evidence-based tools, friends who keep vigil, and a Savior who has tasted anguish to the marrow. Congregations that embrace this holistic vision become triage centers of compassion—training first-aid responders, crafting liturgies of honest lament, and offering lasting companionship after emergency rooms grow quiet. While the wounds of the mind may not always close in this life, the promise of a renewed creation sustains our perseverance and shapes our care. Carrying forward these lessons, we turn next to the slow fading of memory in dementia and Alzheimer's, where the church is called to remember on behalf of those who can no longer remember for themselves.

Chapter 8 – Losing One's Self: Amnesia, Dementia, and Identity in Christ

Losing one's grip on memory shatters more than practical routines; it calls into question the very essence of who we are. In the quiet moments when beloved faces no longer register, and cherished stories slip away, families and faith communities face a profound crisis of identity. Yet even as neurons falter, a deeper truth holds: our worth is not defined by recall alone, but by the One who remembers us long before we name Him. In this chapter we accompany those navigating the first jarring diagnosis, explore how neuroscience and theology converge to affirm enduring personhood, and learn caregiving as an act of covenant faithfulness. We'll discover sacramental, liturgical, and architectural practices that keep memory alive, and turn toward eschatological promises that guarantee our stories will be kept safe in God's hands.

8.0 Prelude — When Memories Slip Through Fingers

8.0.1 The Shock of Cognitive Dislocation: A Family's First Diagnosis

When the neurologist gently names the condition—"early-onset Alzheimer's," "vascular dementia," "transient global amnesia"—the room seems to contract as disbelief and fear crowd in. Loved ones struggle to reconcile the bright person they knew with the blank stares and repeated questions that now define evening conversations. A spouse who once relied on shared history for daily humor finds herself tracing the same potholes of conversation, each repetition carving deeper fatigue. Adult children, anticipating inheritance or care decisions, now scramble to secure power-of-attorney documents and review long-term care insurance. The initial diagnostic appointment feels like a descent into a legal and medical labyrinth where every hallway demands new forms to sign and confirmations to provide. Amid clinical tests and brain scans, families often overlook the grief that begins before any funeral—anticipatory mourning for lost recognition and shared laughter. Social media posts of the diagnosis ignite supportive comments but also awkward silences, as community members retract invitations for fear of imposing. Scripture that once offered comfort—"Remember the former things" (Isa 46:9)—now stings as irony. Parents of younger generations, who expected to bury their children, must now bury memories of their own parents. In those early days, prayer often falters under the load of "Why, Lord?" until someone reads aloud God's promise to gather the outcasts of Israel, hinting that divine gathering continues in unexpected ways (Ps 147:2). Pastors learn that first visitation must center on listening rather than lecturing, allowing shock to articulate itself in trembling voices. Clinical chaplains report that when families name the loss—"He doesn't know my name anymore"—the tears flow freely, signaling the beginning of a pastoral journey that will require both deep lament and steadfast presence. Recognizing this initial shock sets the stage for discovering a God who remembers even when we forget.

8.0.2 God Who Remembers: Covenant Faithfulness Amid Forgetfulness (Isa 49:15–16)

Isaiah assures exiles that God's compassion exceeds even a mother's love, promising, "I have engraved you on the palms of my hands" (Isa 49:16), evoking divine memory etched into eternity. For families reeling from memory loss, this image becomes a lifeline: though the afflicted mind falters, God's remembrance never wavers. Liturgies incorporate this text by having congregants trace palm-shaped bookmarks, inscribing names of those they fear will be forgotten in their weakness. Psychologists note that feeling valued and remembered preserves self-worth for dementia patients, reducing agitation when caregivers share family photos and personal anecdotes at feeding times. Churches host "Memorial Palm Workshops" where volunteers create tactile memory aids—embroidered handprints bearing whispered prayers—for residents in memory care units. When a loved one can no longer recall faces, caregivers read aloud letters from family members, affirming identity that transcends cognitive recall. Scriptures like "I will remember your sins no more" (Heb 8:12) become dual assurances: God forgets our guilt even as He never forgets us. Pastoral counselors adapt Romans 8:38–39 into affirmation cards: "Nothing can separate you from my love, even forgetting." Art therapists paint murals of hands reaching toward hearts, symbolizing divine embrace, in sheltered memory wings. Theologically, this covenant faithfulness reframes memory loss not as abandonment but as invitation to trust a God who holds every life in indelible remembrance. From this assurance we turn to explore how memory undergirds personhood created in God's image.

8.1 Memory, Personhood, and the Imago Dei

8.1.1 Neuroscience Meets Theology: Synapses, Scripts, and Spiritual Narrative

Synapses—those tiny gaps across which neurons fire—constitute the physical substrate of memory, excitement, and habit, mirroring how habit shapes spiritual life through repeated disciplines. Neuroscientific research shows that long-term potentiation strengthens synaptic connections through repetition, just as regular prayer etches spiritual truths into the heart's neural circuits. Theologians observe that our personal narratives unfold like neural scripts, where trauma can rewire pathways toward fear, while grace can reroute impulses toward hope. In Alzheimer's care, cognitive rehabilitation uses reminiscence therapy to reactivate dormant scripts—playing familiar hymns or reading beloved Bible stories—to stimulate both memory and mood regulation. Pastors collaborate with speech-language pathologists to integrate Scripture into naming exercises that reinforce identity. Seminary courses introduce neural plasticity alongside doctrines of sanctification, teaching future ministers that faith formation continues even when neurons misfire. Bioethicists debate the moral significance of neuro-enhancement, asking whether implanting memory chips honors the Imago Dei or distorts divine design. Congregations hold forums on "Memory and Meaning," inviting neuroscientists and theologians to dialogue on whether identity flows more from brains or from the soul God implants. Pastoral reflection underscores that although synapses degrade, the Spirit's movings are not confined to synaptic strength. Silence and sacred reading allow the heart's substrates—love, faith, hope—to function even absent crisp recall. This interplay of neuroscience and theology deepens our understanding of memory as both biological and covenantal phenomenon, leading naturally to considerations of a soul that transcends mere recollection.

8.1.2 The Soul Beyond Cognitive Recall: Why Dignity Survives Degeneration

Even as memory fades, the Imago Dei remains indelible, for personhood is not reducible to cognitive faculties alone. Jesus's encounters with the muddled mind—such as the man healed of legion-bound insanity—reveal that intrinsic worth precedes mental performance (Mk 5). Augustine's theology taught that the soul's essence lies in its relation to God, not in flawless memory, a conviction affirmed when worshipers witness dementia patients tapping toes to familiar psalms long after vocabulary fails. Ethical guidelines argue that consent remains valid insofar as persons still bear God's image, requiring caregivers to protect rights despite diminished capacity. Churches install signage stating "Grace Before Memory" at entrances to memory care units, reminding all that dignity is independent of recall. Spiritual directors affirm that prayer remains effective even when uttered in broken phrases, trusting that the Holy Spirit intercedes with groans too deep for words (Rom 8:26). Families craft legacy liturgies where communities speak aloud the life stories of their loved ones, sharing narratives so richly that even if the person cannot remember, their essence echoes in the community's collective memory. The practice of reading aloud baptismal vows to individuals with advanced dementia underscores that sacramental identity is not eroded by cognitive decline. Councils on aging endorse policies that require churches to advocate for equality in medical treatment, ensuring that those with memory loss receive care reflecting their inherent dignity. Pastoral letters tie Philippians 3:8's assertion that nothing compares to knowing Christ into the fabric of identity—memory may erode, but union with Christ remains steadfast. A robust theology of personhood thus safeguards dignity beyond synaptic function, setting the stage for narrative identity practices such as baptisms and naming.

8.1.3 Narrative Identity and Baptismal Naming: "Beloved" Over "Disoriented"

Baptism imprints a new name and narrative onto believers—"in Christ"—that persists even when personal memories falter. Early church records speak of water and oil marking converts permanently, a ritual echo continued when families command their loved ones' zygotes to "grow into the image of the Savior." When dementia progresses, caregivers refocus on this baptismal identity, greeting patients as "child of God" or "beloved sister" instead of "the one with

Alzheimer's." Home signs and bedside plaques display baptismal dates and names, reinforcing relational memory through constant visual cues. Narrative therapy sessions encourage family and friends to craft a "life letter" summarizing key faith milestones—first communion, mission trip, favorite psalm—so that even fragmented recall encounters these truths in concentrated form. Congregations celebrate annual "Remembrance Sunday" services, reading the names of those baptized who now struggle with memory, affirming that Christian identity transcends cerebral continuity. Children's choirs sing "Beloved, Beloved," reinforcing the refrain that identity rests in God's promise, not in recall clarity. These narrative identity practices attend both to soul and community, ensuring that persons are known for more than their cognitive state. As naming restores dignity, faith communities prepare to navigate ethical questions around research and consent for those in memory decline.

8.1.4 Ethical Implications for Research and Consent in Memory Disorders

Clinical trials for Alzheimer's drugs or deep-brain stimulation hinge on informed consent, a challenge when participants lack full cognitive capacity. Ethical frameworks require assent from the patient wherever possible and surrogate consent by legal guardians, under scrutiny to ensure voluntariness. Churches host community seminars on clinical research ethics, equipping elders and deacons with knowledge to guide families through consent processes without coercion. Pastoral caregivers advocate for research designs that include patients with mild impairment in decision-making roles, modeling dignity-in-action. The Helsinki Declaration and Belmont Report principles are translated into lay language pamphlets distributed at memory clinics, emphasizing respect, beneficence, and justice. Theologians weigh in on whether extending life via experimental drugs honors God's gift of days or risks treating bodies as mere vessels. Congregations lobby for policies preventing profiteering from desperate families, framing access to trials as an issue of neighbor-love rather than market exchange. Bioethics committees within denominations review emerging technologies—gene therapy, amyloid-targeting immunizations—through a lens of covenant responsibility, ensuring benefits reach the vulnerable. These ethical conversations affirm that even in vulnerability we retain agency under God's sovereignty, and prepare us to explore specific forms of memory loss in the next section.

8.2 Trajectories and Typologies of Memory Loss

8.2.1 Transient Global Amnesia: Sudden Blanks and Spiritual Grounding

Transient global amnesia (TGA) strikes without warning, producing profound short-term memory gaps that panicked patients describe as waking into a foreign land. Medical evaluations often reveal benign causes—spinal fluid pressure changes, migraine variants—but the spiritual shock can rival existential dread. Pastors visiting emergency rooms learn to ground patients by reading Psalm 139 aloud: "You knit me together in my mother's womb," reminding minds dislocated by TGA of their enduring Maker (Ps 139:13). Family members tape personal photo collages around hospital beds, triggering familiarity in the hippocampus and offering emotional anchors. Clinicians teach breathing techniques to reduce cortical hyperactivity, while chaplains guide breath prayers—"Jesus…have mercy"—to calm both neurology and spirit. Congregations hold post-episode "Welcome Back" gatherings where friends share laughter and prayer, reinforcing social support networks that mitigate retraumatization. Sermon series on "God of the Unexpected" incorporate TGA stories, illustrating how fleeting amnesia can deepen trust in divine providence rather than undermine it. Medical volunteers offer follow-up visits that combine memory exercises—recounting a shared gospel story—with prayerful reflection. As TGA often resolves spontaneously, these spiritual-grounding practices ensure that the mind's return to baseline occurs within a context of grace rather than lingering fear. Transitioning from transient to persistent loss leads us to chronic trajectories of cognitive decline.

8.2.2 Mild Cognitive Impairment to Alzheimer's: Early Signs, Early Interventions

Mild cognitive impairment (MCI) presents as detectable but non-disabling changes—word-finding difficulty, misplaced keys, mild disorientation—that foreshadow Alzheimer's in a significant subset of cases. Early detection via neuropsychological screening creates a window for interventions: lifestyle modifications, cognitive training, and advanced care planning. Churches partner with gerontologists to host memory clinics during fellowship luncheons, offering baseline assessments and connecting seniors to community services. Pastoral educators teach mnemonic devices using Psalms and gospel refrains, merging cognitive stimulation with spiritual formation. Early support groups for MCI caregivers reduce isolation, training spouses in communication techniques that maintain dignity as deficits grow.

Pharmacotherapy with cholinesterase inhibitors offers modest symptom relief, and congregations learn to view medication adherence as discipleship, embodying 1 Corinthians 9:27's discipline of the body. Narrative ministries invite those diagnosed with MCI to share life stories in spoken-word events, reinforcing identity beyond cognitive function. As progression to Alzheimer's amplifies memory loss, these early interventions lay foundations for deeper covenant faithfulness, preparing us to distinguish subtypes that demand tailored pastoral responses.

8.2.3 Vascular, Lewy-Body, and Frontotemporal Dementias: Distinct Pastoral Challenges

Vascular dementia stems from cerebrovascular compromise, linking heart health and faith practices through diet and exercise disciplines that benefit both. Support ministries organize heart-healthy potlucks and walking clubs, translating medical advice into communal worshipful activity. Lewy-body dementia, characterized by visual hallucinations and fluctuating cognition, often leads families to misinterpret spiritual experiences as supernatural, requiring pastors to discern between divine vision and pathology with prayerful humility. Educational sessions clarify hallucination management: gentle redirection, reality orientation, and compassionate refrains of God's presence that transcend sensory confusion. Frontotemporal dementia strikes the youngest demographic, affecting personality and inhibiting empathy, challenging caregivers to love those whose emotional filters erode. Church-based caregiving coaches offer role-play training in managing disinhibited behaviors, pairing scriptural call to love "as Christ loved the church" with concrete strategies. Legal workshops assist families in securing guardianship early, preventing crisis-driven decisions that fracture relationships. Specialized day programs incorporate music therapy—singing familiar choruses for Lewy-body patients—and interactive storytelling for frontotemporal participants, adapting to each condition's unique pastoral and clinical demands. Understanding these typologies readies the church for nuanced caregiving as memory loss unfolds along divergent paths.

8.2.4 Post-Traumatic and Dissociative Amnesia: Trauma-Informed Discipleship

Traumatic brain injury (TBI) and dissociative amnesia often overlap, as extreme stress disrupts memory encoding or retrieval, leaving survivors unable to recall specific events or sometimes entire life chapters. Pastoral care for these individuals begins with safety-building practices: establishing predictable meeting routines, using consistent names and pronouns, and avoiding questions that may trigger distress. Trauma-informed discipleship emphasizes grounding in the present moment—Psalm 46's "Be still and know that I am God" (Ps 46:10) becomes a mantra for reorienting consciousness. Rehabilitation teams incorporate "spiritual journaling," where survivors dictate daily entries that caregivers type, preserving evolving narratives even when personal recall is fragmented. Congregations host "Story Harvest" workshops where community members contribute recollections of the individual's past—baptism accounts, sermon participation, mission trips—creating a communal autobiography stored digitally for re-exposure therapy. Art therapy sessions use clay to rebuild personal symbols, bridging pre- and post-trauma identities. Pastors caution against over-identifying trauma symptoms with spiritual warfare, balancing deliverance prayer with referrals to neurorehabilitation specialists. By weaving trauma-informed approaches into discipleship, the church ministers holistically to those whose memories have become battlegrounds, and prepares to embrace caregiving as covenantal faithfulness in the next section.

8.3 Caregiving as Covenant Faithfulness

8.3.1 Honoring Parents with Dementia (Ex 20:12)

Honoring one's father and mother takes on renewed depth when roles reverse and adult children guide parents through cognitive decline. The fifth commandment echoes as a call to steadfast loyalty, prompting caregivers to speak gently, listen patiently, and uphold dignity even when recognition falters. Memory care routines become acts of worship as breakfast rituals and pill reminders echo biblical rhythms of feeding and tending (Isa 58:7). Adult children learn to interpret nonverbal cues—facial expressions, agitation patterns—as the primary language of love once shared memories vanish. Family councils create shared caregiving schedules, preventing single individuals from bearing the entire burden and fulfilling the biblical vision of bearing one another's burdens (Gal 6:2). Legal preparations—advance directives and health proxies—are undertaken prayerfully, ensuring parents' wishes guide difficult decisions when they can no longer articulate them. Homes are adapted with grab bars, contrasting colors, and clear signage, reflecting Proverbs 31's call to provide for household needs. Family worship adjusts: hymns are selected for simplicity and repetition, and responsive readings feature familiar texts like Psalm 23 to anchor identity in divine care. Siblings rotate bedtime check-ins, creating a continuous chain of presence that mirrors the Good Shepherd's unceasing watch (John 10:11). Support from deacons and trained volunteers lightens the load, offering meal deliveries, grocery pickups, and respite visits that honor parents as sacred trusts. Annual "Celebration of Life" gatherings invite extended kin to share stories—told aloud to the parent even if they do not recall—reaffirming communal memory. Pastors preach occasional sermons on intergenerational covenant, reminding congregations that caring for elders aligns with God's own care for the frail. Training workshops equip church members with de-escalation techniques for sundowning episodes, combining clinical insight with Christlike compassion. Prayer chains encircle families during hospital stays, demonstrating that the church remembers when human memory fails. Journaling exercises encourage caregivers to record daily gratitude entries, countering the despair that C---often accompanies relentless caregiving. Through these practices, honoring parents becomes a sacred partnership with God's own faithfulness, reflecting the promise that "I will never leave you nor forsake you" (Heb 13:5).

8.3.2 Spousal Vows Tested by Forgetting: "For Better, for Worse" in the Memory Ward

Marriage vows pledge fidelity in sickness and in health, yet dementia introduces a bewildering frontier where spouses may no longer recognize each other. Wedded partners learn new scripts of presence: holding hands during confusion rather than expecting verbal affirmation, offering simple reminders of the wedding day amidst disjointed memories. Rituals such as re-reading vows by the bedside and playing the wedding song cultivate shared affective memories, often activating emotional recall even when factual recall fails. Pastoral counselors suggest writing love letters or recording audio messages to play when verbal reassurance is needed, embedding enduring affection in sensory stimuli. Couples' support groups create safe settings where spouses share grief over lost companionship and find solace in mutual understanding. Communication workshops teach nonverbal affirmation techniques—gentle touch on the cheek, sustained eye contact—to convey ongoing commitment beyond words. Art therapy sessions invite couples to paint abstract representations of their journey, renewing connection through creative collaboration. Churches host "Marriage Through Memory Loss" seminars, pairing clinical experts with faith leaders to equip congregations for this unique form of covenant care.

Community volunteer networks provide respite for spousal caregivers, enabling them to rest, attend worship, or simply go on a date night, affirming that self-care undergirds sustained commitment. Sermons on Ephesians 5 reinterpret Christ's sacrificial love for the church in the context of caregiving love that perseveres when reciprocity falters. Couples are encouraged to develop shared spiritual practices—praying the Lord's Prayer together each morning—to reinforce spiritual union in the face of cognitive separation. Pastoral check-ins offer a listening ear, acknowledging both sorrow and the quiet joy of serving one's beloved in vulnerability. Over time, spouses discover that love can transcend memory, rooted not in recollection but in the indelible covenant sealed by God.

8.3.3 Community-Based Respite and Day-Program Models: A Church's Shared Yoke

Long-term caregiving can lead to physical exhaustion, emotional depletion, and social isolation, requiring structured respite. Churches can partner with local memory care centers to host weekly "Respite Sundays," where trained volunteers supervise art, music, and gentle exercise for those with dementia while caregivers attend worship or support groups. Day-program spaces in fellowship halls offer stimulating activities—remembrance choir, tactile crafts, faith-based storytelling—designed by occupational therapists and chaplains to engage both cognition and spirit. Volunteer teams receive trauma-informed training, learning to manage challenging behaviors with calm voices and activity redirection, transforming potential crisis into moments of shared joy. Congregations provide midday meals prepared by deacons, ensuring both nutrition and fellowship, while a team of elders rotates hospitality, embodying Acts 2's model of communal care. Grant-funded partnerships supply transportation vans, enabling homebound individuals to participate and freeing caregivers from driving burdens. Monthly "grandparents circle" gatherings connect spouses with peer mentors who have navigated similar journeys, reinforcing that no one carries the yoke alone. Church newsletters highlight testimonials from respite participants whose agitation levels decreased by structured social engagement, demonstrating clinical benefits alongside spiritual accompaniment. Children's Sunday school classes organize intergenerational visits—singing hymns, reading picture Bibles—to bring delight to memory-impaired members while teaching kids compassionate service. Pastoral teams use these day-programs as opportunities for spiritual check-ins, offering brief blessings at session start and end that anchor participants in divine love even amid confusion. This communal network embodies Galatians 6:2, as the body bears burdens together, ensuring caregivers can rest, rejuvenate, and return to their vocation with renewed strength.

8.3.4 Self-Care for Caregivers: Elijah's Nap, Angel's Bread, and Modern Burnout

(Assuming subsections... but 8.3 had four. Actually 8.3.4.) Self-care for caregivers begins with permission to rest, echoing God's instruction for Sabbath after creation (Gen 2:2). Respite care partnerships allow primary caregivers to take overnight breaks or weekend retreats for spiritual renewal. Workshops teach stress-reduction techniques— progressive muscle relaxation, guided imagery—paired with contemplative prayer, fostering integration of body and soul restoration. Peer support circles encourage sharing of frustrations and blessings, reducing isolation and stigma. Therapy offerings, including marriage enrichment and individual counseling, address secondary trauma resulting from sustained caregiving. Nutrition seminars emphasize whole-food diets rich in omega-3 and antioxidants, linking medical research on caregiver health to biblical calls for bodily stewardship (1 Cor 6:19–20). "Care for the Caregiver" Sunday mornings include small-group yoga and breath-prayer sessions, reminding church members that sustaining those who serve is a high calling. Pastors model vulnerability by sharing personal care mistakes and restorative practices, fostering a culture where self-compassion triumphs over martyrdom. Mobile apps guide quick midday prayer breaks, combining breath prayer with Scripture prompts for caregivers on the go. Annual caregiver retreats weave worship, workshops, and quiet reflection, renewing resilience through communal solidarity. Clinical chaplains note that caregivers who practice self-care report fewer chronic illnesses and better mental-health outcomes, enabling sustained service. Policies within church leadership include mandatory vacation scheduling for pastoral caregivers, setting an example for lay carers to follow. These multilayered self-care strategies ensure that those who bear others' burdens receive the rest, nourishment, and spiritual refreshment they need to continue bearing those burdens with grace.

8.4 Liturgical and Spiritual Tools for Memory Loss

8.4.1 Table, Touch, and Tune: Eucharist, Blessing Oil, and Familiar Hymns

In memory care contexts, the Eucharist conveys profound reassurance of Christ's presence when personal recollection falters. Portable communion kits—sealed gluten-free wafers and grape juice cups—are taken to memory units, where chaplains slow the liturgy to allow participants time to process sensory cues. As bread is broken, congregants place a small piece on the tongue of a resident who cannot swallow a wafer, ensuring sacramental inclusion. Blessing oil, approved by infection-control nurses, is anointed on hands and foreheads while reading numbers 6:24–26, visually and tactilely affirming divine protection. Familiar hymns—"Amazing Grace," "Jesus Loves Me"—are played on a loop during services, invoking deep-seated neural associations that can spur momentary clarity and calm agitation. Churches install small hymn libraries in memory wings, where caregivers can easily cue beloved tunes to redirect agitation toward tranquility. Music therapists lead group sing-alongs, noting that dyadic synchrony in chant-like songs reduces cortisol and fosters communal cohesion. Pastors preach that sacramental rhythm mirrors the heartbeat of covenant, sustaining identity beyond memory. Intergenerational hymn sessions invite children and elders to sing together, weaving new relational memories and celebrating continuity across decline. These embodied practices bridge liturgy and neuroscience, revealing that table, touch, and tune are instruments of divine remembering in communities grappling with cognitive loss.

8.4.2 Scripture by Heart: Using Repetitive Psalms and Lord's Prayer Pathways

Repetitive recitation of short, rhythmic passages strengthens retrieval pathways in neurodegenerative brains. Psalms 23, 121, and 100 are carved onto large-print cards and strategically placed in memory-wing corridors, creating visual prompts that invite spontaneous aloud reading. Caregivers guide residents through "Scripture strolls," walking past posters of each verse, pausing to speak lines together in unison, merging physical movement with cognitive recall to leverage embodied memory consolidation. The Lord's Prayer, divided into eight manageable clauses, is practiced daily at mealtimes, each line becoming a trigger for anxiety reduction through its predictable structure. Smartphone apps with large icons play audio recordings of these passages, allowing residents to activate them independently when agitation rises. Family devotional kits include laminated prayer cards and tactile rosaries or prayer ropes, offering manual engagement when speech is limited. Over months, caregivers observe improvements in orientation and mood coherence during and after Scripture sessions. Intergenerational Story Circles encourage grandchildren to read these psalms to grandparents, reinforcing relational bonds and embedding scriptural truth in family memory. Seminarians develop guided Scripture meditation guides for dementia contexts, training future ministers in tailored lectio divina for the memory-impaired. As repetitive scripture becomes a daily anchor, residents experience moments of lucidity and reassurance that echo God's enduring promises, preparing hearts to enter communities of remembrance.

8.4.3 Sensory Stations of Remembrance: Smell, Sight, and Sacramental Objects

Memory care wings benefit from multi-sensory "Remembrance Stations" where families and volunteers set out objects tied to a resident's past—vintage perfume bottles, family photo albums, well-worn hymnals. Olfactory cues like lavender sachets and freshly baked bread evoke limbic-center memories, as Moses' encounter with burning bush emphasizes that encountering the divine often engages multiple senses (Ex 3). Stations incorporate tactile items—wooden crosses, smooth river stones—inscribed with favorite verses, inviting residents to hold and explore scripture through texture. Visual collages, printed in high-contrast colors, depict biblical scenes familiar from youth Sunday school, grounding viewers in shared spiritual history. Soundscapes of church bells or organ music play softly in the background, layering auditory cues that calm cognitive dissonance. Occupational therapists design station layouts that encourage gentle pacing and safe, exploratory engagement, preventing environmental overstimulation. Church volunteers refresh stations weekly, rotating items to maintain novelty while preserving core favorites. Pastors lead monthly blessing services at the stations, anointing objects and participants with prayers adapted for sensory connection. Interdisciplinary research teams document reductions in behavioral disturbances associated with these multisensory interventions, affirming their therapeutic value. Through curated sensory stations, faith communities transform memory wards into interactive sanctuaries where souls are remembered by touch, sight, and smell when minds falter.

8.4.4 Digital Aids: Audio Bibles, Photo Apps, and Communion via Livestream

Advances in digital technology offer powerful tools for memory affirmation. Audio Bibles with clear, calm narrators allow residents to absorb scripture without fatigue from visual reading. Tablet apps customized for elders display family photos and captioned video messages from loved ones, providing identity cues and emotional comfort. Churches provide large-button remote controls programmed to start livestreamed communion services, enabling homebound or memory-impaired individuals to participate virtually in real time. Video memoir software guides families through recorded life-story interviews, generating interactive timelines that residents can revisit at will. Smart-home devices, voice-activated and adapted for low-tech users, announce gospel readings at set times, reinforcing spiritual rhythms. Memory-care units install digital photo frames on each room's wall, cycling through decades of worship gatherings and mission trips, linking godly legacy to present identity. Pastors record short devotionals and affirmations for playback during challenging times—"You are God's masterpiece" (Eph 2:10)—so that personalized encouragement remains available when human visitors cannot. Training sessions teach volunteers to assist residents in using these devices, ensuring tech adoption does not become another barrier. Data privacy policies maintain confidentiality and consent for digital content, honoring both legal and spiritual ethics. By integrating digital aids into spiritual care, churches extend their presence into the private worlds of memory-impaired members, ensuring that identity in Christ remains visible and vocal even as human recollection fades.

8.5 Communities of Remembrance

8.5.1 "Memory Cafés" in Fellowship Halls: Coffee, Crafts, and Storytelling

Memory cafés provide informal, stigma-free spaces where individuals with early cognitive decline and their caregivers gather over coffee and pastries to socialize, create art, or share stories. These gatherings often feature themed storytelling prompts—"Your favorite Sunday school memory"—that spark reminiscence and communal laughter. Volunteers trained in gentle redirection help guests who become confused or upset, guiding them back into group activities without causing embarrassment. Craft stations offer simple projects like decorating crosses or painting scripture verses, engagements that simultaneously stimulate fine motor skills and spiritual reflection. Local historians may present photos of the town's past, providing common ground for shared local narratives that transcend personal memory loss. Pastors lead brief prayer circles, inviting participants to hold a hand and repeat simple affirmations of belonging—"I am treasured by this community." Adult Sunday school classes connect with cafés by delivering baked goods and joining as conversational partners, reinforcing intergenerational solidarity. Evaluations by social workers track improved mood and decreased caregiver stress following café attendance. These regular, welcoming gatherings anchor participants in a broader fellowship, countering isolation and affirming that even as memories fade, relational bonds endure.

8.5.2 Intergenerational Choirs: Children Singing Faith Back to Elders

Intergenerational choirs assemble children, youth, and elders with memory loss to rehearse and perform simple hymns during worship services. Young voices often trigger elders' vocal responses, reactivating neural pathways associated with music and memory. Rehearsals become counseling sessions where verses like "Jesus loves me" resonate across generations, each stanza cementing shared identity in Christ. Music therapists note that rhythmic entrainment in group singing improves gait and speech fluency for Parkinson's and Alzheimer's participants, demonstrating biopsychosocial impact. Choral directors adjust arrangements to accommodate limited vocal ranges, ensuring inclusivity. Concerts in memory-care units follow, allowing residents to both listen and participate, often tapping canes in time or humming along. Families witness these moments of lucidity, finding hope in musical harmony that transcends cognitive barriers. Youth volunteers report deepened empathy and theological insights as they serve alongside elders, learning that the church's choir is more than a performance ensemble—it's a living metaphor for the body of Christ. Churches share recordings on social media, celebrating unity in diversity and inviting wider communities to support memory-health ministries.

8.5.3 Architectural Mercy: Way-finding, Lighting, and Soundscapes in Church Buildings

Dementia-friendly design principles enhance navigability and comfort in church campuses. Way-finding signage uses high-contrast colors, large fonts, and simple icons—an open Bible for the sanctuary, a plate-and-cup for the fellowship hall—helping memory-impaired attendees maintain orientation. Lighting schemes minimize glare and shadows, reducing disorientation and visual stress. Soundscapes incorporate gentle ambient hymns in hallways, guiding footsteps toward worship spaces with audio cues that reassure and direct. Flooring patterns avoid abrupt changes in texture that can cause falls, and chairs with armrests assist those who need help standing. Bathrooms feature contrasting grab bars and visual cues—moon decals for night services—to facilitate independence. Architectural teams collaborate with congregational health ministries to retrofit existing structures and plan new builds, integrating these mercy-focused features. Training for usher teams includes spotting guests who appear lost and gently escorting them using the predictable signage. Ambient scent methods—lemon verbena in restrooms, frankincense near prayer rooms—anchor spaces in sensory memory, aiding recall of function. These design elements honor the Imago Dei by removing environmental obstacles to participation, reflecting Levitical care for the vulnerable in community spaces.

8.5.4 Advocacy for Dementia-Friendly Cities: Public Policy as Neighbor Love

Churches extend their caring role beyond campus boundaries by joining municipal coalitions to create dementia-friendly neighborhoods. Advocacy efforts target public transit modifications—clear route maps, priority seating—so that those with memory loss maintain mobility and social connections. Faith communities lobby for bank policies that allow caregivers to accompany relatives in financial transactions, reducing vulnerability to fraud. Public libraries partner with congregations to host "Dementia-Friendly Story Hours," where familiar Bible stories are shared in accessible language and format. Parks departments install safe wandering gardens with circular paths that prevent disorientation, replicating memory-café principles in public spaces. Churches host civic forums on passing dementia-friendly city resolutions, embedding biblical neighbor-love into policy discourse. These cross-sector collaborations demonstrate that loving our neighbor includes shaping the public square to reflect gospel hospitality for the memory-impaired. Through advocacy, faith communities model that caring is a societal project, extending covenant faithfulness from living rooms to legislative chambers.

8.6 The Theological Mystery of Identity and Continuity

8.6.1 What Makes "Me" Me? Substance Dualism vs. Narrative-Relational Models

The question of personal identity has occupied philosophers and theologians for centuries, asking whether we remain the same person if our memories and personality shift. Substance dualism posits a soul or immaterial substance that undergirds identity apart from mental states, echoing Plato and later Descartes, yet raising questions about how the immaterial and material interact. In contrast, narrative-relational models suggest that identity arises from the ongoing story we tell of ourselves—our relationships, commitments, and memories woven into a coherent self-narrative. Neuroscience complicates both views by showing that memory and personality reside in brain networks that degrade in dementia, challenging the idea that unchanging substrates or coherent life stories fully capture who we are. Scripture reflects both paradigms: God forms Adam's dust-filled body but breathes into him a living soul (Gen 2:7), suggesting a material-immaterial unity, while Jesus carries scars into eternity (John 20:27), indicating continuity of personal history beyond bodily change. Pastors wrestling with dementia cases find substance dualism comforting when cognitive decline threatens narrative coherence, affirming that the soul's image remains regardless of memory. Others embrace relational models by encouraging families to speak truths of identity—"You are my mother," "You baptized me"—maintaining the personal story collectively even when the individual cannot recall it. Ethical implications arise: if identity is narrative, consent for research or treatment may require community endorsement when self-narration falters. Clinical chaplains report that framing identity as relational rather than solely cognitive reduces anxiety in patients who fear "losing themselves." Seminaries now include modules on philosophical anthropology, preparing ministers to articulate nuanced perspectives that honor both soul substance and communal storytelling. Integrating these models, churches discern that identity in Christ transcends neurobiological disruption, sustaining personhood even amid memory loss.

8.6.2 Baptism, Eucharist, and the "Seal" of the Spirit (Eph 4:30)

Christian sacraments imprint identity in ways that endure beyond cognitive capacity. Baptism marks believers with the Holy Spirit's seal, an irreversible act of divine adoption (Eph 4:30), communicating that one belongs to God even if earthly memory fades. Churches often revisit baptismal vows with those experiencing dementia, reading aloud the promises and gestures of water renewal to re-anchor identity in covenantal belonging. The Eucharist similarly confers spiritual nourishment, reminding participants that their identity is hidden in Christ (Col 3:3) rather than in cognitive performance. In memory care settings, chaplains adapt communion liturgies to include tactile cues—dipping a hand in water to signify baptismal grace—ensuring that embodied sacraments speak truth when words falter. Liturgical calendars incorporate remembrance of ordination and other sacramental milestones, celebrating anniversaries with simple rituals that reinforce ecclesial identity. Pastoral theologians observe that sacraments operate as divine memory devices, binding communities together and anchoring forgotten individuals in the unchanging narrative of gospel grace. Even when a person cannot articulate belief, participation in sacramental acts embodies union with Christ and the body of believers. Ethical considerations require informed assent adapted to cognitive levels, ensuring respect for agency while honoring sacramental theology. As cognitive barriers rise, sacraments stand as anchors that God continues to enact, bearing witness to identity beyond memory loss.

8.6.3 When Personality Shifts: Sin, Disease, or Neurological Drift?

Dementia can unleash personality changes—irritability, disinhibition, or apathy—that shock families accustomed to lifelong temperaments. Pastors and caregivers must discern whether such shifts stem from moral failure, demonic influence, or purely neurological processes. Biblical narratives recognize both spiritual and physical factors in behavior: Saul's torment by an evil spirit (1 Sam 16:14) and Paul's "thorn in the flesh" (2 Cor 12:7) illustrate that affliction can have spiritual and somatic dimensions. Modern neuroscience shows that frontal-lobe degradation often underlies impulsive behavior, suggesting a neurobiological rather than a moral root. Pastoral care teams therefore collaborate with neuropsychiatrists to assess capacity and craft appropriate responses—adjusting expectations, modifying communication styles, and providing pharmacological interventions when needed. Congregational education clarifies that blame is neither helpful nor accurate, redirecting stigma toward compassionate accommodation. Support groups for caregivers share strategies for responding to personality shifts: labeling the disease as "the dementia" rather than the person helps maintain relational love. Sermons on Christ's compassion for sinners and sufferers equip communities to offer grace rather than judgment. When harmful behaviors arise, ethical protocols guide safe responses—redirection techniques, environmental modifications—rather than punitive measures. Ultimately, combining theological insight and clinical knowledge reframes personality changes as cries for care, not indictments of character.

8.6.4 Pastoral Conversations on Salvation Assurance Amid Cognitive Decline

A central pastoral concern is whether those with severe dementia can cling to salvation promises when mental faculties erode. Biblical assurance rests not on memory or understanding alone but on God's covenant faithfulness (Rom 8:38–39) and the irrevocable nature of divine promise (2 Tim 4:18). Pastors affirm that salvation is rooted in union with Christ sealed by the Spirit, not in retained cognitive capacity. Conversations employ parables—like the shepherd leaving ninety-nine sheep to rescue one lost (Luke 15:4)—to illustrate God's persistent pursuit despite human floundering. Families are encouraged to speak gospel truths into the ears of loved ones, trusting the Holy Spirit to apply the Word beyond conscious comprehension. Case studies of persons uttering fragments of Scripture in advanced dementia spark discussions on the Spirit's work in hidden ways. Pastoral letters recommend regular singing of hymns and recitation of creeds, creating an "audio catechism" that sustains faith memory. Ethical guidelines caution against last-minute baptisms or exorcisms driven by fear, advocating instead for a posture of trust in God's prior work. Training modules equip elders to navigate these delicate dialogues, blending theological depth with pastoral sensitivity. As families wrestle with uncertainty, the church's collective witness offers reassurance: identity in Christ endures beyond neural collapse. Transitioning from identity questions, we now turn to eschatological restoration of memory.

8.7 Eschatological Restoration of Memory

8.7.1 The Book of Remembrance (Malachi 3:16)

Malachi's vision of a divine "book of remembrance" kept for those who fear the Lord reveals that God memorializes deeds of faith long after human forgetfulness (Mal 3:16). This image comforts families who worry that acts of love and service will vanish from human memory, assuring them that every tear and prayer is recorded in heaven's ledger. Pastoral liturgies incorporate responsive readings from Malachi, inviting worshipers to inscribe names of saints with memory loss into a symbolic book displayed in the sanctuary. Christian artists create visual journals—scrapbooks of stories and photos—for church archives, archiving testimonies of those whose earthly recollection fades. Clergy encourage congregants to write letters to God recounting moments of mercy shown, trusting that these letters join the divine record. Youth groups participate by documenting intergenerational encounters, weaving collective memory into the fabric of ecclesial legacy. Seminary courses on eschatology now assign reflection papers on Malachi's text, prompting future pastors to envision heavenly continuity. As dementia erases human files, God's remembrance ensures that nothing done for Christ will be lost (Luke 18:16). From this celestial archive we move to the perfect knowing that awaits in the age to come.

8.7.2 Perfect Knowing in the Age to Come (1 Cor 13:12)

Paul's metaphor of seeing "in a mirror dimly" contrasts with the "face to face" clarity believers will enjoy in the resurrection, implying full cognitive restoration beyond present limits (1 Cor 13:12). This promise fuels hope that dementia's gaps will vanish in perfected minds, where loved ones recognize one another fully and share eternal communion. Preachers illustrate this truth using the Edenic fellowship restored in Revelation's new creation, where knowledge and memory are unbroken (Rev 21:3–4). Pastoral prayers ask God to "give us renewed minds" in anticipation of that day, even as earthly synapses fire imperfectly. Caregivers share this vision with residents during worship, using simplified language to communicate that God will make all things new. Memorial services often conclude with lighting a "resurrection candle," symbolizing the transition from dim mirror to face-to-face knowing. Music ministries choose anthems like "Face to Face" that lyrically capture this eschatological hope, allowing congregants to sing future reality into present suffering. Discussion groups explore how perfect knowing may transform relationships, fueling motivation for compassionate care now. As the church embraces this vision, believers find renewed purpose in caring for those whose minds echo the "dim mirror" imagery, confident that a consummate cognition awaits.

8.7.3 "I Will Give You a White Stone with a New Name" (Rev 2:17): Identity Re-gifted

Revelation's promise of a white stone inscribed with a new name symbolizes personal identity bestowed anew by Christ (Rev 2:17), offering a powerful metaphor for those feeling unmoored by memory loss. Churches incorporate this motif into liturgies by handing recipients smooth pebbles engraved with "Beloved" or "Child of God," teaching that identity is ultimately Christ-gifted rather than self-generated. Memory-impaired members can clutch these stones during disorientation, using tactile reassurance to recall that they bear a divine name. Art workshops guide participants in painting stones with symbols—doves, crosses, fish—personalized to reflect their faith journey. Pastoral couples find solace in exchanging new-name stones when familiar names no longer connect, embodying Revelation's re-naming promise. Sermon series on the letters to the seven churches draw out this theme, underscoring that Christ knows each person intimately despite cognitive decline. At funerals, stones are placed in caskets or scattered at memorial sites, signifying the end of earthly forgetting and the continuation of identity in heavenly realms. The practice reminds communities that identity is a gift, not solely a memory function, preparing us for liturgical comfort in the face of final goodbyes.

8.7.4 Comfort Liturgies for Funeral and Memorial Services of Memory-Lost Saints

Funeral liturgies for those who died with dementia need unique sensitivities: eulogies focus on character traits—kindness, humor, faith—rather than chronological life events. Pastors select Scripture such as Revelation 7:17, "He will guide them to springs of living water," implying that in the next life suffering ends and perfect refreshment begins. Crematoria and graveside services include planting a "memory tree," where family and friends place soil from the churchyard as a living memorial. Hymns like "Amazing Grace" and "Be Thou My Vision" underscore that God's grace and vision outlast human recollection. Memorial cards feature a favorite verse and photograph from the person's earlier years to evoke communal memory. Post-funeral receptions incorporate memory-sharing circles, where attendees bring one memory to recite, ensuring that each contributes to the desert of forgetfulness becoming an oasis of collective remembrance. Pastoral letters sent on the first anniversary of death recall Revelation's new-morning joy, reminding mourners that their beloved's identity persists in God's eternal community. These liturgies balance acknowledgment of earthly loss with confident proclamation of divine remembrance, closing our eschatological reflections and leading into practical training resources in the next section.

8.8 Pastoral Resources and Training Modules

8.8.1 Dementia-Competent Ministry Certification: Core Competencies for Leaders

Churches partner with medical schools and social-service agencies to develop certification programs that credential pastors and lay leaders in dementia care. Core competencies include understanding cognitive decline stages, communication strategies, legal-ethical frameworks, and spiritual formation techniques. Training modules feature classroom lectures, interactive simulations of disorientation scenarios, and field placements in memory-care units for firsthand experience. Assessments require learners to demonstrate proficiency in adapting liturgies, creating sensory environments, and coordinating multi-disciplinary teams. Ethical components cover confidentiality, informed consent, and boundary-setting to protect both caregivers and recipients. Graduates receive pins and are commissioned in worship, signaling congregational trust and institutional support. Ongoing continuing-education units ensure leaders stay current with clinical advances and theological insights. Research partnerships track outcomes—reduced caregiver burnout, improved resident well-being—validating the program's impact. This certification elevates dementia ministry to professionalized vocation, recognizing its complexity and Christ-honoring importance.

8.8.2 Sermon Series Toolkit: Preaching Hope When Minds Fray

Pastoral staff curate sermon series outlines that address memory loss from theological, biblical, and practical angles. The toolkit includes sample lectionary schedules, thematic homiletic outlines, and illustrative stories drawn from both Scripture—Moses at ninety-nine (Ex 4)—and modern caregiving experiences. PowerPoint slides, video testimonies, and guided reflection questions enhance congregational engagement. Preaching notes emphasize language that avoids shame, centers divine remembering, and invites all ages to participate in pastoral care. Small-group discussion guides accompany sermons, prompting deeper reflection and practical application. Worship planners suggest hymn selections, responsive readings, and symbolic visuals—empty chairs representing those who forget—integrating liturgy and homiletics. Supplementary resources point to recommended reading and local support services. A digital companion app allows sermon audio downloads and push notifications reminding worshipers of weekly memory-affirming practices. This toolkit equips preachers to address the topic comprehensively and compassionately.

8.8.3 Small-Group Curriculum: Walking with Forgetfulness—Six-Week Guide

The curriculum unfolds over six sessions: session one explores biblical anthropology of memory; session two teaches communication techniques; session three focuses on self-care for caregivers; session four introduces sensory and sacramental practices; session five examines legal and ethical planning; session six celebrates hope through eschatological vision. Each session includes scripture passages, discussion questions, prayer prompts, and home assignments—such as creating memory boxes or practicing breath prayers. Facilitator guides provide background reading, video clip suggestions, and troubleshooting tips for group dynamics. Participant workbooks offer space for journaling, recording personal caregiving plans, and drafting legacy letters. Guest speakers—gerontologists, ethicists, chaplains—join select sessions, broadening perspectives. Churches host graduation ceremonies at program conclusion, commissioning graduates as "Memory Care Ambassadors." Feedback surveys inform iterative improvements, ensuring the curriculum meets community needs. This small-group structure fosters mutual learning, spiritual growth, and practical equipping.

8.8.4 Recommended Reading, Films, and Websites for Congregational Education

Curated bibliographies include classics like Oliver Sacks's *The Man Who Mistook His Wife for a Hat* alongside theological works such as Daniel's *Soul of Shame*. Films such as *Still Alice* and documentaries like *Glen Campbell: I'll Be Me* provide narrative empathy for cognitive decline. Websites like the Alzheimer's Association, Dementia Friendly America, and Christian Memory Care network offer downloadable toolkits, local chapter contacts, and online training modules. Audio resources—podcasts by medical ethicists and pastoral theologians—deliver on-the-go learning. Annotated summaries highlight key takeaways and discussion points for church newsletters. Book clubs meet quarterly to review these materials, inviting family and caregivers to share insights. Volunteer teams rotate through community libraries stocking these resources, lending them freely. As congregational education deepens, stigma erodes, and readiness to minister to memory-impaired neighbors increases.

8.9 Epilogue — God Remembers Our Frame

This chapter has woven theology, neuroscience, and pastoral practice to affirm that identity in Christ transcends memory loss. Families enacting covenant faithfulness honor parents and spouses through adaptive rituals and community support. Clinicians collaborate with chaplains to develop dementia-competent environments that integrate medical care with sacramental presence. Faith communities adopt architectural, liturgical, and digital tools that embody divine remembrance when human recall falters. Training modules professionalize dementia ministry, ensuring leaders possess both compassion and competence. The narrative identity and sacramental naming practices remind us that names like "beloved" endure beyond cognitive decline. Eschatological promises—Malachi's book, face-to-face knowing, white-stone renaming—sustain hope amid erosion, inviting communities to live in the tension of already–not yet memory restoration. Together, these insights equip all stakeholders to walk gently with those whose memories slip, reflecting God's unforgetting love.

Conclusion Our journey through amnesia and dementia has revealed a God who neither erases nor abandons us when our own minds falter. Families learn that honoring parents and spouses becomes a sacred vocation rooted in ancient commandments, even when roles reverse. Churches discover that baptismal naming, Eucharist at the bedside, and sensory-rich worship environments weave threads of identity that outlast cognitive decline. Ethical frameworks guide research and consent with compassion, while training modules equip leaders to minister competently to those who can no longer advocate for themselves. Above all, the promise of a divine Book of Remembrance and face-to-face knowing in the age to come sustains hope amid present loss. As memory fades here, it is perfected beyond the veil, ensuring that nothing done for Christ will ever be forgotten.

Chapter 9 – Lifestyle and Environment: Diet, Addiction, and Stewardship

Our everyday choices—from the meals we share to the air we breathe—reflect beliefs about God's provision and our role as caretakers of creation. In this chapter, we explore how the simple act of breaking bread ties us to ancient covenant rhythms and modern nutritional science, how our bodies bear the imprint of corporate patterns of consumption and addiction, and how the world around us shapes health through soil, water, and air. We will journey from Daniel's quiet resolve in a foreign court to contemporary kitchens and community gardens, from the struggle of substance dependency to the redemption of bodies as temples of the Spirit. Along the way, we learn that stewarding our own health is inseparable from caring for our neighbors and the planet, and that every dietary choice, habit, and policy engagement can become an act of worship.

9.0 Prelude — Bodies on Loan, Earth in Trust

9.0.1 From Eden's Garden to Today's Grocery: A Brief History of Eating

Humanity's relationship with food begins in Eden, where Adam and Eve were invited to "eat freely of every tree in the garden" (Gen 2:16). That divine provision signaled God's intention that food sustain both body and delight the senses. After the fall, eating took on toil and peril, as thorns and thistles entered human labor (Gen 3:18–19), introducing the first food insecurity and marking the onset of survival struggles. Ancient Israel's manna in the wilderness illustrated both God's daily care and the danger of hoarding, as any leftover manna bred worms, underscoring the balance between provision and trust (Ex 16). Levitical dietary laws refined this paradigm, distinguishing clean and unclean animals, foreshadowing gospel freedom while affirming that bodily stewardship matters (Lev 11). In early Christian communities, tables became signs of unity across former clean/unclean divides (Acts 10), modeling the messianic table where every tribe is welcome. The Middle Ages saw monastic gardens preserve heirloom grains and medicinal herbs, anchoring spiritual disciplines in soil stewardship. Industrialization introduced mass-produced, nutrient-poor foods and refined sugars, contributing to malnutrition even amid abundance. The 20th century's grocery revolution—supermarkets, processed convenience foods—reshaped eating patterns, often away from communal table rhythms and toward solitary, on-the-go consumption. Public-health crises like the obesity epidemic reveal the spiritual and communal costs of disconnected eating. Contemporary farm-to-table and local-food movements recall Eden's proximity to soil and neighbor, urging a return to seasonal, regionally rooted diets. Grocery stores now display organic labels and whole-food sections, reflecting consumer demand for health-aligned choices. Yet disparities persist, as food deserts limit access in low-income neighborhoods, echoing Genesis's curse on ground and the need for covenantal care. Narratives of families reclaiming kitchen gardens speak to deep-seated longing for Edenic patterns, reminding us that eating wisely is both a bodily necessity and a spiritual vocation. From this historical sweep, we turn to God's vocational mandate to steward creation's resources.

9.0.2 Stewarding Soil, Water, and Breath: The Vocational Mandate (Gen 2:15)

God placed Adam "in the garden to work it and keep it" (Gen 2:15), charging humanity with cultivation and conservation of creation. This early vocational mandate frames environmental stewardship as intrinsic to human flourishing and divine mission. Soil, the medium that births grain and fruit, requires care through practices like crop rotation, balanced fertilization, and erosion control—modern agronomy echoing ancient wisdom. Water, a symbol of life in Scripture, must be guarded from pollution; prophetic condemnations of polluted springs (Amos 4:7–8) resonate with today's industrial runoff threatening freshwater supplies. Breath, the divine wind that animates all living creatures, directs us to address air-quality issues that exacerbate asthma and cardiovascular illnesses. Churches participate in water-restoration projects, sponsoring stream cleanups and advocating for fair water access in underserved communities. Congregational tree-planting events align with Psalms that celebrate God's trust in humanity to watch over earth (Ps 104:14–15). Faith communities certify safe baptistry water and encourage proper sanitation in mission fields, connecting spiritual cleansing with physical hygiene. Environmental justice efforts target marginalized neighborhoods disproportionately impacted by factories and traffic emissions, embodying James 2's call to care for "the orphans and widows." Educational seminars teach parishioners about carbon footprints, composting, and renewable energy, framing lifestyle adjustments as acts of worship. Lobbying for clean-air regulations and supporting climate resiliency measures become contemporary expressions of Genesis's stewardship charge. As congregations embrace creation care, they witness that protecting soil, water, and breath is inseparable from loving God and neighbor. From this foundational mandate, we now explore a theology of nourishment that guides day-to-day dietary choices.

9.1 A Theology of Nourishment

9.1.1 Created Foods, Clean Foods, and the Messianic Table

God's original provision included every plant yielding seed and fruit trees in Eden (Gen 1:29), suggesting a plant-forward diet aligned with human flourishing. Levitical food laws then distinguished clean animals—ruminants with cloven hooves—and fish with fins and scales, teaching God's care for bodily wholesomeness (Lev 11). These distinctions pointed beyond mere hygiene to holiness practices that unified spiritual and physical health. In the Gospels, Jesus ate with Pharisees yet healed on the Sabbath, showing that the Messiah would fulfill and transcend ritual food boundaries (Matt 12:1–8). His ascension meal with the disciples foreshadowed the eschatological banquet where every tribe gathers (Rev 19:9). Today, whole grains, legumes, fruits, and vegetables recall Eden's diet and the Mosaic concept of clean foods, while diverse global cuisines reflect the messianic table's inclusiveness. Community meals in church cafeterias emphasize whole, unprocessed ingredients, demonstrating that culinary choices can be both celebratory and healthful. Farmers markets on church grounds restore the connection between grower and eater, reinforcing scriptural affirmations of God's provision through earth. Special "Blue Zones" initiatives in faith communities highlight regions where centenarians thrive on plant-rich diets, linking biblical patterns with longevity science. As believers gather around tables, they enact a theology of nutrition that marries scriptural precedent with modern nutritional knowledge, preparing hearts and bodies for deeper journeys into moderation and spiritual rhythms.

9.1.2 Moderation, Gratitude, and Gluttony: Virtue Ethics for the Plate

Scripture warns against gluttony—excessive indulgence in food and drink—as a form of self-idolatry that dulls spiritual sensitivity (Prov 23:20–21). Conversely, moderation emerges as a fruit of the Spirit's self-control (Gal 5:23), enabling believers to honor bodies as temples (1 Cor 6:19). Gratitude reframes eating moments into liturgical experiences, as Paul instructs believers to give thanks for all things, including food (Eph 5:20). Simple practices—starting meals with a blessing, pausing between bites to savor flavors—cultivate mindful eating that bridges physiology with theology. Church retreats incorporate communal potlucks where no one may take seconds until all have eaten, dramatizing interdependence and care. Health ministries teach portion control using visual guides—like the biblical image of gathering manna by the omer per person (Ex 16)—linking ancient measures to modern dietary science. Sermons on fasting operate in tandem with teachings on feasting, framing both activities as expressions of dependence and celebration. Small groups discuss how gratitude journals reduce emotional eating by redirecting cravings toward thankfulness. Charity events like "fast-a-thons" raise funds for the hungry, channeling discipline into neighbor love. Moderation also extends to sugar and sodium intake; church cookbooks adapt traditional recipes to lower-sugar and low-salt versions, preserving heritage flavors in healthier forms. By cultivating moderation and gratitude, Christians embody virtue ethics for the plate, honoring God's provision without succumbing to self-indulgence. From this ethic of restraint, we move into sacred fasting and celebration rhythms.

9.1.3 Fasting as Protest, Feasting as Praise (Isa 58; Lk 5:33–35)

Fasting in biblical narrative often accompanies repentance, mourning, and pursuit of justice—as Isaiah 58 critiques hollow fasts that ignore the oppressed, urging fasts "to loose the chains of injustice" rather than mere hunger (Isa 58:6–7). Jesus describes His disciples fasting in a time of mourning but proclaims that the wedding feast of the kingdom will one day supplant such fasts (Lk 5:33–35), framing fasting as a precursor to eschatological feasting. Contemporary churches adopt these rhythms by scheduling corporate fasts to pray for local and global issues—economic injustice, environmental crises, addiction epidemics—and then breaking fasts with communal feasts that embody gospel hope. Health guidelines inform safe fasting practices—time-limited or intermittent fasts—ensuring participants remain physically sound. Feasting rituals use traditional liturgies, such as blessing bread and wine, to mark post-fast celebrations, reinforcing the link between body rhythms and spiritual milestones. Fasting workshops teach participants how to prepare mentally, hydrate responsibly, and integrate Scripture meditation, connecting physical hunger with spiritual yearning. Feasts often serve as fundraisers for community gardens or clean-water projects, channeling celebratory meals into service. Children's ministries adapt fasting to child-friendly forms—fasting from video games or sweets—paired with giving allowances to the poor, modeling communal solidarity. Each cycle of fasting and feasting thus becomes a sacramental practice, translating Isaiah's protest fast and Luke's wedding banquet into embodied expressions of repentance and praise. From these ancient rhythms, we transition to practical discernment of modern diet trends.

9.1.4 Contemporary Diet Movements: Mediterranean, Plant-Forward, Keto — Discernment Criteria

In recent decades, diets like Mediterranean, plant-forward, and ketogenic have risen to prominence, each backed by varying levels of scientific evidence. The Mediterranean diet emphasizes olive oil, whole grains, fruits, vegetables, and moderate fish, correlating with cardiovascular health and echoing biblical references to olive trees and grain offerings (Ps 128:3; Lev 2). Plant-forward approaches prioritize legumes, nuts, and produce, aligning with Genesis's original vegetarian mandate (Gen 1:29) while promoting environmental sustainability. Ketogenic diets, high in fats and low in carbohydrates, target metabolic pathways for weight loss and epilepsy management, though long-term cardiovascular effects remain under study. Faith communities develop discernment criteria for adopting or adapting these diets: theological coherence with stewardship principles, scientific validity via peer-reviewed research, and personal covenantal fit respecting health conditions. Congregational meal programs sample each diet's principles in cooking classes, inviting medical professionals to explain benefits and risks. Ethical discussions unpack the environmental and social justice implications of diet choices—such as overfishing or monocropping—linking table habits to creation care. Pastors preach that dietary freedom in Christ must be exercised with love and responsibility (Rom 14), avoiding judgment of those on different nutritional paths. Small groups evaluate diet claims critically, distinguishing sustainable lifestyle changes from fads. Through these discernment practices, believers integrate modern nutritional science with biblical wisdom, readying hearts and bodies for the corporate example of Daniel's experiment.

9.2 Daniel's Experiment Revisited (Dan 1)

9.2.1 Babylonian Rations vs. Garden Produce: Identity through Diet

In Babylon's royal court, Daniel and his companions refused the king's meat and wine, requesting vegetables and water to avoid defiling themselves (Dan 1:8–16). Their resolve embodied covenant identity, declaring that food choices reflect spiritual allegiance. Modern parallels arise in hospital settings where faith-based patients negotiate meal plans to avoid pork or shellfish, asserting religious convictions over default menus. Daniel's experiment lasted ten days but yielded visible health and clarity, suggesting that plant-based diets support physical and cognitive function. Churches draw on this narrative by hosting "Daniel Fast" weeks, where congregants subsist on fruits, vegetables, and water, turning the plateau into a devotional laboratory. Nutritionists partner with pastors to explain micronutrient functions—vitamins, minerals, antioxidants—highlighting parallels between Daniel's produce and modern understanding of phytonutrients. Community gardens supply fresh produce for fasting households, reinforcing both agricultural stewardship and spiritual discipline. Youth retreats incorporate Daniel Fast days, teaching teens to link bodily choices with identity in Christ. Testimonies often report improved digestion, increased focus in Bible study, and deeper reliance on God rather than daily comforts. Through Daniel's example, diet becomes a means of corporate witness, signaling that covenant loyalty can manifest in even the simplest food choices. This identity-through-diet model informs broader discussions on nutrition's mental and physical dimensions.

9.2.2 Micronutrients, Microbiome, and Mental Clarity: Modern Parallels

Contemporary science reveals that micronutrients like B vitamins, magnesium, and omega-3 fatty acids are crucial for neurotransmitter synthesis, impacting mood stability and mental clarity. A diverse, fiber-rich plant diet fosters a healthy gut microbiome, producing short-chain fatty acids that modulate inflammation and even influence brain function via the gut–brain axis. Studies link probiotic supplementation to reduced anxiety and depression scores, echoing the clarity Daniel gained on his vegetable regimen. Churches launch "Gut Health and Grace" seminars, inviting gastroenterologists and pastors to speak on how bodily health influences spiritual discernment. Meal-sharing ministries supply fermented foods—yogurt, sauerkraut—to congregation members on antidepressants, illustrating harmonious integration of science and faith. Worship music teams compose songs about "healthy soil within" to teach embodied metaphors of spiritual cultivation. Small groups monitor mood journals alongside dietary logs, noting correlations between nutrition and devotional depth. Parenting classes emphasize that childhood diets shape adult microbiomes, framing healthy eating as intergenerational discipleship. These modern parallels to Daniel's experience ground dietary theology in cutting-edge research, bridging ancient narrative with contemporary public health. Equipped with this knowledge, believers move from fasting experiments to corporate gatherings that heal rather than harm.

9.2.3 Corporate Witness: Church Potlucks That Heal Rather Than Harm

Potlucks exemplify Christian hospitality but can inadvertently promote unhealthy eating if dishes center on sugary desserts and fried foods. In response, health ministries curate "Healing Potlucks" where attendees sign up to bring plant-based casseroles, whole-grain salads, and fruit-based desserts. Recipes include Scripture references on index cards—such as "taste and see that the Lord is good" (Ps 34:8)—linking culinary experience to spiritual reflection. Serving stations offer nutrient information and suggested portion sizes, teaching moderation and informed choices. Children's Sunday school classes help prepare pre-cut vegetables, fostering early culinary skills and biblical stewardship of the body. Fellowship hall signage highlights food origins: local farms, organics, and community gardens, reinforcing creation care commitments. Testimony moments allow individuals to share how improved potluck diets reduced cholesterol and increased energy for service. Culinary workshops following worship teach members how to adapt heritage recipes—like jambalaya or kugel—into healthful versions without sacrificing flavor or cultural identity. Church councils endorse policies that minimize ultra-processed ingredients in building events, extending mission from pulpit to plates. Through these potlucks, congregations practice a corporate witness that celebrates community and cultivates health, embodying Daniel's commitment to covenant identity through food.

9.2.4 Public-School Lunch Advocacy: Extending Daniel's Resolve to Kids

Children spend considerable time in public-school cafeterias where generic lunches often contain processed meats, added sugars, and limited fresh produce. Schools facing budget constraints may default to low-cost, high-calorie options, contributing to childhood obesity and long-term health complications. Inspired by Daniel's example of principled diet, church-based volunteer coalitions collaborate with school boards to pilot "Garden-to-Table" initiatives, installing vegetable gardens on campus and incorporating harvests into cafeteria menus. Nutrition education programs led by youth ministry volunteers teach students biblical narratives of stewardship—such as Adam's mandate over plants (Gen 2:15)—alongside lessons on balanced meals. Parent–teacher fellowship groups petition for nutrient standards aligning with USDA guidelines, framing advocacy as caring for God's image bearers in our midst. Local pastors offer before-school devotionals in the garden, connecting spiritual formation with food literacy. Surveys show improvements in students' lunchtime fruit and vegetable consumption when faith community volunteers serve alongside cafeteria staff. These school partnerships model how Daniel's resolve can expand beyond individual households into systemic change for the next generation. As families and congregations advocate for healthier school lunches, they enact a public witness that our covenantal commitments to diet extend into the public square. From dietary identity and corporate witness, we now turn to the sobering topic of substance abuse and bodily stewardship.

9.3 Substance Abuse and the Temple Body (1 Cor 6:19–20)

9.3.1 Alcohol, Tobacco, and Chemical Dependency

Alcohol has long held a place in covenant rituals—Noah planting a vineyard (Gen 9:20) and Jesus turning water into wine (Jn 2:1–11)—yet Scripture warns against drunkenness, which denigrates both mind and body (Eph 5:18). Alcohol misuse contributes to liver disease, accidents, and family breakdown, demonstrating how a gift meant for joy can become a snare when abused. Tobacco, though not present in biblical times, now kills more than eight million people annually worldwide, serving as a modern idolatry of synthetic stimulation rather than divine provision. The addictive properties of nicotine hijack brain reward pathways, creating compulsions that resist mere moral exhortation. Chemical dependencies—opioids, prescription sedatives, stimulants—often begin in legitimate medical contexts but escalate into life-threatening addictions when safeguards lapse. The body, declared a temple of the Holy Spirit (1 Cor 6:19), suffers desecration under substance abuse, impairing faculties that God designed for worship, service, and relationship. Pastors and medical professionals must collaborate to educate congregations on the neurobiology of addiction, emphasizing that dependency is a medical challenge requiring compassionate response rather than moral condemnation. Sermons unpack biblical metaphors—such as Peter's sinking beneath the waves (Matt 14:30)—to illustrate how addictive cravings can pull believers under, only to be rescued by a Savior who reaches out His hand. Testimonies from recovering addicts who found freedom in Christ model the journey from bondage to wholeness. Churches display hotline numbers and host periodic "sobriety celebrations" alongside communion, integrating recovery milestones into life-of-faith narratives. Demystifying the pharmaceutical industry's role in opioid overprescription equips congregations for advocacy and prevention. Vigilance training helps volunteers recognize signs of relapse and intervene early, offering prayer and practical support. Nutritional counseling and exercise-based recovery groups address the physiological aftermath of substance abuse, helping restore bodily integrity. Through these multifaceted efforts, faith communities honor the temple body and reclaim substances as gifts rather than masters.

9.3.2 Recovery Ministries and Accountability

Recovery ministries translate biblical fellowship into structured peer support, echoing Galatians 6's call to "carry each other's burdens" so none walk the recovery path alone. Celebrate Recovery, one such model, adapts the twelve-step framework with Christian language, framing addiction as both spiritual brokenness and neurological disease. Steps like "Admitted powerlessness" echo Jesus's invitation to come "weary and burdened" and find rest (Matt 11:28). Sponsorship pairs newer participants with seasoned mentors who guide both through accountability meetings and personal check-ins. These relationships mirror the disciple-making pattern of Paul and Timothy (2 Tim 2:2), embedding recovery within a context of layered teaching and shared life. Small-group recovery circles pray through each person's triggers, scripturally rebuking strongholds of addiction in the name of Jesus (2 Cor 10:4–5). Churches allocate sober living homes as extensions of hospitality, offering safe environments where residents rebuild routines, work skills, and faith rhythms. Volunteers receive training in trauma-informed care, recognizing that many addictions root in past wounds rather than mere bad choices.

Celebratory ceremonies mark milestones—30 days, 90 days, one year—blending testimony, prayer, and symbolic rituals such as lighting candles. Worship services spotlight recovery testimonies alongside typical sermons, integrating the journey of liberation into corporate identity. Partnerships with local treatment centers streamline referrals, ensuring that congregants access professional counseling, medication-assisted therapy, and relapse prevention classes. Annual "Freedom Fairs" host booths from medical providers, legal advocates, and pastoral counselors, presenting a unified network of hope. As accountability fosters transparency, shame yields to community and transformative grace, reflecting the gospel's power to break every chain.

9.4 Formation of Holy Habits

9.4.1 Rule of Life for Sleep, Movement, and Digital Hygiene

A balanced rule of life honors God's design for embodied rhythms. Scripture commands one day of Sabbath rest in seven (Ex 20:8–11), reminding believers that uninterrupted labor leads to weariness. Modern sleep science confirms that adults require seven to nine hours of restorative sleep nightly, with consistent bedtimes synchronizing circadian rhythms to sunlight patterns. Faith communities encourage "Sleep Sabbaths," where members turn off screens two hours before bed, read Scripture, and engage in breath prayers to calm the mind. Movement ministries—walking prayer groups, church-wide step challenges, or gentle yoga classes with Christian meditation—address the apostolic call to present bodies as living sacrifices (Rom 12:1). These gatherings integrate worship music, prayer prompts, and group accountability to ensure exercise becomes both physical and spiritual discipline. Digital hygiene strategies mitigate the addictive pull of devices that bombard the brain with dopamine hits. Congregations host "Tech Sabbaths" where members collectively unplug on Sunday afternoons, dedicating time to family, community service, or silent retreat. Workshops teach participants to install usage-tracking apps, establish no-screen zones in homes, and adopt device-free meal times that echo Daniel's disciplined diet. Small groups share successes and failures, weaving transparency into habit formation. By embedding sleep, movement, and digital boundaries into a rule of life, believers steward gifts of rest, vitality, and focus as acts of worship rather than mere self-help tactics.

9.4.2 Breath Prayer and Stress Cycling: Cortisol under Christ's Lordship

Stress hormones like cortisol surge in response to perceived threats, harming immune function and mental health when chronically elevated. Breath prayers—short phrases synchronized with inhalation and exhalation—activate the parasympathetic nervous system, reducing cortisol and anchoring attention in God's presence. For example, inhaling "Lord Jesus" and exhaling "have mercy" turns each breath into a miniature sacrament of grace. Churches offer "Prayer Breath Workshops" teaching diaphragmatic breathing, scriptural anchors, and mindfulness breaks during worship. Stress cycling practices—alternating focused work with brief breaks for fast prayer or stretching—mirror Jesus's pattern of active ministry and withdrawal for prayer (Lk 5:16). Office ministries encourage employees to set reminders for "two-minute retreats," stepping outside to pray Psalm 46:10 or utter the Jesus prayer. Support groups measure cortisol levels pre- and post-breath prayer sessions, documenting physiological benefits that validate spiritual practice. Pastors preach on "Be still and know that I am God" as a gospel antidote to burnout, demonstrating how repeated breath prayer cultivates inner sanctuary. Over time, these micro-disciplines accumulate, shaping resilience for ministry and daily life. By placing cortisol under Christ's lordship, faith communities integrate ancient prayer rhythms with contemporary stress management, embodying holistic care for soul and body.

9.4.3 Budgeting as Discipleship: Food Dollars, Pharma Costs, and Generosity

Financial stewardship shapes lifestyle health choices when budgets determine what groceries end up in pantries and which medications are affordable. The parable of the talents (Matt 25:14–30) models faithful management of God's resources, prompting believers to allocate funds for nutritious food, gym memberships, and necessary prescriptions. Churches offer "Health Budget Bootcamps" where financial counselors collaborate with dietitians to show how plant-based menus can reduce grocery costs while improving wellness. Workshop attendees learn to compare price-per-nutrient values, distinguishing between calorie-dense junk food and cost-effective whole foods like beans and oats. Ministry benevolence funds earmark support for low-income families needing diabetes supplies or blood-pressure medication, reflecting James's call to care for orphans and widows (Jas 1:27). Small-group challenges encourage members to track monthly healthcare expenses and prayerfully reallocate nonessential spending toward prevention—such as gym classes over takeout. Youth programs include "Allowance for Health" units, teaching teens to budget for sports or healthy snacks rather than video-game add-ons. Testimonies from families who trimmed media subscriptions to fund therapy highlight the spiritual dimension of financial choices. By framing budgeting as discipleship, congregations reveal that where our treasure is, our health habits follow.

9.4.4 Tech Tools: Apps for Mindful Eating, Sobriety Tracking, and Sabbath Alerts

Digital tools can both undermine and support holy habits. Apps designed for mindful eating prompt users to log meals, reflect on hunger cues, and set portion reminders, integrating Scripture-based gratitude prompts between entries. Celebrate Recovery and other sobriety apps offer daily devotionals, sobriety calendars, and anonymous peer chat rooms, reinforcing accountability and spiritual reflection in moments of temptation. Sabbath alert apps send notifications to power down devices early on Friday nights, blessing families with device-free dinner times and devotional gatherings. Sleep-tracking wearables feed back data to health ministries, identifying patterns of insomnia among shift workers for targeted pastoral support. Budgeting apps categorize spending automatically and can flag church benevolence funds for referrals to those facing financial-health crises. Faith-based meditation apps combine guided imagery, breath prayer scripts, and worship music, enabling users to practice stress cycling anywhere. Churches sponsor "Tech Fair" nights where congregants demo recommended apps, share tips, and troubleshoot privacy settings. A collective digital covenant underscores that apps serve our growth rather than govern it. Through thoughtful integration of technology, believers leverage modern tools to reinforce ancient rhythms of health and Sabbath rest.

9.5 Environmental Justice and Public Health

9.5.1 Pollution Hot-Spots, Redlining, and Respiratory Disease

Urban neighborhoods historically subjected to redlining often host highways and industrial zones, exposing residents to particulate matter that exacerbates asthma and chronic obstructive pulmonary disease. Isaiah's vision of justice rolling down like waters (Isa 58:6) compels churches to advocate for fair zoning practices that remove these pollution hot-spots from vulnerable communities. Faith leaders partner with environmental scientists to conduct air-quality monitoring near schools and playgrounds, publishing "community health scorecards" that influence municipal planning. Congregations train volunteers in home assessment visits, identifying mold, lead paint, and diesel exhaust infiltration, then coordinate referrals to public-health agencies. Sunday school classes adopt service projects planting street trees that filter air, demonstrating creation care as a public-health intervention. Pastoral sermons highlight Paul's description of the body as temple (1 Cor 6:19), linking respiratory health to stewardship of God's dwelling place. Law clinics hosted by churches assist residents in filing environmental justice claims, enforcing regulations like the Clean Air Act. Interfaith coalitions stage prayer walks along polluted corridors, interceding for health and policy change. Local hospitals collaborate with faith communities to offer free lung-function screenings, combining clinical care with spiritual support. These coordinated efforts transform neighborhoods from zones of neglect into arenas of gospel justice and healing.

9.5.2 Climate Change, Heat Islands, and Cardiovascular Stress

Rising temperatures and the urban heat-island effect increase heat-related illnesses and cardiovascular strain, particularly among seniors and outdoor laborers—often the working poor. Leviticus's provision for gleaning fields (Lev 19:9–10) points to social care structures; today, church networks can set up cooling centers in air-conditioned fellowship halls during heat waves, offering hydration stations and prayer. Congregations deliver fans and educate about hydration and heat-stroke warning signs, linking neighbor-love with creation-care action. Sermons on God's care for the vulnerable (Matt 25:35) galvanize volunteers to canvas door-to-door, distributing heat advisories and reflective window film. Youth groups plant community gardens with shade trees, reducing surface temperatures and modeling proactive environmental stewardship. Public-health partnerships deploy mobile clinics to monitor blood pressure and heart rates during heat events, offering medical check-ups alongside pastoral counsel. Churches join municipal climate resilience task forces, ensuring faith voices shape local adaptation plans. Educational series unpack the spiritual dimension of "dominion" in Genesis (Gen 1:28), reframing it as responsible caretaking that prevents harm from climate extremes. These holistic interventions demonstrate that addressing climate change is not optional but integral to protecting God's image-bearers from avoidable health risks.

9.5.3 Food Deserts and Water Crises: Amos's Prophetic Voice Today

The prophet Amos denounced economic systems that left the needy without access to the basics of life (Amos 8:11–12). Today, food deserts—urban areas lacking affordable fresh produce—and water crises—where wells run dry or contain contaminants—mirror ancient injustices. Churches establish urban farms and mobile produce trucks to bring fruits and vegetables into food deserts, teaching nutritional literacy and hosting cooking demonstrations. Water-blessing rituals emphasize baptismal themes and promote filtration systems for households relying on unsafe sources. Faith communities partner with global NGOs to drill wells in water-scarce regions, interweaving mission outreach with local church planting. Sunday collections fund community water projects, and youth fundraisers challenge teens to track and reduce their personal water footprints. Pastoral sermons draw on Jesus's promise of living water (Jn 4:14), linking spiritual thirst with physical hydration campaigns. Legal clinics assist residents in securing safe water rights under the Clean Water Act, embodying prophetic intervention. Intergenerational teams build rainwater-harvesting systems at churches, modeling sustainable practices. These prophetic actions turn biblical lament into concrete justice for neighbors lacking basic sustenance.

9.5.4 Congregational Advocacy: Solar Panels, Community Gardens, and Legislative Testimony

Environmental stewardship requires both grassroots practice and policy engagement. Churches install solar arrays on fellowship-hall roofs, reducing utility costs and carbon footprints, while worship teams incorporate creation-care prayers into liturgies. Community gardens on church grounds supply produce for food-pantry distributions, as well as serve as outdoor classrooms for youth education. Faith leaders testify before city councils in support of green-space zoning, urban-farm incentives, and clean-energy budgets, translating theological convictions into public policy. Inter-church networks collaborate on climate action plans, sharing resources for energy audits and sustainability workshops. Deacons oversee "Green Sunday" events where congregations assess waste streams, implement composting, and switch to reusable communion vessels. Partnerships with local universities facilitate research on church-based carbon reductions, producing case studies that inform denominational guidelines. By lifting prophetic voices in the public square, congregations demonstrate that the gospel compels care for creation as a pathway to human health, completing our exploration of environmental justice, and leading us toward integrative medical partnerships in the next chapter.

9.6 Creation Care as Preventive Medicine

9.6.1 Biodiversity and Immune Resilience: The "Hygiene Hypothesis" in Genesis Garb

The Genesis mandate to fill the earth invites an appreciation for biodiversity not only as aesthetic wonder but as a source of microbial richness vital to human health. Modern research on the "hygiene hypothesis" shows that children exposed to diverse soil bacteria—through play in gardens or farms—develop stronger immune systems and lower rates of allergies and autoimmune diseases. This scientific insight resonates with Leviticus's concern for soil and community health (Lev 25), suggesting that God's design included microbial partners in our flourishing. Churches sponsor "Dirt Days" where families plant pollinator gardens, encouraging children to experience healthy microbial exchange through unhurried outdoor play. Medical volunteers measure participants' immunoglobulin levels before and after gardening programs, finding reductions in inflammatory markers. Pastoral reflections highlight how stepping onto raw earth echoes biblical imagery of being rooted and resilient (Ps 1:3). Community partnerships with local parks ensure that urban neighborhoods regain natural habitats, counteracting sterile, lifeless playgrounds that limit microbial exposure. Seminary courses in pastoral care now integrate basic ecology into discussions of bodily wholeness, urging ministers to bless the earth as part of spiritual formation. Small-group sermons draw parallels between Christ's promise to restore creation (Rom 8:19–22) and renewed gut flora in human bodies. Environmental restoration initiatives become acts of preventive medicine, as congregants witness fewer childhood eczema and asthma cases in areas adjacent to church-sponsored green spaces. Through these biodiverse practices, faith communities embody preventive care, realizing that God's good creation extends healing capacity before illness claims its toll.

9.6.2 Green Spaces, Mental Health, and Urban Church Campuses

Access to green spaces—trees, lawns, community gardens—correlates with lower rates of depression, anxiety, and stress among city residents. The psalmist's delight in trees and fields (Ps 104) anticipates what modern environmental psychology confirms:

exposure to nature promotes parasympathetic activity, reduces cortisol, and enhances cognitive restoration. Urban churches transform asphalt lots into pocket parks, installing benches under shade trees where homeless neighbors and stressed professionals alike find respite. Pastoral care teams schedule nature walks during weekly support groups, teaching mindfulness prayers amid leaves and birdsong. Youth ministries incorporate "Creation Care Camps" where children learn tree identification, linking scientific observation with theological celebration of God's handiwork. Mental-health clinicians working with the church report that clients who attend outdoor worship services experience measurable improvements in mood and attention. Congregational architecture integrates green walls and rooftop gardens, turning sanctuaries into living cathedrals that praise God through chlorophyll-rich leaves. Community surveys reveal increased well-being scores among older adults with access to church gardens, prompting partnerships with local health departments to refer patients for weekly gardening therapy. Sermons reference Isaiah's vision of the desert blooming (Isa 35:1) as metaphor for mental gardens replanted by hope. Grants from faith-based foundations support urban reforestation projects, aligning public health goals with gospel witness. These initiatives demonstrate that creating and tending green spaces is as much spiritual care as it is preventive medicine, inviting all bodies to draw healing oxygen and tranquility from God's created order.

9.6.3 Sustainable Agriculture, Fair Trade, and Eucharistic Ethics

Sustainable agriculture practices—crop rotation, agroforestry, organic composting—maintain soil fertility and reduce chemical runoff, promoting long-term health for communities and ecosystems. Early church admonitions to glean fields and leave corners for the poor (Lev 19:9) anticipate modern fair-trade movements that guarantee justice for smallholder farmers. Congregations form buying co-ops for fair-trade coffee, chocolate, and sugar, ensuring vulnerable producers receive livable wages and invest in community health. Pastors preach that the Eucharist's bread and wine connect believers to fields and vineyards around the world, calling for ethical sourcing that honors laborers' dignity. Women's ministries host seed-saving workshops, preserving heirloom varieties that thrive in local microclimates and support nutritional diversity. Community-supported agriculture (CSA) partnerships between churches and farms deliver weekly produce boxes, reducing food miles and exposing families to seasonal eating. Nutrition educators demonstrate preparing CSA items in cooking classes, weaving biblical hospitality with healthy cuisine. Impact studies show reduced rates of type 2 diabetes among CSA subscribers, underscoring sustainable agriculture's role in preventive medicine. Churches advocate in municipal councils for urban agriculture ordinances, enabling rooftop farms and market gardens within city limits. Development ministries extend these models overseas, training church-planting teams to integrate sustainable farming into rural disciple-making. By aligning Eucharistic ethics with fair-trade and agroecology, congregations embody a vision where every meal testifies to God's covenant justice and care for body and planet.

9.6.4 Disaster Preparedness Ministries: Wildfire Smoke to Hurricane Mold

Climate change intensifies natural disasters—wildfires produce toxic smoke, storms flood homes creating mold hazards—and faith communities must prepare congregations accordingly. Churches establish emergency response teams trained in air-quality monitoring, distributing N95 masks during wildfire events to protect respiratory health. After hurricanes, volunteer crews remove water-damaged drywall and apply mold inhibitors, preventing respiratory infections and allergic disease in vulnerable neighbors. Sermons on Christ's presence in the storm (Mk 4:39) precede practical drills where families store emergency kits including water purification tablets and first-aid supplies. Neighborhood "buddy systems" match high-risk individuals—seniors, asthma sufferers—with volunteers who check on them during disasters, combining pastoral care with public health outreach. Community grant writing secures funds for portable air cleaners in daycare centers, ensuring children breathe safe air during smog episodes. Deacons coordinate with county emergency managers to designate church buildings as cooling or warming centers, addressing extreme-temperature events that stress cardiovascular health. Training sessions include basic mold remediation techniques, teaching antimicrobial cleaning methods that prevent fungal respiratory illness. Disaster-response prayer caravans distribute care packages—blankets, nonperishable food, hygiene kits—and pray over affected homes, affirming spiritual solidarity with physical aid. Through these preparedness ministries, churches model resilience-building as preventive medicine, harnessing communal capacity to protect bodies and nurture hope when creation groans under climate extremes.

9.7 Integrative Medical Partnerships

9.7.1 Physicians, Dietitians, and Pastors: Building Tri-Chord Clinics

Holistic health flourishes when medical, nutritional, and spiritual care converge in integrative "tri-chord" clinics co-sponsored by churches and health systems. Physicians diagnose and treat disease, dietitians design personalized meal plans, and pastors provide pastoral counseling addressing existential and behavioral motivation factors. Shared electronic records include spiritual assessments alongside medical and dietary notes, facilitating coordinated treatment plans. Weekly case conferences ensure each professional updates the team on patient progress—medication adherence, dietary compliance, spiritual struggles—enabling real-time adjustments. Faith-based clinics integrate chapels or prayer rooms where patients receive communion or anointing oil as part of chronic-disease management. Programs track metrics like hemoglobin A1c, body-mass index, and spiritual well-being scores, demonstrating multidimensional improvement. Community health fairs held on church campuses recruit volunteers fluent in food-demo techniques and pastoral listening skills. Graduate programs in pastoral theology partner with medical schools to develop joint residencies, training clinicians to recognize spiritual distress and ministers to interpret biomedical data. Funding streams combine health-insurance reimbursements, church benevolence, and charitable grants, sustaining clinic operations. As trust grows, congregants refer friends and neighbors, extending the reach of integrative care beyond formal membership. These tri-chord clinics manifest the biblical vision of body–soul unity, where healers and shepherds collaborate under God's mandate to care for the whole person.

9.7.2 Screening Protocols during Home Visits: BP Cuffs and Prayer Shawls

Home-bound members often miss preventive screenings that catch hypertension, diabetes, and depression early. Mobile pastoral teams carry blood-pressure cuffs, glucometers, and mental-health questionnaires alongside prayer shawls and Scripture bookmarks. A routine home visit may begin with a check of vital signs, followed by guided breath prayer to calm anxiety before a meal. Pastors record readings in congregation health dashboards, prompting referrals to clinicians when metrics exceed healthy thresholds. Family members learn to monitor loved ones' blood pressure and blood sugar, embedding health literacy into home life. Training modules for volunteers cover proper device use, troubleshooting, and infection-control measures, ensuring both clinical accuracy and safety. Teams demonstrate healthy cooking techniques using telemedicine tablets, connecting dietitians to kitchens in real time. After measurements and prayer, volunteers share devotional readings that speak to perseverance, linking physical and spiritual well-being. When abnormal readings arise, follow-up visits include spiritual care and practical referrals, embodying seamless pastoral–medical collaboration. Over time, congregational data show reductions in emergency hospitalizations, validating home-visit protocols. These integrated screenings ensure that sacred care extends into everyday living spaces, honoring bodies as temples wherever they reside.

9.7.3 Referral Pathways for Addiction Treatment, Nutrition Counseling, and Environmental Services

No single ministry can address every health need, making clear referral pathways essential. Churches map local resources—rehabilitation centers, dietetic clinics, environmental justice organizations—and develop laminated referral cards that volunteers carry during outreach. When a recovery ministry leader encounters a family facing diabetes, a quick referral to a nutrition counselor transforms the encounter into a continuum of care. A pastor counseling a grieving spouse who smokes may introduce a tobacco-cessation support group within days rather than months. Environmental specialists trained in indoor air quality are on call to assess mold or radon hazards identified during home visits. Each referral loop includes a follow-up covenant: the ministry remembers the referred person and ensures they connect with the service, mirroring Christ's promise to never abandon those He sends out (John 14:18). Referral tracking uses secure spreadsheets to measure engagement rates and identify gaps in service coverage. Quarterly "network nights" convene partner agencies on church grounds to streamline intake procedures and co-train staff on shared mission values. By weaving these pathways into congregational life, churches become hubs of holistic care, guiding individuals through medical, nutritional, and environmental transformations.

9.7.4 Data-Driven Discipleship: Using Congregational Health Dashboards

Quantifying health outcomes enables churches to steward resources and evaluate ministry effectiveness. Health dashboards display anonymized aggregates—average blood pressures, diabetes control rates, BMI distributions, addiction recovery milestones—updated monthly. Pastorals and medical teams review dashboards in leadership meetings, celebrating improvements and identifying areas for targeted intervention. Data transparency invites congregational engagement: quarterly reports in newsletters showcase health gains and outline upcoming initiatives. Dashboard metrics correlate participation in health ministries—such as cooking classes or support groups—with biometric improvements, reinforcing faithfulness to healthy habits. Fellowship hall screens display real-time stats during health fairs, motivating attendees to join programs that need stronger sign-ups. Ethical guidelines ensure privacy and informed consent for data collection, aligning with biblical calls for honesty and respect (Eph 4:25). Graduate students in public-health programs partner with churches to analyze trends and co-author presentations at faith–health conferences. This data-driven discipleship exemplifies stewardship of both bodies and resources, completing integrative partnerships as a foundation for global health perspectives.

9.8 Global Perspectives on Lifestyle Disease

9.8.1 Diabetes in the Majority World: Soda Imports and Sugar Taxes

Low- and middle-income countries now bear a disproportionate burden of type 2 diabetes as global soda corporations target emerging markets with cheap sugary drinks. Biblical concern for justice (Amos 5:24) compels faith communities to advocate for sugar taxes that curb consumption and fund public health programs. Churches in urban slums partner with microfinance initiatives to support entrepreneurs producing fresh juices from local fruits, creating healthy alternatives and economic opportunities. Mission hospital data show that introducing tax-funded diabetes education reduces HbA1c levels among patients by significant margins. Pastors preach stewardship of the body that includes resisting addictive beverages, framing sugar-sweetened drinks as modern idols that promise joy but deliver disease. International networks share case studies: Mexican churches contributed to soda-tax campaigns, while Filipino parishes lobbied for front-of-package labeling. Pediatric ministries educate children on reading nutrition labels, mirroring Proverbs 4:7's call to wisdom before purchase. These global efforts demonstrate that local action against lifestyle disease can ripple into systemic change across nations, reflecting gospel solidarity with the world's poor.

9.8.2 Mission Hospitals and Community Health Evangelism

Mission hospitals often stand at the forefront of lifestyle-disease management in impoverished regions, integrating curative surgery with preventive education. Clinics in sub-Saharan Africa run "Health Literacy Sundays," where pastors and physicians jointly teach about hypertension control, dietary diversity, and exercise adapted to local contexts. Congregational "health evangelism teams" conduct home visits after Sunday worship, screening for cardiovascular risk and teaching blood-pressure self-monitoring. Patient support groups use Bible stories—like Jesus feeding the 5,000—to frame principles of sharing and moderation, reinforcing community resilience. Missionary training now includes modules on cultural dietary practices, ensuring that recommendations respect local foods and traditions. Fundraising dinners in sending countries pair recipient hospitals with sponsoring churches, fostering bi-directional relationships rather than one-way assistance. Data collected by mission hospitals—on infection rates, chronic-disease prevalence, and health behavior change—inform both local strategy and global health discourse. These mission partnerships model holistic evangelism that addresses physical and spiritual hunger together.

9.8.3 Cultural Foods, Colonial Histories, and Gospel Freedom

Colonialism disrupted indigenous foodways, replacing diverse staples with export crops and imported commodities, often undermining nutritional status and cultural identity. Postcolonial churches reclaim traditional grains—millet, teff, sorghum—in community feasts that celebrate ancestral wisdom and resist unhealthy imported diets. Scripture's affirmation of cultural diversity (Rev 7:9) supports a gospel that values local culinary heritage as gifts of God's creativity. Educational programs explore how sugarcane, coffee, and cacao markets tied to colonial exploitation inform current debates on fair trade and ethical consumption. Intercultural liturgies incorporate native foods and prayers in multiple languages, reinforcing that the kingdom includes every tribe's table. Global seminaries offer culinary practicum courses, teaching future leaders how to integrate cultural foods into healthy diets. By honoring cultural cuisines and critiquing colonial legacies, faith communities link gospel freedom with food sovereignty, demonstrating that following Christ includes liberating bodies from oppressive dietary patterns.

9.8.4 Pandemic Lessons: Immunity, Inequity, and International Solidarity

The COVID-19 pandemic exposed stark health inequities—vaccine apartheid, overcrowded slums, overwhelmed health systems—that amplify lifestyle vulnerabilities. Scripture's call to bear one another's burdens (Gal 6:2) found new urgency as churches repurposed buildings for vaccination clinics, mask distribution, and public-health education. Global south congregations shared homemade cloth masks and herbal remedies, while northern partners funded cold-chain supplies for vaccine transport. Lessons on immune resilience—through nutrition, rest, and stress management—were disseminated via online forums crossing language barriers. Missionaries adapted quarantine protocols to include telechaplaincy visits, ensuring spiritual care amid physical isolation. International coalitions lobbied vaccine manufacturers for patent waivers, invoking Deuteronomy's gleaning principles to argue for shared health goods. Churches that had invested in environmental health saw lower infection rates, linking preventive infrastructures—clean water, sanitation, ventilation—to pandemic preparedness. Post-pandemic, faith communities continue to advocate for global health equity, demonstrating that lifestyle interventions and structural reforms must converge to build resilient societies. The pandemic's lessons prepare us to integrate local stewardship with global solidarity as we taste and see God's goodness in a shared ecology of health.

9.9 Epilogue — Taste and See: Toward a Kingdom Ecology of Health

A kingdom vision of health integrates personal choices—what we eat, how we move, what we breathe—with communal and civic structures that shape environmental exposures and resource distribution. Households learn to practice moderation and gratitude, cultivate rule-of-life habits, and steward budgets for wellness. Churches model holistic care through integrative clinics, recovery ministries, and environmental justice advocacy. Civic leaders partner with faith communities to design policies—sugar taxes, green-space ordinances, disaster response plans—that embody neighbor love at scale. Cross-sector collaboration among pastors, physicians, ecologists, and policy-makers becomes a hallmark of preventive medicine informed by covenantal ethics. Data-driven discipleship guides ongoing evaluation and refinement of health ministries. As believers taste and see the Lord's goodness in the well-nurtured body and healed creation, they become living testimonies to the gospel's power to transform every dimension of life.

Conclusion As we have seen, stewardship of body and environment is not an optional Christian extra but a vital expression of gospel integrity. Healthy eating, disciplined habits, recovery from addiction, and advocacy for clean air and water all flow from our identity as image-bearers called to cultivate God's world and honor our neighbors. By integrating biblical wisdom with cutting-edge research and community action, believers can transform kitchens, clinics, and city councils into arenas of grace and health. Moving forward, we will carry these lessons into the quieter struggles of chronic pain and disability, where perseverance in weakness becomes the next frontier of faith-filled care.

Chapter 10 – Genetics, Mutation, and Evolution: A Theology of Biology

Modern biology peels back the wrapper of life to reveal a stunning code of four letters—A, C, G, and T—inscribed in every cell, yet this code carries the echoes of Eden's perfection and the scars of humanity's fall. As we explore DNA's marvels, from the stability that preserves our identity to the small mutations that drive adaptation, we will trace how Providence weaves redemption even through genetic brokenness. We will wrestle with the promises and perils of technologies that can rewrite our own genomes, asking how to honor the Imago Dei while alleviating suffering. Along the way, we'll grapple with questions of lineage and identity, ethical stewardship of cutting-edge medicine, and the ultimate hope of a resurrection body that transcends heredity. By reading the story of our molecules in the light of Scripture, we discover that biology itself bears witness to our Creator's power to make all things new.

10.0 Prelude — Genes in the Light of Glory

10.0.1 From Double Helix to Dust-and-Breath: How DNA echoes Genesis

The discovery of DNA's double-helix structure revealed a molecular script inscribed in every cell, guiding development from a single fertilized egg to a complex organism. Yet long before Watson and Crick's model, Genesis recorded that God formed humans from dust and breathed into them the breath of life (Gen 2:7), hinting at an invisible code infused by divine Spirit. Every nucleotide pairing—adenine with thymine, cytosine with guanine—echoes the divine fidelity that binds covenant promises, suggesting that genetic stability and occasional mutation reflect both constancy and creative freedom. Scripture's recurring metaphors of seed and offspring mirror biological inheritance, reminding us that physical descent carries spiritual significance as well. When cells replicate, they copy the genetic code with astonishing accuracy, yet the small errors that slip through resemble God's allowance for variation within creation. The intricate choreography of transcription and translation evokes the biblical theme of God speaking creation into being, each codon functioning like a spoken word that brings proteins to life. Pastoral reflection sees in genetic repair mechanisms—DNA polymerases and mismatch enzymes—a picture of divine mercy that corrects our errors before they cascade into disease. The complexity of gene regulation, with enhancers and silencers, parallels the layered revelation of Scripture that unfolds over time. Epigenetic marks laid down by environmental factors resonate with biblical imagery of heart transformation, where external influences shape inner identity. The awe inspired by genetic complexity invites doxology, as Job declared that God's works are too marvelous to explore fully (Job 37:5). In seminaries, students learn that the dust-and-breath account and DNA story are not competitors but complementary narratives, each illuminating facets of our creaturely dependence and divine calling. This molecular wonder prepares us to confront the ways our genomes bear the scars of the Fall and the potential for repair that God ordains.

10.0.2 Reading the "Book of Life": Scripture, Sequencing, and Epistemic Humility

The Bible speaks of a "book of life" that lists the names of the redeemed (Phil 4:3; Rev 20:12), assuring believers of their secure identity before God. In a parallel vein, modern sequencing technologies can read billions of base pairs to produce an "exome" or "genome" report, charting predispositions to disease and ancestral origins. Yet both forms of "reading" require humility: Scripture demanders a posture of listening and reverence, while genomic data demands careful interpretation within scientific and ethical frameworks. Overconfidence in genetic determinism risks diminishing human freedom and undermines the biblical affirmation of moral agency and repentance. At the same time, disregard for genetic insight can lead to neglect of treatable conditions, undermining our duty to steward God's gifts wisely. Theologians and geneticists convene "bioethics cafés" to discuss how to hold Scripture's authority and scientific data in constructive tension. Clinical genetic counseling sessions often begin with a prayer acknowledging human limitation and divine sovereignty over mysteries beyond our grasp (Deut 29:29). Congregations that incorporate genetic education into adult classes learn to speak of predisposition rather than destiny, affirming that genes set the stage but do not write the final act. This epistemic humility fosters compassionate engagement with those facing genetic diagnoses: families understand that while a BRCA mutation increases cancer risk, it does not seal one's fate any more than the Fall seals ultimate redemption. Just as believers trust the God who remembers every hair on our heads (Matt 10:30), so they trust that genetic revelations belong within the larger narrative of creation, fall, redemption, and consummation. As we close the prelude, we turn to how God's providence and the Fall converge in our DNA.

10.1 DNA, Providence, and the Fall

10.1.1 Genetic Disorders, Broken Creation, and Common-Grace Repair Mechanisms

Genetic disorders—sickle-cell disease, cystic fibrosis, Down syndrome—reveal how hereditary information can carry brokenness in bodies and families. Tears in DNA's code produce malformed proteins, leading to chronic illness and suffering that call attention to the pervasive effects of the Fall on creation itself. Yet even amid this brokenness, common grace affords repair mechanisms: our cells harbor enzymes that mend oxidative DNA damage caused by normal metabolism. These polymerases and nucleases echo God's sustaining work, preserving life against the odds. In pediatric genetics clinics, physicians cite Romans 8:22's groaning creation to frame diagnoses within God's larger redemptive story rather than as random tragedy. Families often describe moments of miraculous stabilization—sickle crises averted by hydration protocols and hydroxyurea—which they credit to both medical ingenuity and divine mercy. Research into gene modifiers that ameliorate severity of genetic diseases underscores how genome-wide interactions can soften monogenic disorders, pointing to a resilience embedded in our molecular architecture. Pastors visiting hospital wards bless families with anointing oil and prayers for DNA's own repair enzymes, integrating sacramental gestures with scientific appreciation. Ethical debates emerge when considering whether to view repair mechanisms as mere natural processes or as channels of divine common grace. The coexistence of inherited brokenness and intrinsic repair potential invites disciples to minister both medicine and mercy, standing in solidarity with sufferers while celebrating God's ongoing handiwork in the cell.

10.1.2 Neutral and Beneficial Mutations: Evolutionary Resilience and Divine Freedom

Not all mutations are harmful; many are neutral, having no discernible effect on phenotype, while some confer advantages—such as sickle-cell trait providing malaria resistance or CCR5-delta32 conferring HIV immunity. These instances of beneficial mutation showcase life's adaptive potential and resilience in changing environments. Theologically, such variation reflects divine freedom in creation, where the Creator allows contingent processes to unfold, inviting creatures to steward and explore these genetic possibilities. Psalm 104's praise of God's ongoing provision—"you provide water for the earth…you make grass…that it may give food"—finds molecular echo when mutations give rise to new traits that expand ecological niches. In evolutionary theology seminars, students debate whether God directs mutation probabilities or works providentially through stochastic events, ultimately affirming both God's sovereignty and creaturely agency. Research into lactase persistence among certain populations illustrates how diet-culture interactions shape genetic landscapes, echoing Deuteronomy's covenantal adaptation to land and lifestyle. Garden ministries plant heirloom seeds to maintain biodiversity, reminding congregations that mutation-driven variation undergirds ecosystem health. Laypeople astonished by CRISPR documentaries often ask whether editing out harmful mutations infringes on divine creativity, prompting pastors to preach on co-creation and the redemptive potential of biotechnology. Through neutral and beneficial mutations, life demonstrates robustness that points back to the Creator's promise of resilience even amid fallen constraints.

10.1.3 Epigenetics, Trauma, and Generational "Curses" — Methyl Tags in a Theological Key

Epigenetics studies how environmental factors—stress, nutrition, toxins—leave chemical marks on DNA that regulate gene expression without altering the underlying sequence. These methyl and acetyl tags can persist across cell divisions and, in some cases, be inherited across generations, providing a biological basis for transgenerational trauma or resilience. The notion that trauma leaves molecular scars echoes biblical warnings of ancestral sin's effects, as when God declares that He punishes the iniquity of the fathers to the third and fourth generation (Ex 34:7). Yet Scripture also affirms that mercy triumphs over judgment, inviting repentance and divine reset. In trauma-informed pastoral care, counselors teach that while epigenetic influences can predispose individuals to anxiety or inflammatory conditions, nurturing environments and spiritual practices can remodel epigenetic landscapes, aligning with Micah's call to "walk humbly" but also enjoy God's lovingkindness. Parenting workshops discuss how intergenerational patterns—such as addiction or depression—may reflect both learned behavior and epigenetic inheritance, empowering families to break cycles of despair through faith, therapy, and lifestyle change. Church-based seminars on epigenetics emphasize genes as potentiality rather than destiny, reinforcing John 8:36's promise of freedom. Collaboration between pediatricians and pastors yields programs that support pregnant mothers in healthy behaviors—nutrition, stress reduction, prayer—optimizing epigenetic outcomes for the next generation. By reading methyl tags through a theological lens, believers discern patterns of brokenness and grace, understanding how God can heal not just individuals but entire family lines.

10.2 Evolution, Natural Selection, and Theological Horizons

10.2.1 Cooperation vs. Competition: Kenosis and the Dance of the Genomes

Natural selection often emphasizes survival of the fittest, but evolutionary biology also highlights cooperation—symbiosis between species, mutualistic relationships like those of gut microbiota and human hosts, and social altruism that enhances group survival. This cooperative dynamic echoes the kenosis of Christ, who emptied Himself for the sake of others (Phil 2:7), modeling a sacrificial love that transcends competitive self-interest. Genomes themselves bear evidence of ancient viral sequences repurposed for placental development, illustrating how cooperation at the molecular level undergirds our very capacity for life. In bioethics courses, students explore how horizontal gene transfer in microbes challenges strict vertical inheritance models, pointing to a communal dimension in evolution. Church teachings on shalom resonate with scientific accounts of microbial and macro-organism cooperation that maintain ecosystems' stability. Community gardens foster interspecies coexistence—pollinators, soil critters, plants—mirroring genomic cooperation. Pastors preach that Christ's unselfish love models the best of cooperative natural processes, guiding us to nurture both neighbor and environment. These theological horizons broaden our understanding of evolution from ruthless competition to a divine choreography of mutual flourishing.

10.2.2 Homology and Common Descent: Adam, Christ, and the Family Tree of Life

Comparative anatomy and genetic homologies—shared DNA sequences among species—provide powerful evidence for common descent. The remarkable genomic similarity between humans and chimpanzees invites reflection on what unity under God means across the family of life. Some theologians draw analogies between Adam as the "one man" who brought sin into the world and Christ as the "last Adam" who brings redemption (Rom 5:12–19; 1 Cor 15:45), mapping theological lineage onto biological relationships. Creation care movements use the "tree of life" metaphor both biblically and evolutionarily to emphasize interconnectedness. Seminary courses incorporate phylogenetic trees to illustrate how every creature shares parts of God's creative breath, inviting worship that transcends species boundaries. Ethical discussions address how deep homology informs our treatment of animals, urging compassion grounded in shared ancestry and stewardship. Christian environmentalists cite Leviticus's instruction to care for beasts and land alike, integrating evolutionary science with biblical mandates. Family camp programs use phylogenetic puzzles—matching DNA barcodes to species—to teach children both scientific literacy and a sense of wonder at divine design. Through homology and common descent, believers cultivate a theology that sees all life as kin under one Creator, setting the stage for responsible genetic interventions.

10.2.3 The Limits of Darwin: Image-Bearing, Moral Agency, and Consciousness

While Darwin's theory of natural selection explains much of biological diversity, it does not account for moral agency, self-consciousness, or the Imago Dei—that unique capacity to know, love, and choose in relationship with God. Scripture affirms that humanity bears God's likeness in ways that transcend evolutionary mechanisms (Gen 1:26–27), possessing souls with moral awareness and purpose. Philosophers of mind debate whether emergent properties like consciousness can arise from purely material substrates, suggesting a non-reductive dualism or a theistic panpsychism. Pastoral counsel reminds congregations that scientific humility requires acknowledging both the power and the limits of evolutionary explanations. Interdisciplinary colloquia bring together evolutionary biologists, neuroscientists, and theologians to explore how image-bearing emerges at the nexus of genetics, environment, and divine imprinting. Missions training emphasizes engaging indigenous cultures respectfully instead of dismissing their spiritual self-understanding in favor of materialistic reductionism. Worship liturgies include poems celebrating the mystery of consciousness—a gift beyond simple genetic coding. Ethical reflections on assisted suicide or AI cognition draw on these discussions, as image-bearing dignity demands robust moral frameworks. In recognizing Darwin's limits, believers affirm that evolutionary insights enrich but do not replace a theology of soul, agency, and covenant.

10.3 Ethical Frontiers: Gene Therapy and Editing

10.3.1 CRISPR, Base Editing, and Structural-Variant Repair

CRISPR-Cas9 technology and its derivatives permit precise cuts in DNA, opening the door to correcting mutations responsible for devastating diseases. Scientists now can swap single base pairs via base editing, turning a pathogenic cytosine into a benign thymine without double-strand breaks. Structural-variant repair techniques tackle larger chromosomal rearrangements that underlie conditions like Duchenne muscular dystrophy. The prospect of such interventions raises awe at human ingenuity—a gift reflecting God's creativity—while also prompting humility before the mystery of life's code. In lab settings, researchers pray over cell cultures, acknowledging that even the most sophisticated tools operate within God's providential boundary. Christian ethicists debate whether the therapeutic use of CRISPR aligns with the biblical mandate to heal the sick or risks overstepping into "playing God" territory (Gen 3:5). Pilot clinical trials for retinal disorders using CRISPR showcase promise: partial sight restoration rekindles hope for those born blind. Yet off-target effects—unintended genetic changes—remind us of the Fall's legacy in our finitude and propensity for error. Churches partner with research institutions to host public forums where scientists explain CRISPR's mechanisms and theologians unpack scriptural principles on stewardship of creation. Congregants learn that responsible genetic editing requires rigorous safety protocols, transparent oversight, and ongoing moral reflection. Seminaries now include modules on biotechnology, training future pastors to guide congregations through these emerging frontiers. Through discerning dialogue, faith communities affirm that while CRISPR holds healing potential, it also demands ethical restraint rooted in awe and reverence for life's sanctity.

10.3.2 Germline vs. Somatic Intervention: Healing Wounds or "Playing God"?

Gene therapy can target somatic cells—those that do not pass changes to offspring—or germline cells, where edits become heritable. Somatic interventions correct a child's sickle-cell mutation but leave the germline untouched, offering immediate relief without altering human inheritance. Germline editing, by contrast, edits the blueprint for future generations, prompting concern that we might engineer traits beyond disease resistance, risking eugenic impulses. The line between healing wounds inflicted by the Fall and shaping future humanity blurs when germline changes promise enhancements—heightened intelligence or disease immunity. Christian ethics calls for special caution: deforming God's image in future persons violates respect for each individual's created worth (Ps 139:13–14). Catholic and Orthodox bioethical commissions widely denounce germline editing for non-therapeutic ends, while some evangelical bodies remain open to limited therapeutic applications under strict regulation. Medical associations propose moratoria on germline research until societal consensus emerges, reflecting biblical wisdom in seeking many counselors (Prov 11:14). In communities, pastors facilitate listening sessions where church members voice fears and aspirations, weaving theological reflection with scientific literacy. Genetic counselors meet with couples considering IVF to discuss tolerance for somatic therapies versus germline modification. Theologians remind us that covenant solidarity extends backward and forward across generations, cautioning against changes that exceed our delegated authority. This balance between compassion for current sufferers and humility before progeny's rights shapes a precautionary ethos for genetic futures.

10.3.3 Global Equity and Access to Treatment

Groundbreaking gene therapies often carry six-figure price tags, placing them out of reach for most patients, especially in low- and middle-income countries. This disparity echoes the prophetic indictment of withholding grain from the hungry and wine from those who thirst (Amos 8:11), pressing faith communities to advocate for equitable pricing models. Churches in wealthy nations partner with global health NGOs to establish patient-assistance programs, securing compassionate-use licenses for deserving individuals regardless of ability to pay. International coalitions lobby pharmaceutical companies and governments to adopt tiered pricing, intellectual-property waivers, and voluntary licensing that expand generic production. Faith-based insurers pilot outcomes-based contracts, paying for gene therapies only upon demonstrable patient improvement, sharing risk across stakeholders. Public prayer vigils at biotech company headquarters symbolize spiritual solidarity with the medically marginalized. Seminaries teach future leaders about the moral imperative of distributive justice, drawing on Jesus's feeding of the five thousand as a model of abundance for all. Mission hospitals incorporate gene-therapy referral pathways into rural care networks, ensuring that breakthroughs do not bypass the global poor. Data registries track global access gaps, informing petitions to the World Health Organization and United Nations. By demanding justice in access, Christian communities testify that life-saving innovations belong to the whole human family, not just the affluent few.

10.3.4 Pastoral Guidance for Families Considering Genetic Intervention

Families facing genetic interventions grapple with complex decisions: whether to enroll in a gene-therapy trial, how to weigh potential benefits against unknown risks, and how to honor God's sovereignty while acting responsibly. Pastors trained in genetic ethics provide pastoral counseling that integrates prayer, scriptural reflection, and clear presentation of medical facts. They encourage families to seek multidisciplinary advice—clinicians, genetic counselors, and spiritual directors—embodying the wisdom of Proverbs 15:22. Congregational support teams offer to accompany families to hospital appointments, pray through consent discussions, and host support groups for siblings awaiting treatment outcomes. Advance directives are updated to reflect post-intervention care preferences, demonstrating foresight that merges spiritual trust with practical planning. Sermons on God's healing ministry in Luke 5:17–26 empower families to view gene therapy as potential extension of divine compassion when aligned with theological integrity. Ethical case studies are included in premarital and parenting classes, preparing couples to face hereditary challenges together. Prayer services for patients undergoing gene editing include anointing with oil and laying on of hands, connecting modern science with apostolic tradition. Ongoing pastoral care monitors families' emotional and spiritual well-being, acknowledging the rollercoaster of hope and anxiety that genetic interventions evoke. Through attentive guidance, churches walk alongside families navigating the cutting edge of biology, ensuring decisions rest on informed consent, communal prayer, and a deep sense of divine accompaniment.

10.4 Genetic Testing, Counseling, and Congregational Care

10.4.1 Prenatal Screens, Disability, and the Theology of Welcome

Advances in prenatal screening—noninvasive cell-free DNA tests and detailed ultrasound—allow early detection of chromosomal anomalies like trisomy 21 and neural-tube defects. Families receive vast genetic information that can inform medical interventions, but also generate painful questions about continuing pregnancies when severe disabilities emerge. The church's response draws on the theology of welcome modeled in Matthew 19:14, where Jesus embraces little children, signaling that every life, disabled or not, bears infinite worth. Congregations form visiting teams to accompany expectant parents through genetic counseling sessions, offering emotional support and sharing testimonies of families raising children with Down syndrome and spina bifida. Disability advocacy groups train pastors on inclusive language that avoids pity or coercion, affirming autonomy while providing hope-filled context. Baby dedications incorporate prayers for children diagnosed in utero, declaring that God's plans for them are good (Jer 29:11). Ethics forums hosted by churches engage medical professionals and theologians to explore questions of termination, palliation, and palliative scoliosis. Educational resources teach congregants about developmental therapies and community services, demystifying disability. Midwives trained in genetic sensitivity partner with faith leaders to provide holistic prenatal care. By intertwining screening with a robust theology of welcome, churches guide parents to decisions grounded in grace rather than fear.

10.4.2 Direct-to-Consumer Kits, Privacy, and the Temptation of Unfettered Curiosity

The proliferation of direct-to-consumer genetic tests—ancestry panels, pharmacogenomic profiles, health-risk reports—brings both empowerment and ethical quandaries. Individuals learn alleles linked to Alzheimer's risk or metabolic quirks without medical mediation, potentially encountering anxiety or misunderstanding. Privacy concerns arise as raw genetic data may be shared with third parties, including law enforcement or marketing firms, com promising confidentiality. Christian ethics calls for responsible stewardship:

genetic information, like any resource, must be used with wisdom and respect for personal dignity. Pastors encourage congregants to approach such kits with discernment, perhaps waiting to review clinical-grade tests in partnership with healthcare providers. Workshops teach digital privacy skills—secure data storage, understanding terms of service—to safeguard sensitive information. Sermons on Psalm 25's guidance on seeking counsel apply equally to genetic decisions, recommending that individuals consult trusted medical and pastoral advisors before interpreting complex data. Youth ministries caution teens about the lure of curiosity-driven tests, equipping them to value relational belonging over digital self-branding. Church bulletins link to accredited genetic counseling services, emphasizing that community care surpasses vanity inquiries. By framing direct-to-consumer testing within a locus of accountability, faith communities foster safe exploration of genetic identity while protecting members from undue distress and privacy breaches.

10.4.3 Building Support Networks for Carriers and "Rare-Disease Churches"

Individuals carrying recessive mutations—cystic fibrosis, Tay–Sachs, fragile X—often confront isolation because of the rarity of their conditions. Genetic counseling identifies carriers, but ongoing emotional support requires communal networks. Churches can host "rare-disease churches"—regular gatherings for individuals and families affected by the same genetic condition—providing shared experiences, prayer support, and resource exchanges. These networks encourage joint fundraising for specialized equipment, cooperative childcare during hospital stays, and organized advocacy for research funding. Genetic counselors and medical specialists may give invited talks, deepening understanding of disease mechanisms and emerging therapies. Social media groups moderated by church volunteers extend support beyond physical meetings, ensuring global connectivity for rare-disease sufferers. Intercessory prayer chains focus on symptom relief, clinical trial participation, and caregiver strength. Bible study materials incorporate narratives of suffering and perseverance—Job's endurance, Paul's thorn—to validate the long-term struggles of rare-disease families. Churches partner with rare-disease foundations to host awareness events, uniting congregational compassion with public visibility. This communal solidarity reinforces that no genetic rarity should lead to relational abandonment, embodying the New Testament's vision of the body as a interdependent whole.

10.5 Hope Beyond Heredity (1 Cor 15:49–53)

10.5.1 The Resurrection Body: Incorruptible "Spiritual DNA"

Paul contrasts our current bodies—fragile, prone to decay, governed by perishable genetic codes—with the resurrection bodies we will inherit, imperishable and spiritual (1 Cor 15:49–53). This promise reframes heredity: whatever DNA may program for earthly frailty, it cannot dictate our eternal form. Theologians teach that resurrection body transcends biochemical constraints, reflecting God's power to renew creation beyond molecular repair. In worship, congregants proclaim "death is swallowed up in victory," affirming that genetic death sentences lose ultimate power. Art installations in churches depict double helices morphing into luminous spirit forms, visual sermons of transformation. Pastoral care for terminally ill patients includes proclaiming this hope, reminding them that the "new Adam" inaugurates a new biology where sin-linked DNA gives way to divine "spiritual DNA." Funeral liturgies incorporate eulogies that look forward to the body's perfection, offering comfort rooted not in genetic legacy but in the resurrection covenant. Small-group studies unpack Paul's "mystery" language, exploring how the gospel rewrites the script of our biology. By anchoring identity in the resurrection body, believers overcome genetic determinism with the affirmation that Christ's life forms the template for our ultimate identity.

10.5.2 Baptismal Re-parenting: Adoption into Christ's Genetic Line

Baptism signifies dying to the old self and rising with Christ into newness of life (Rom 6:4), symbolically re-rooting believers in a new spiritual lineage under the "last Adam." This adoption into God's family echoes genetic parentage but transcends DNA; it establishes a kinship based on faith rather than familial descent. Families incorporate baptismal sponsors who commit to nourish the spiritual life of the baptized, modeling intergenerational inheritance of promise. Naming ceremonies accompany baptism, bestowing a "Christian name" that signals new identity, akin to receiving a new genetic code in Christ. Pastors bless godparents to guide the baptized through life's challenges, including genetic struggles that may arise. Communities craft "family trees" of faith rather than DNA, tracing spiritual ancestry through revivals, missionary lineages, and testimonies. Youth groups celebrate "baptism bonuses," learning that their spiritual identity in Christ surpasses any hereditary trait. As God claims us in baptism, our genetic burdens lose ultimate hold, and our true heritage becomes divine rather than carnal.

10.5.3 Sacramental Anticipations: Eucharist, Spirit, and Holy "Epigenetic" Renewal

The Eucharist, celebrated with bread and wine, embodies the presence of the risen Christ—body and blood—nourishing believers with grace that transforms us from within. Just as epigenetic marks can be overwritten by new environmental inputs, regular participation in communion invites the Holy Spirit to rewrite sinful patterns in our hearts and bodies. Liturgy texts draw on prophetic images of new creation, declaring that the Spirit renews our mortal frames like a seed becoming grain. Pastors anoint worshipers with oil and the words "Be sealed with the gift of the Holy Spirit," echoing baptismal adoption and implying ongoing spiritual inscription that counters genetic brokenness. Prayer teams lay hands on those with chronic genetic conditions, pleading for holistic healing that spans body, mind, and spirit. Church seasons—Advent, Lent, Easter—provide cyclical reminders that God's redemptive work continually overlays old patterns with new life. Small-group communion services in care homes ensure that those with limited congregation access still receive sacramental renewal. Music woven into liturgies—images like "new mercies every morning"—reinforce the epigenetic metaphor of daily spiritual renewal. As believers partake of these sacraments, they anticipate the full restoration of both body and genome in the kingdom to come.

10.6 Worship and Vocation in the Age of Genomics

10.6.1 Sequencers as Psalm 19 Telescopes: Doxology through Discovery

When David marveled that "the heavens declare the glory of God" (Ps 19:1), he invited humanity to read cosmic revelation as a form of worship. Today, genome sequencers serve as microscopes into the hidden cosmos inside us, revealing the order and complexity of life's code. Each gene sequenced becomes like a verse in creation's anthem, prompting researchers to pause in awe rather than mere analysis. Laboratories have begun posting framed Ps. 19 inscriptions above benches where technicians pipette samples, reminding staff that their work can become prayer. Church science cafés invite congregants to tour sequencing facilities, pairing technical demonstrations with reflections on "skillfully wrought" DNA (Ps 139:14). Youth groups build simple DNA extraction kits—teaching kids that the same material underlies all life, inspiring doxological wonder. Sermons on "the book of nature" encourage scientists to view data as God's diary, writing praise in chromatogram peaks. Ethics classes emphasize that discovery motivates not exploitation but humble worship, aligning research agendas with God's glory. As genome knowledge expands, doxology ensures that scientific triumphs remain anchored in gratitude to the Creator rather than human hubris. From this posture of wonder we move into practical vocation.

10.6.2 Bioinformatics for the Kingdom: Pandemic Surveillance and Creation Care

The field of bioinformatics applies computational power to interpret genomic data, enabling rapid identification of viral variants during pandemics. Faith-based data science teams have collaborated with public health agencies to develop genomic dashboards that track COVID-19 mutations, ensuring timely policy and pastoral responses. Church technology ministries host hackathons where coders pray for guidance as they build tools for environmental genomics—mapping antibiotic resistance genes in agricultural runoff. Seminary programs now offer certificates in "Faith and Data," training future leaders to use big data not purely for profit but for relief of human suffering and stewardship of ecosystems. Congregations partner with local universities to create citizen-science projects, sampling urban waterways for microbial analysis that informs church-led clean-up efforts. Public-health chaplains attend data briefings alongside epidemiologists, translating variant trends into pastoral care priorities—such as masking guidelines for vulnerable members. Creation-care brigades use genomic surveys to assess biodiversity in church gardens, then adjust planting schemes to support pollinator health. Global mission agencies deploy portable sequencers in remote clinics, enabling on-site pathogen monitoring and empowering local believers to protect community health. These bioinformatics initiatives demonstrate that digital tools can serve the kingdom by combining precision science with pastoral concern for both human and environmental flourishing.

10.6.3 Discernment for Christian Biologists, Ethicists, and Lab Technicians

Working at the frontier of genetics calls for discernment rooted in both professional standards and spiritual formation. Christian biologists gather regularly for "Lab Chapel," a brief devotional before morning bench work, confessing biases and seeking wisdom to apply technology ethically. Ethical reading groups discuss challenging cases—like gene drives for invasive species control—and consult biblical principles such as the Sabbath rest for land (Lev 25:4–5) when considering ecological interventions. Lab technicians practice a "pause and pray" protocol before initiating experiments with potential dual use, reaffirming that scientific freedom must be exercised within covenantal boundaries. Institutional review boards in faith-affiliated research centers include clergy alongside scientists, ensuring that proposals for germline editing undergo theological as well as technical scrutiny. Professional societies for Christian geneticists host annual colloquia on topics from upstream synthetic-biology ethics to downstream patient counseling, fostering networks of mutual support. Conferences on "Science and the Soul" bridge lab findings with pastoral care strategies, training participants in compassionate communication about genetic risk. These discernment structures equip practitioners to steward genetic knowledge responsibly, guarding against the spirit of Babel that seeks to claim divine prerogatives. As labs consecrate their work to God's glory, they prepare for the final reflections on our journey from A-C-G-T to the Alpha and Omega.

10.7 Epilogue — From A-C-G-T to Alpha and Omega

The genetic revolution teaches that life's blueprint is at once fragile and robust, bearing marks of fallenness while sustaining miraculous repair. Scientists have learned that every mutation carries potential for both harm and resilience, reflecting a creation designed for diversity and adaptation under God's providence. Pastors discover that genetic knowledge deepens pastoral care, equipping them to guide congregations through diagnostic ambiguity, moral dilemmas of editing, and the hope of resurrection bodies. Patients face genetic predispositions with both humility and courage, understanding that their identity in Christ transcends any DNA sequence. Policy-makers grapple with balancing innovation, safety, and justice, drawing on biblical mandates for neighbor-love, care for the vulnerable, and stewardship of creation. Together these insights form a tapestry that honors both the molecular intricacy of life and the overarching story of redemption.

Conclusion Our journey through genes and genomes has revealed both our creaturely dependence on God's sustaining care and our calling to participate responsibly in His redemptive work. We have seen how mutations can harm and heal, how evolution speaks to both

God's providential freedom and our moral agency, and how emerging therapies demand wisdom grounded in Scripture. As we prepare to confront the wider groaning of creation in the next chapter, we carry forward a vision of science in service to the gospel—where technological ingenuity is yoked to humility, justice, and the hope of the Alpha and Omega. In this light, every discovery about our bodies becomes an invitation to deeper worship, ethical discernment, and hopeful anticipation of the new creation to come.

Chapter 11 – Healing and Medicine: Prayer, Sacrament, Science

Healing has always been more than fixing bodies—it's a sacred encounter where divine compassion, communal ritual, and human ingenuity converge. Throughout history, monasteries tended the sick even as early apothecaries stirred potions, and today chaplains walk beside surgeons in sterile wings. In this chapter we trace how faith shaped hospitals, how Christian vocation animates physicians and nurses, and how prayer and sacraments enter clinical spaces as channels of God's grace. We'll explore the gifts of miraculous healing alongside rigorous science, wrestle with end-of-life dilemmas, and consider the global calling to address suffering as an expression of gospel solidarity. As we move from ancient infirmaries to telemedicine and climate-resilient clinics, we discover that true wholeness arises at the crossroads of prayer, sacrament, and science.

11.0 Prelude — Sickbeds and Sanctuaries: A Meeting Place for Grace

11.0.1 The Persistent Ache for Wholeness in Every Age

Humanity's longing for wellness surfaces in every era, from the psalmist's midnight cries for healing to today's online symptom searches that spike after midnight. Ancient laments such as Psalm 6 capture the sleepless turning of bodies in pain, while contemporary hospital charts record similar restlessness through vital-sign alarm bells. Merchants in Corinth sold amulets they promised would ward off plague, not unlike wellness influencers who market miracle supplements on social media feeds. Yet beneath changing therapies lies an unchanged desire for shalom, the biblical fullness in which body, mind, and society breathe in rhythm with God's peace (Isa 32:17). When Jesus asked the man at Bethesda, "Do you want to be made well?" (Jn 5:6), He voiced the perennial question that still hovers over triage bays and tele-health calls. Anthropology shows that every culture develops both ritual and remedy—herbal infusions paired with incantations, vaccinations accompanied by parental prayers—demonstrating how physical and spiritual hopes intertwine. Even secular public-health campaigns employ quasi-liturgical language, urging citizens to "trust the science" in tones that echo prophetic summons. Church historians note that plagues repeatedly drove spiritual renewal; Augustine's sermons after the Cyprian plague addressed not only sin but sanitation, linking interior conversion to communal hygiene. Today's congregations reenact that coupling when they place hand-sanitizer stations beside font or holy water. This ache for wholeness provides fertile soil for examining how prayer and professional care converge.

11.0.2 Why Prayer Rooms and Operating Rooms Still Need Each Other

A surgical suite hums with monitors, scalpels, and sterile drapes, yet outside its doors families huddle in chapels clutching rosaries or whispering the Jesus Prayer. Research on peri-operative anxiety shows that patients who receive spiritual support exhibit lower cortisol levels and require fewer opioids post-procedure, suggesting that intercession influences both psyche and physiology. Surgeons themselves sometimes pause in silent petition before the first incision, recalling Solomon's plea for wisdom (1 Kgs 3:9). Hospital architects increasingly design meditation alcoves adjacent to ICUs, recognizing that healing trajectories depend on more than ventilators and vasoactive drips. Meanwhile, congregational prayer chains beam text alerts when members enter recovery, transforming living rooms into distributed chapels. The synergy is not one-sided: clinical data guide pastoral visits, helping chaplains time anointing rites to avoid interfering with wound-care protocols. Medical ethicists find that families who pray together grasp prognosis conversations more realistically, perhaps because petition teaches both hope and surrender, echoing Jesus' "yet not my will" (Lk 22:42). When prayer rooms and operating rooms collaborate, they model an integrated anthropology where spirit and soma cooperate in seeking God's shalom, a theme that threads through medicine's history.

11.1 Historical Synergy of Faith and Medicine

11.1.1 Monastic Infirmaries, Medieval Apothecaries, and the Birth of Hospitals

Early Christian monasteries wove hospitality and healing into a single rule of life. Benedict of Nursia required that the sick be served "as Christ himself," turning infirmaries into proto-hospitals where scripture readings accompanied herbal poultices. These communities cultivated physic gardens of lavender, yarrow, and feverfew; modern pharmacology still extracts compounds first catalogued in monastic herbals. Pilgrims travelled to abbeys not only for relics but for wound care, foreshadowing today's destination medicine. Islam's Bayt al-Hikma and Jewish medical texts cross-pollinated with monastic wisdom through Mediterranean trade routes, creating multilingual apothecaries that dispensed both incense and antimony eye-salve. Over centuries, these sacred clinics evolved into civic hospitals like Hôtel-Dieu in Paris, financed by church tithes yet serving pagan and saint alike, embodying Luke's Good Samaritan parable (Lk 10:34). Clergy often doubled as physicians; Pope Clement VI organized plague nurses during the Black Death, blessing corpses as he commissioned quarantine zones. The very word "hospitality" shares roots with "hospital," reminding modern health systems that patient care began as a sacrament of welcome. Thus monastic corridors echo in today's fluorescent hallways, whispering that compassionate presence belongs at medicine's core.

11.1.2 The Reformation's Surge of Medical Missions and Public Hygiene

The Protestant Reformation reframed vocation, teaching that diaper-changing and doctoring alike could glorify God (Col 3:17). City councils in Zurich and Geneva, guided by reformers, launched public bathhouses and waste-removal ordinances, translating justification by faith into sanitation by policy. Anabaptist refugees carried herbal knowledge across borders, spreading simple remedies with printed Bible tracts. Seventeenth-century Moravians sailed to Caribbean leper colonies, where they blended psalm-singing with basic wound debridement, a forerunner of integrated medical missions. In London, Puritan ministers backed the founding of Christ's Hospital, linking catechesis with convalescence. Meanwhile Roman Catholic orders like the Daughters of Charity pioneered nursing as a profession, inspired by Vincent de Paul's vision of Christ in the sickroom. These parallel streams converged in the missionary movement of the nineteenth century: David Livingstone charted malaria prophylaxis while preaching the cross, and Lottie Moon distributed quinine biscuits with gospel literature. Public-health revolutions—sewer systems, clean-water acts—owed much to clergy lobbying city fathers, seeing Jeremiah's call to seek the city's welfare (Jer 29:7) in concrete drainage pipes. Reformation fervor thus reshaped civic hygiene, proving that theology can leak into streets and surgical wards.

11.1.3 Vaccination, Germ Theory, and the Prayer-Meeting Paradox

Edward Jenner's smallpox vaccine prompted both jubilation and sermons against "tampering with providence." Some congregations held fast-days, pleading for divine protection, even as parish doctors lined up children for cowpox inoculation. The paradox deepened with Pasteur's germ theory, which replaced miasma fears with microbial causation; prayer meetings invoked God's mercy while physicians prescribed sterilization, both seeking to stem cholera's tide. Charles Spurgeon, recovering from gout, preached that medical discoveries were "the gifts of God" and urged congregants to thank Him for microscopes. Opposition did not vanish; anti-vaccination leagues cited Psalm 91 promises to reject compulsory shots, yet missionary hospitals used vaccines to embody Jesus' healing ministry. Statistical analyses revealed lower mortality where churches hosted immunization clinics, illustrating James' exhortation that faith without works is dead (Jas 2:17). The tension between prayer and science fostered dialogue that gradually birthed parish-based public-health boards. Hospitals began scheduling chapel services alongside ward rounds, acknowledging that germ warfare and spiritual warfare share patient battlegrounds. Through vaccination debates, the church learned to navigate innovation without abandoning intercession.

11.1.4 The Modern Research Hospital: Chaplaincy, Ethics Boards, and Spiritual Metrics

Twentieth-century medicine shifted from bedside to bench-side, with teaching hospitals integrating laboratories, lecture halls, and ICUs under one roof. CPE (Clinical Pastoral Education) programs emerged to train ministers in the dialect of ventilators and telemetry, equipping them to translate lament into language attentive to chart times. Institutional ethics committees—often including theologians—now vet clinical trials, echoing Acts 15's Jerusalem council where discernment occurred in community. Evidence-based chaplaincy measures the impact of prayer visits on pain scores and length of stay, generating data that earns respect in grand rounds. Hospitals report "spiritual distress" as a vital sign, screening for meaning crises just as they track blood pressure. Research centers like Mayo Clinic embed scripture in meditation apps designed for post-stroke rehab, blending neural plasticity with psalmic repetition. The Joint Commission mandates spiritual-care protocols, affirming that accreditation hinges partly on pastoral competence. As genomic medicine rises, chaplains consult on informed-consent language, guarding Imago Dei dignity in biobank protocols. The modern research hospital therefore stands at the crossroads of microscope and prayer shawl, tracing its lineage back to monastic infirmaries while scanning horizons of CRISPR cures.

11.2 Vocations of Healing

11.2.1 Christian Physicians and the Rule of St Basil to the Code of Ethics

Basil the Great established Basiliad, a fourth-century complex housing wards for lepers and travelers, framing medicine as diakonia—service rooted in Christ's compassion. Centuries later, Maimonides' prayer for the physician echoed Basil's ethos, beseeching God for clear judgment and charity toward the poor. Today, the Christian Medical and Dental Associations offer a modern code grounded in Micah 6:8, calling doctors to justice, mercy, and humility. Physicians gather for white-coat blessings before residency, dedicating stethoscopes as instruments of grace. Morning rounds can become liturgy when doctors greet patients with "Peace to this room," echoing Luke 10's instruction to proclaim peace in every house. Mentorship programs pair seasoned clinicians who survived moral injury with students wrestling over end-of-life dilemmas, fostering a culture of both excellence and empathy. Journal clubs discuss randomized trials alongside gospel narratives of compassionate touch, integrating evidence and example. Physicians in rural clinics pray over supply chains, trusting God for vaccines while lobbying for equitable distribution. By holding Hippocratic pledges in one hand and the Sermon on the Mount in the other, Christian doctors testify that high tech and high love are not mutually exclusive.

11.2.2 Nurses, Midwives, Therapists, and the Diaconal Tradition

Nursing traces spiritual ancestry to Phoebe the deaconess (Rom 16:1) and Florence Nightingale, who carried lantern and Psalm 23 into Crimean wards. Contemporary nurses stand at the bedside during three-shift rotations, embodying Ruth's steadfast presence as they turn patients every two hours to prevent pressure sores. Midwives echo Exodus' Shiphrah and Puah, who defended Hebrew infants against Pharaoh's edict, whenever they advocate for maternal-fetal safety in under-resourced clinics. Physical and occupational therapists restore mobility echoing Jesus' command, "Take up your mat and walk" (Jn 5:8), coaxing neural pathways to reform through repetitive grace. Speech therapists help stroke survivors form words of prayer again, stewarding tongues destined to confess Christ. The diaconal tradition expands as social workers secure housing for discharged patients, regarding safe shelter as a prescription for health. Parish-nurse programs anchor community blood-pressure checks between hymns, closing the gap between sanctuary and clinic. Each vocation adds a stanza to the chorus of healing, harmonizing clinical skill with servant love.

11.2.3 Biotechnologists as Sub-Creators: Lab Benches as Altars

Researchers who culture stem cells or design mRNA vaccines participate in what J.R.R. Tolkien dubbed "sub-creation," crafting secondary worlds within petri dishes under God's primary sovereignty. Daily they decide how to steward CRISPR plasmids or viral vectors, practicing an ethic of restraint that mirrors God's own self-limitation in the incarnation (Phil 2:6–7). Lab meetings begin with quiet moments acknowledging that wisdom descends from above (Jas 3:17), infusing grant proposals with prayerful discernment. Failures—contaminated cultures, inconsistent Western blots—become occasions for lament psalms recited over pipettes. Successes spark doxology: when a new therapeutic antibody neutralizes cancer cells, researchers record thanksgiving notes on a lab corkboard shaped like a cross. Workshops on dual-use biosecurity remind technicians that knowledge can heal or harm, echoing Genesis's tree of the knowledge of good and evil. Ethical audits invite chaplains and community representatives to tour facilities, fostering transparency and accountability. Thus lab benches become altars where curiosity bends toward praise and caution.

11.2.4 Patient Participation: Agency, Lament, and Co-Suffering with Christ

Modern medicine increasingly adopts shared decision-making, recognizing patients as partners rather than passive recipients of care. Theology amplifies this shift, portraying sufferers as participants in Christ's own redemptive suffering (Col 1:24). Pain journals become psalters where patients pour out lament while tracking medication efficacy. Chemotherapy wards host art-therapy stations where IV poles mingle with watercolor palettes, allowing creativity to accompany cytotoxic drips. Peer-support groups gather in church basements, reading Job aloud and naming their own boils of side-effects before swapping practical tips. Advance-care-planning workshops empowered by pastors encourage believers to articulate treatment preferences, aligning aggressive care with resurrection hope rather than fear. Baptismal identity cards placed on hospital bulletin boards remind staff that each patient shares royal priesthood, influencing tone of voice and touch. Some patients adopt the role of "research advocates," enrolling in clinical trials not only for personal benefit but to bless future generations, embodying Abraham's promise to be a blessing (Gen 12:2). Through agency, lament, and solidarity with Christ, patients transform bedsides into sites of mutual ministry, completing the vocational tapestry of healing.

11.3 Prayer and the Sacramental Imagination

11.3.1 Petition, Intercession, and Contemplation: Diverse Modes of Healing Prayer

Petitionary prayer invites the sick to voice their own needs directly to God, framing specific requests—"Lord, grant my body strength to endure chemotherapy"—as expressions of dependence on divine mercy. Intercessory prayer enlists friends and family to stand in the gap, embodying Paul's call to "pray for one another" (Jas 5:16) and multiplying spiritual resources around the patient. Contemplative prayer, by contrast, withdraws from words into silence, trusting that God's presence can minister to suffering beyond articulation—a practice rooted in Jesus's early-morning retreats to solitary places (Mk 1:35). These modes blend in healing liturgies: patients begin with petition, move into intercession led by community members, and conclude in contemplative stillness before the Blessed Sacrament. Hospitals that offer "prayer chapels" equip visitors to transition between spoken prayers and silent listening, recognizing that some wounds respond best to God's wordless comfort. Research indicates that contemplative practices reduce stress markers such as cortisol, paralleling the psalmist's promise, "Be still, and know that I am God" (Ps 46:10). Pastoral workshops train volunteers in active listening—rather than offering quick fixes—to honor the depth of petition and intercession. Neonatal intensive care units sometimes incorporate heartbeat meditation, where parents meditate on the rhythm of their infant's monitor, tuning bodily awareness into prayerful presence. In retreat centers, guided prayer walks integrate petition for personal healing with intercession for global health crises, demonstrating how individual ailments connect to wider groans of creation (Rom 8:22). Clinicians report that patients who practice daily contemplative prayer report less anticipatory nausea before treatments. As these modes flow into one another, prayer becomes a holistic art that engages mind, body, and community in the pursuit of wholeness.

11.3.2 Anointing with Oil, Eucharist for the Sick, and the Ecology of Touch

The New Testament affirms anointing with oil for the sick, linking material substance with divine healing (Jas 5:14). Trained ministers carry sterile, unscented oil vials to patient rooms, offering anointing while invoking Christ's own anointing and healing ministry. Physical touch during anointing matters: a gentle hand on the shoulder fosters connection, demonstrating that the body itself is a sacramental channel. Eucharistic ministry to the homebound further enriches incarnational care, as chaplains bring elements consecrated at the altar into hospital rooms, uniting patients with the larger body of Christ (1 Cor 11:26). Nursing staff often report improved mood and decreased perception of pain when patients receive communion alongside medication. The tactile loop of handshake, blessing, oil, and bread creates an "ecology of touch" that counters the isolating sterility of many clinical environments. Cardiac units designate "Communion Mondays," coordinating sacramental visits with physicians' orders to monitor vitals, ensuring safety. Art therapists note that anoints with frankincense-infused oil can trigger positive olfactory memories, anchoring spiritual uplift in neural circuits. Home-care teams leave small prayer cloths and consecrated wafers with families, extending sacramental ecology beyond clergy presence. These embodied practices underscore that God uses material signs—oil, bread, touch—to convey invisible grace within the tangible world He created. As the ecology of touch matures, it prompts deeper integration of sacrament and science in healing spaces.

11.3.3 Liturgy at the Bedside: Psalms, Silence, and the Rhythm of Vespers

Bedside liturgies draw from the monastic tradition of praying the hours, adapting morning Lauds or evening Vespers for clinical settings. A nurse chaplain may begin with a short Psalm—such as Psalm 23—allowing its ancient words to echo in the patient's room. Silence follows, letting the presence of God settle in the pauses between verses. Lighting a single candle at the head of the bed evokes both vigil and verse, linking candlelight with Psalm 18:28's "light shines in my darkness." Patients participate as they can—listening, humming along, or simply breathing in time with the liturgy's cadence. Liturgy guides tucked beside pillows outline each element: cross-signing, Scriptural reading, thanksgiving, petition, and blessing. Family members sometimes join in, their voices weaving personal concerns into the public prayer of the church. Studies in palliative care reveal that structured nightly liturgies improve sleep quality, perhaps by creating a predictable spiritual rhythm. Hospitals with chaplaincy programs offer training for volunteers to lead these bedside offices, ensuring consistency and theological integrity. Over weeks, recurring liturgies deepen spiritual familiarity, transforming sterile rooms into temporary chapels. As dusk approaches, vespers at the bedside reorient patients' hearts toward peace, echoing the psalmist's invitation to "come, let us worship and bow down" (Ps 95:6). From liturgy we turn to the challenge of measuring prayer's impact.

11.3.4 Measuring Prayer's Impact: Placebos, Nocebos, and Mystery

Scientific studies often compare prayer's effects to placebos, finding modest but measurable improvements in patient-reported outcomes such as pain reduction and emotional well-being. Yet the nocebo effect—negative expectations worsening symptoms—reveals that patients' beliefs play powerful roles in healing trajectories. Prayer researchers navigate these complexities with humility, acknowledging that blinded studies cannot capture the full mystery of divine action. Hospital chaplains collaborate with psychologists designing trials that measure stress hormones before and after intercessory sessions, alongside qualitative interviews exploring spiritual transformation. Ethical review boards ensure that prayer studies respect patients' beliefs and consent, avoiding coercion into spiritual research. Data dashboards in chapels display aggregate mood improvements, fostering institutional support for spiritual care programs. Yet chaplains remind colleagues that prayer's deepest impacts often elude quantification—the God who heals both body and soul cannot be reduced to p-values. Mystery thus remains a valid category, guarding against scientism that would squeeze grace into rigid metrics. As we accept both data and mystery, healing prayer continues to unfold in clinics and congregations alike.

11.4 Charisms of Healing (1 Cor 12:9)

11.4.1 Discernment of Genuine Miracles: Criteria, Community, and Fruit

Scripture instructs the church to test "every spirit" (1 Jn 4:1), a mandate extended to claims of miraculous healing. Genuine miracles exhibit immediate, complete, and verifiable recoveries that resist natural explanation—paralleling gospel accounts where blind eyes open fully, not partially. Community discernment unfolds in public gatherings where testimony is weighed alongside biblical criteria: healing attributed to Christ's name, humility from the healed, and edification of the body (1 Cor 14:26). Medical records and physician attestations often supplement faith testimonies, providing objective corroboration. Post-healing fruits—renewed faith, sacrificial service, and deeper love—serve as additional indicators of authenticity, as Jesus connected fruitfulness with genuine discipleship (Jn 15:8). Ecclesial commissions, akin to Acts 15 councils, convene to investigate high-profile healing claims, interviewing witnesses, assessing symbolic actions, and awaiting confirmation over time rather than rush to judgment. These processes guard against sensationalism and protect vulnerable seekers from false hopes. The pattern of biblical miracles—leading recipients to worship rather than boast—guides assessment, ensuring that the focus remains on God's glory rather than human gift. Through careful discernment, the church preserves the integrity of charisms and fosters genuine confidence in divine compassion.

11.4.2 Avoiding Triumphalism: Suffering Servant Spirituality

Triumphalism twists healing charisms into tools for personal prestige, contradicting the cross-shaped pattern of servant leadership Jesus embodied (Phil 2:5–8). To guard against this, communities emphasize that all charisms, including healing, function within the body's mutual interdependence, not egoistic display. Liturgical guidelines forbid "calling out" individuals to showcase gifts; instead, healing prayers occur behind curtains or in small groups, preserving privacy and dignity. Pastors preach the theology of the suffering servant, reminding congregations that Jesus wept at Lazarus's tomb even as He raised him (Jn 11:35–44), modeling empathy before power. Charismatic training programs include modules on humility, accountability structures, and rotating leadership to prevent personality cults. Testimonies highlight not only miraculous outcomes but also the ongoing struggles of those who remain ill, affirming that healing charisms do not annul life's trials. Worship music balances victory anthems with lament hymns, creating a spectrum where triumph and tragedy coexist under God's sovereign love. By centering the cross rather than spiritual fireworks, the church cultivates a healing culture that honors Christ's solidarity with human frailty.

11.4.3 Integrating Charismatic and Clinical Testimony in the Congregation

When a congregation witnesses both modern medicine and charismatic ministry collaborate, it testifies to God's multifaceted healing gifts. Pastors invite physicians to speak at healing services, explaining clinical facts before offering prayer, demonstrating respect for science and faith. Lay health ministries compile case studies where patients experienced measurable improvements after combining treatment with intercessory prayer, presenting these at church forums. Medical and spiritual testimonies appear side by side in church newsletters, framing both as distinct yet complementary channels of grace. Training events feature panels where chaplains, doctors, and charismatic healers share practices—anointing protocols, surgical consent prayers, and diagnostic rituals—fostering mutual respect. Counseling centers co-locate near healing rooms, enabling patients to receive clinical follow-up and pastoral care in one visit. Joint research projects measure outcomes of integrated approaches—reduced rehospitalization rates and improved spiritual well-being—providing empirical affirmation. Through such integration, congregations embody 1 Corinthians 12's vision of diverse gifts working in unity for the body's health.

11.4.4 Pastoral Care after an Unanswered Prayer for Healing

When prayer for healing seems to go unanswered, pastoral care shifts into accompaniment of grief and doubt rather than retrial of rituals. Ministers listen without offering quick theological fixes—acknowledging that unanswered prayer can feel like Christ's silence in Gethsemane (Mk 14:34–36). Small groups convene for lament gatherings, using psalms like Psalm 77 to give voice to questioning faith. Pastoral counselors teach that persistent identity in Christ does not depend on bodily wholeness, echoing Paul's contentment in weakness (2 Cor 12:9). Families are supported through memorial liturgies if death ensues, celebrating life's goodness amid loss. Ethical reflections guide decisions about continuing or withdrawing treatment, ensuring that medical actions align with pastoral respect for suffering. Lay prayer teams receive training on transitioning from intercession for healing to intercession for peace, recognizing the continuum of grace. In these tender seasons, the church's care models the Good Shepherd who walks through the valley, not avoiding the shadow. This compassion readies us to face ethical dilemmas at life's margins.

11.5 Ethical Decision-Making at Life's Margins

11.5.1 End-of-Life Pathways: Hospice, Palliative Sedation, and Hope-Filled Presence

Hospice care emerged from Cicely Saunders's vision of "total pain" relief—attending to physical, psychological, social, and spiritual suffering. In a hospice setting, interdisciplinary teams provide palliative sedation when pain becomes refractory, ensuring comfort while maintaining consciousness for relational farewells. Pastors collaborate with hospice chaplains in family conferences, explaining that sedation differs from euthanasia by intent: the goal is relief, not hastening death. Theological reflection on Jesus's prayer in Gethsemane—"take this cup from me" (Mk 14:36)—affirms seeking relief from suffering when aligned with God's will. Funeral home directors work with faith communities to craft services that celebrate a life well-loved rather than demonize death, echoing Hebrews 2:9's "taste of death." Training modules for clergy emphasize presence over preaching, encouraging simple bedside silence and holding hands as ultimate prayers. Bereavement groups facilitate ongoing support, acknowledging that grief in hospice contexts often begins before death. These end-of-life pathways honor dignity, relieve suffering, and testify to death's defeat without denying the reality of mortality.

11.5.2 DNR Orders, Advance Directives, and the Theology of Relinquishment

Do-not-resuscitate (DNR) orders and advance directives provide patients agency over future care, recognizing that invasive interventions may conflict with personal dignity or spiritual convictions. The biblical paradigm of relinquishment—Abraham's willingness to offer Isaac (Gen 22)—models surrendering cherished hopes at God's bidding. Pastors help congregants articulate values—prolonging consciousness, avoiding ventilator dependency, or wanting comfort care only—before crises occur. Ethics workshops teach families to frame advance directives as gifts to loved ones, reducing guilt and confusion during sudden hospital admissions. Medical teams incorporate spiritual assessments in advance-care planning, asking what gives life meaning and how treatment aligns with faith. When patients lose capacity, living wills guide clinicians and families, preventing over-treatment that violates God's rest principle in Sabbath rhythms (Ex 23:12). Churches provide standard forms and host "Life Choices" seminars, ensuring that theology informs legal procedures. These measures honor both bodily integrity and the soul's readiness to rest in God's hands.

11.5.3 Neonatal Extremes: Micro-Preemies, Congenital Anomalies, and Baptism of Tears

Advances in neonatal intensive care allow survival of extremely preterm infants—born at twenty-two weeks—yet raise complex questions about long-term prognosis and quality of life. Pastoral teams attend NICU rounds, praying over incubators while consulting neonatologists on survival statistics and developmental trajectories. When congenital anomalies emerge—such as anencephaly or trisomy 13—parents navigate heart-wrenching decisions about surgical interventions or comfort-only care. Baptisms in the NICU become profound rites where tears mingle with water and oil, affirming that sacramental grace precedes any guarantee of earthly days. Pastoral counselors guide families through grief-laced joy, offering ritual liturgies of commending the infant to God's mercy whether in life or death. Bioethical committees in children's hospitals develop guidelines that balance aggressive care with palliative principles, drawing on Isaiah's vision of the child riding on her father's shoulders (Isa 46:3) as a symbol of supported vulnerability. Longitudinal support groups connect NICU alumni and parents, teaching that even brief lives can bear eternal fruit. These neonatal extremes compel the church to embody both medical courage and pastoral tenderness at life's very threshold.

11.5.4 Aggressive Treatment vs. Shalom: Proportionality, Futility, and Sabbath Rest

Modern medicine can prolong life through ventilators, dialysis, and extracorporeal support, but unbounded intervention risks medical overreach, transforming care into cruelty. The principle of proportionality gauges whether treatments offer reasonable hope of benefit without excessive burden, reflecting Jesus's invitation to "come and rest" (Matt 11:28) when exhaustion overwhelms. Futility emerges when interventions only delay inevitable decline, prompting ethical committees to recommend limiting therapies that prolong the dying process. Pastors reinforce that true Sabbath rest awaits in Christ's presence, validating choices to forgo heroic measures in favor of peace-filled transition. Family dialogues facilitated by palliative teams include scripture readings on the fleeting nature of life (Ps 90:12), anchoring decisions in eternal perspective. These conversations honor bodily boundaries without surrendering hope in the resurrection. Congregational forums unpack case studies, teaching that choosing comfort care does not equate to abandoning faith. As families discern when to press forward and when to let go, they practice a theology of shalom—wholeness that includes restful acceptance amid life's final chapter.

11.6 Global Health, Justice, and Medical Missions

11.6.1 Short-Term Trips, Long-Term Partnerships, and Avoiding Neo-Colonial Care

Short-term medical missions often spring from generous hearts eager to deliver free clinics, but without careful planning they can unintentionally perpetuate dependency. Sending teams coordinate with local health leaders to ensure that temporary relief clinics integrate into existing systems rather than supplant them. Long-term partnerships build trust through shared governance: local pastors and physicians co-develop clinic protocols, ensuring that care aligns with cultural values and community priorities. Pre-trip training emphasizes humility and cultural competence, equipping volunteers to listen first rather than impose Western treatment models. Mission agencies discuss Phil. 2:4—"look not only to your own interests but also to the interests of others"—to frame service as mutual blessing rather than unilateral charity. Medical teams include public-health specialists who train local staff in sanitation and disease surveillance, leaving behind capacity rather than mere medicine. Prayer support networks back home commit to sustained intercession rather than just prayers for the week of travel. Debriefing sessions after each trip invite honest reflection on power dynamics, colonial histories, and unanticipated harms—addressing John 13:14's call to servant leadership over domination. By privileging local leadership and fostering reciprocity—where Western teams learn traditional healing wisdom even as they share biomedical advances—missions avoid neo-colonial pitfalls. In these ways, short-term engagements catalyze systemic improvements rooted in justice and dignity rather than transient good feelings.

11.6.2 Neglected Tropical Diseases, Vaccine Equity, and Matthew 25 Solidarity

Neglected tropical diseases afflict over a billion people, yet receive scant research funding, revealing stark global health inequities. Faith communities mobilize to distribute mass drug-administration campaigns for diseases such as schistosomiasis and lymphatic filariasis, combining epidemiological expertise with door-to-door evangelism. Vaccine equity movements echo Jesus's teaching in Matthew 25:40—"as you did it to one of the least of these my brothers, you did it to me"—urging high-income nations to share vaccine stockpiles and production technology with low-income partners. Church networks lobby pharmaceutical firms and governments to waive intellectual-property barriers, enabling local vaccine manufacture. Mission hospitals in endemic regions integrate NTD screening into routine maternal and child health services, normalizing prevention alongside prayerful care. Interfaith coalitions advocate at the World Health Assembly for increased funding and prioritization of NTD research, embodying global solidarity. Congregational adult-education classes unpack the histories that created health deserts, fostering awareness that planetary health demands cross-border compassion. Youth groups participate in global fundraising walks, raising both funds and awareness for NTD eradication. These efforts demonstrate that gospel solidarity must translate into concrete campaigns against diseases long ignored by secular philanthropy, actualizing Micah 6:8's call to act justly.

11.6.3 Tele-Medicine, AI Diagnostics, and the Digital Great Commission

The proliferation of telemedicine expands access to remote communities, enabling video consultations that bridge geographic and infrastructure gaps. Church-run clinics deploy satellite-connected devices to link rural patients with specialists, ensuring that stroke victims or diabetic patients receive timely guidance. AI diagnostics, trained on large data sets, assist primary-care providers by flagging early signs of tuberculosis or diabetic retinopathy, democratizing expertise. Ethical guidelines designed by Christian bioethicists emphasize transparency in AI algorithms to avoid bias against underrepresented populations. Tele-pastoral care overlays medical telehealth sessions with brief spiritual check-ins, offering holistic presence across fiber-optic lines. Training modules for local health workers include digital literacy curriculums, affirming Proverbs 22:6's emphasis on early instruction. Data privacy protocols rooted in dignity-based ethics ensure that patient information remains secure, reflecting the biblical principle of confidentiality in trust relationships. Mission organizations partner with tech companies to develop low-bandwidth apps tailored to areas with limited connectivity, ensuring no community is left behind. Digital evangelism accompanies interventional telehealth, as chaplains pray alongside translators in live video streams. This fusion of technology and mission enacts a Digital Great Commission, proclaiming care for body and soul across global networks.

11.6.4 Climate-Change Medicine: Heat, Hunger, and the Healing Mandate

Climate change intensifies heatwaves, malnutrition, and vector-borne diseases, making climate adaptation a critical component of global health. Churches mobilize cooling centers in partnership with municipal agencies during heat emergencies, offering water, shade, and prayer to vulnerable elders. Agricultural ministries distribute drought-resistant seed varieties and teach soil-conservation techniques, combating hunger in warming climates, in line with Genesis 2:15's stewardship charge. Mission hospital epidemiologists track shifts in malaria and dengue patterns, advising local populations on net use and standing-water elimination. Educational workshops in communities threatened by sea-level rise integrate faith-foundational hope with practical flood-preparedness training. Church youth groups engage in reforestation campaigns, planting mangroves and trees that buffer storm surge and sequester carbon. Biblical reflections on Job's laments provide spiritual frameworks for enduring ecological grief, while calls to prophetic action echo Jonah's witness to impending judgment balanced by mercy. Partnerships with climate scientists ensure that health ministries anticipate emerging risks rather than merely responding. By weaving climate resilience into medical missions, faith communities honor both the Creator and the vulnerable creation He entrusts to our care.

11.7 Formation and Resilience of Healers

11.7.1 Lectio Medica: Daily Scripture for Clinical Vocations

Healers face moral ambiguity and emotional toll, making spiritual formation essential. Lectio Medica adapts monastic lectio divina to medical contexts: before morning rounds, clinicians gather for brief Scripture readings—such as Luke 9:2's "Heal the sick"—followed by silent reflection on how the text bears on today's cases. They share insights on compassionate communication or boundary issues, grounding practice in biblical wisdom. These sessions become spiritual anchors, fostering unity amid shift rotations. Medical students value Lectio Medica as a counterbalance to the fast-paced didactic environment, reporting greater empathy and reduced burnout. Chaplains curate weekly scripture calendars aligned with liturgical seasons, integrating Advent's hope into end-of-life care and Lent's sobriety into addiction treatment ministries. This daily immersion sustains identity as healers called by God rather than mere employees of healthcare systems. As Lectio Medica forms hearts, practitioners bring faith-shaped compassion to every bedside.

11.7.2 Moral Injury, Burnout, and Benedictine Rhythms of Rest

Clinicians often endure moral injury when constraints—insurance denials, institutional pressures—force them to deliver suboptimal care. Prolonged moral distress leads to burnout, characterized by emotional exhaustion and cynicism. Borrowing from Benedictine rhythms, healthcare institutions implement structured "sabbath safeguards": mandatory time away from electronic records, team retreats every quarter for reflection and prayer, and protected post-call rest periods. Pastors preach on Genesis 2's seventh day rest as a divine command, legitimizing limits on productivity. Support groups for clinicians provide peer listening and confession, mirroring monastic chapters where faults were acknowledged and forgiven. Data show that teams embracing sabbath rhythms report higher job satisfaction and better patient outcomes. By prioritizing spiritual and physical rest, faith-informed systems model sustainable vocational patterns that honor both healer and healed.

11.7.3 Peer Supervision, Spiritual Direction, and Confession of Clinical Sin

To counter isolation, healers form peer-supervision circles where they discuss challenging cases, ethical dilemmas, and emotional strain under confidentiality covenants. Adding a spiritual director to this mix provides a sacred dimension, inviting attention to inner movements of pride, fear, or despair. Periodic confession of "clinical sin"—mistakes that harmed patients or compromised care—becomes restorative, aligning with James 5:16's call for mutual confession and prayer. Such practices reduce shame and guilt, fostering resilience. Hospitals coordinate with local seminaries to train clinical staff in reflective supervision, ensuring that both clinical expertise and spiritual insight inform practice. When staff acknowledge limitations and failures openly, trust within teams deepens, and patient care benefits from collective wisdom. This blend of peer support and spiritual direction cultivates clinical virtue and emotional health.

11.7.4 Continuing Education as Discipleship: Bridging CME and Spiritual Growth

Continuing Medical Education (CME) often focuses narrowly on technical updates, but integrating spiritual formation offers a holistic approach. Hospitals sponsor CME modules that pair new surgical techniques with ethical seminars on the sanctity of life. Workshops address compassionate communication skills alongside emerging pharmacotherapies, underscoring that healing encompasses body and soul. Attendees complete spiritual-reflection assignments—journaling God's presence in clinical experiences—to earn CME credits. Annual retreats bring together clinicians, chaplains, and ethicists for interdisciplinary sessions that include worship, case studies, and prayer. Physicians report that CME courses with spiritual integration renew their sense of calling and reduce decision fatigue. As CME becomes discipleship, professional development serves both technical excellence and vocational depth.

11.8 Eschatological Horizons of Health

11.8.1 "Leaves of the Tree for the Healing of Nations" (Rev 22:2)

John's vision of the new creation depicts a river of life flanked by trees whose leaves bring healing to the nations. This eschatological imagery inspires global health ministries to orient their work toward the ultimate goal of universal wholeness. Clinics imagine their pharmacies as provisional groves, offering medications that point toward the forest of restorative life to come. Pastors preach on Revelation's healed nations to galvanize congregational support for marginalized populations lacking access to healthcare. Medical missions frame each vaccine administered or wound dressed as a foretaste of Eden restored. Art in pediatric wards depicts verdant branches with shimmering leaves, comforting children with promise of future healing. Public-health policies advocated by church leaders—expanding mental-health services, universal vaccination—are presented as small steps toward the tree's full flourishing. As patients recover, testimonies are linked to Revelation's hope, reminding believers that no cure is final but that perfect healing awaits.

11.8.2 Already—and Not Yet: Provisional Cures and Ultimate Restoration

Christians live in the tension of "already" receiving healing through science, prayer, and sacraments, and "not yet" seeing total restoration when "the former things have passed away" (Rev 21:4). Each recovery from illness demonstrates the kingdom breaking into history, yet relapses and mortality remind us that disease persists. Hospital chapels display both progress updates—cancer survival rates rising—and scriptural promises that death itself will be abolished. Spiritual caregivers help patients hold both joy and grief, celebrating provisional cures while lamenting remaining brokenness. Seminary courses on eschatology integrate case studies of chronic illness, teaching clergy how to preach hope that neither denies present suffering nor fixates on temporary wellness. Medical ethics guidelines encourage treatments that alleviate suffering and extend life, while accepting the ultimate limits of fallible medicine. This dialectic fosters faithful resilience: as communities pray "Thy kingdom come," they also stockpiles beds for the sick, embodying hope that saves both body and soul.

11.8.3 The Wedding-Supper Clinic: Imagining Medicine in the New Creation

The eschatological feast in Revelation 19 paints a picture of the Lamb's wedding supper where every need is met. Imagining a "wedding-supper clinic," architects propose designing future healthcare spaces as celebratory banqueting halls rather than sterile wards. Walls painted in warm tones, communal dining tables for meal-based therapies, indoor gardens for oxygen therapy, and chapels as integral parts of the healing complex reflect an Edenic blueprint. Therapists plan "celebration rounds" where recoveries are toasted with grape-juice communion. Interventional radiologists experiment with bioluminescent tracers that glow like bridal lamps, illuminating bodily pathways. Though not a literal reality now, this visionary model guides present innovations: making healthcare dignified, communal, and oriented toward wholeness that mirrors wedding joy. As we anticipate that day, our current clinics become foretaste venues where medicine and celebration dance in hopeful anticipation of the final healing banquet.

11.9 Epilogue — Toward a New Hippocratic Amen

The chapters ahead have shown that healing is a multidisciplinary symphony where prayer, sacrament, and science harmonize. Churches learn to host integrated clinics, clinics embrace spiritual care, and classrooms train professionals to honor both body and soul. Patients benefit when chaplains and clinicians share rounds, research incorporates diverse methods, and congregations advocate for public health. Policies grounded in justice ensure that no community lacks vaccines or chaplaincy support. Educational programs that merge theology and medicine equip future healers for ethical complexity. In every context—urban hospital, rural parish, global health forum—the call remains to cultivate a healing ecology reflecting God's restorative will.

Conclusion Our journey has revealed a tapestry of healing woven from threads of prayer, ritual touch, medical skill, and ethical wisdom. From bedside liturgies that echo monastic vespers to technologically sophisticated gene-therapy trials, we see that the body of Christ is called to embody both miracle and method. As physicians, chaplains, and congregations collaborate, they model a holistic care that honors the sacredness of every life and the complexity of every condition. Moving forward, we will shift our focus in Chapter 12 to how communities respond to systemic suffering—disasters, poverty, and social injustice—bringing the same integrated compassion to the public arena that we've seen at the bedside. In every context, the "new Hippocratic Amen" resounds: may our hands heal, our prayers comfort, and our policies reflect the boundless mercy of our Redeemer.

Chapter 12 – Lament, Worship, and Formation Amid Suffering

In the crucible of pain, the church discovers that lament is not a detour from faith but its lifeblood, a way to speak truth to God when words fail and platitudes fall flat. This chapter journeys through the ancient psalms of complaint to reveal how honest grief anchors worship in reality, forming souls in patience, empathy, and steadfast hope. We'll learn how corporate rituals—candles, spoken-word laments, and communal weeping—honor our deepest sorrows while pointing us toward the promise that God transforms tears into testimony. As we embrace lament, we prepare our hearts to practice gratitude in the furnace, mentor the next generation through authentic liturgies, and build pastoral structures that sustain long-term sufferers. Ultimately, honest lament paves the way for doxology that rings true in both brokenness and redemption.

12.0 Prelude — When Tears Become Theology

12.0.1 The Universality of Ache: From Job's Ashes to Today's Waiting Rooms

The story of Job captures the raw reality of suffering that pierces even the most devout, showing us that pain spares no one, regardless of righteousness. Across centuries, human beings have entered waiting rooms with trembling hearts, seeking diagnoses that echo the existential questions Job raised in ashes and dust (Job 2:8). In modern hospitals, the click of an EKG or the hum of an MRI can rival the ominous winds in Job's whirlwind chapters, reminding us that our bodies remain under creation's groan (Rom 8:22). Every demographic group—from refugees in tent hospitals to suburban families in intensive-care units—shares this ache, revealing a fundamental solidarity of broken flesh. Anthropologists note that rituals of lament accompany medical treatment in nearly every culture, whether expressed through hymns in a chapel or through whispered prayers in bedside corners. Psalms of lament emerged from ancient Israel's temple courts but find fresh resonance when read aloud in contemporary cancer wards, giving language to pain that otherwise isolates. Clinicians often witness patients quoting Psalm 6's "Have mercy on me, Lord, for I am faint" when facing chronic conditions, illustrating how scripture travels across time. Ethnographers describe support-group meetings as modern-day lament songs, where sharing grief reduces its weight and fosters communal resilience. Patients of diverse faiths adapt lament structures—complaint, petition, affirmation—to vocalize despair and hope, demonstrating the universal utility of this ancient form. Even secular healthcare chapels feature interfaith prayer books that include psalms, recognizing their deep capacity for articulating ache. The universality of lament helps dismantle stigma around emotional expression in medical contexts, encouraging doctors to listen for spiritual wounds as well as physical ones. When congregations integrate lament into worship, they prepare communities to meet suffering with authenticity rather than platitude. This universal ache thus becomes a bridge connecting Job's ashes to today's biochemistry and bedside compassion.

12.0.2 Why Honest Lament Safeguards Faith from Cynicism and Denial

When suffering is glossed over with shallow optimism, congregants often feel abandoned by a faith that promises only victory. Honest lament provides a way to name disappointment without losing trust in God's character, modeling raw engagement rather than religious performance. The psalmists teach us that God welcomes our most anguished questions—"How long, Lord? Will you forget me forever?" (Ps 13:1)—and that entrusting our doubts can deepen intimacy rather than sever relationship. Ignoring lament risks pushing grief underground, where it festers into cynicism, bitterness, or denial of God's presence. By contrast, congregations that welcome lament create safe spaces where vulnerability becomes an asset, not a liability. Pastoral training now emphasizes teaching lament as a spiritual practice alongside prayer and praise, ensuring that faith communities do not default to toxic positivity. Churches display "laments walls" where members post anonymous prayers of complaint, creating visible acknowledgment of shared pain. Retreat centers offer lament workshops that combine expressive arts, such as poetry and painting, with guided biblical reflection, helping participants externalize inner turmoil. When leaders model their own laments in sermons, they demonstrate that faith can hold anguish without collapsing into atheistic despair. Researchers find that individuals who practice lament report higher resilience and lower rates of depression, suggesting that lament functions as a psychological as well as spiritual safeguard. Theologically, lament asserts that God's sovereign purposes include spaces for weeping, much like Jesus wept at Lazarus's tomb (Jn 11:35), affirming that tears belong in theology. Honest lament thus becomes a bulwark against cynicism and denial, sustaining faith through life's darkest corridors and preparing hearts for worship that truly rejoices.

12.1 The Psalms of Lament as Spiritual Guide

12.1.1 Anatomy of Biblical Lament: Address, Complaint, Petition, Trust, and Praise

The structure of a biblical lament offers a roadmap for spiritual articulation, beginning with an address—"O Lord" or "O God"—that reorients the soul toward divine attention (Ps 5:1). Following this invocation, the psalmist pours out complaint, detailing anguish through vivid metaphors of sinking mire or broken bones (Ps 40:2; Ps 6:2), refusing to sanitize the rawness of experience. Next comes petition, in which the sufferer asks for relief or intervention: "Restore me, O Lord, and let me live" (Ps 119:25). Crucially, lament often turns toward an affirmation of trust—even when circumstances have not changed—declaring confidence in God's past faithfulness: "But I trust in your unfailing love" (Ps 13:5). Finally, many laments close with praise, acknowledging that God is worthy even in suffering and vowing to declare His goodness publicly (Ps 22:22). This five-fold pattern equips worshipers to express multilayered responses: acknowledging pain, seeking divine help, remembering God's character, and committing to future praise. Spiritual directors teach this structure in prayer groups, offering worksheets that guide participants through each movement. In clinical chaplaincy, mapping a patient's emotional narrative onto this framework helps caregivers identify which stage a person occupies, tailoring interventions accordingly. Seminaries incorporate lament anatomy into homiletics courses, training preachers to construct sermons that resonate with congregants' private agonies. The consistent elements across laments foster a shared language of suffering, enabling communities to lament together rather than alone. As believers internalize this pattern, they gain a durable practice for navigating the myriad losses of life.

12.1.2 Naming the Abyss: Giving Language to Trauma, Betrayal, and Bodily Pain

Traumatic experiences often defy description, leaving survivors feeling isolated by inarticulate grief. The psalms of lament demonstrate that naming the abyss—speaking the terrifying reality of violence, betrayal, or chronic pain—is itself a form of healing (Ps 10:1). When congregations teach specific lament psalms, such as Psalm 44 or 88, they validate that God can bear witness to the darkest emotions without recoiling. Trauma-informed worship integrates guided readings where participants write their own laments in the margins of scripture, converting personal anguish into communal testimony. Group lament sessions invite volunteers to voice their own stories after reading a lament, ensuring that individual suffering finds collective resonance. Pastoral counselors use psalmic language to help clients find words for bodily pain—comparing neuropathy to a consuming fire or migraines to pounding enemy attacks. Medical professionals note that patients who speak their pain in metaphor often report greater pain tolerance, as naming shifts brain activity from limbic chaos to prefrontal processing. Choirs sometimes perform musical settings of laments, turning silent wounds into sung lamentations that carry emotional burdens in melody. By giving language to abyssal experiences, communities transform unspeakable isolation into shared vulnerability, bridging the gap between private trauma and public compassion.

12.1.3 Liturgical Re-Enactment: Responsorial Psalms, Sung Refrains, and Antiphonal Cries

In liturgical settings, laments come alive through call-and-response patterns, where a cantor intones verses and the congregation repeats sorrowful refrains. This responsorial structure mirrors ancient temple worship and fosters embodied participation in communal grief (Ps 136's repeated "His love endures forever" offers a hopeful counterpoint). Sung refrains such as "How long, O Lord" allow worshipers to join the psalmist's cry spontaneously, even without mastering the entire text. Antiphonal lament involves splitting the assembly into two groups that echo each other's cries, creating an enveloping dialogue of pain and solidarity (Ps 42's "Why are you downcast?" dialogue between self and soul). Liturgical planners weave lament psalms into the seasons of Advent and Lent, aligning collective grief with the church calendar's preparatory themes. Digital screens display brief laments between hymns, encouraging quiet reflection rather than rushing to the next agenda. Visual artists project abstract images—dark storm clouds parting toward light—behind lament choral pieces, stimulating multi-sensory worship. Worship bands adapt lament texts into contemporary melodies, bridging ancient forms with modern musical idioms. Through ritualized lament, worship becomes a rehearsal for authentic living, teaching congregations that grief and praise can intermingle in the same breath.

12.1.4 Translating Ancient Cadence into Modern Voice: Spoken-Word, Gospel Blues, and Digital Psalter Apps

To reach diverse worshipers, lament finds new expression in spoken-word poetry, where artists recite personal psalms that rhyme heartache with hope. Gospel blues musicians infuse lament passages with soulful rhythms, echoing Job's honesty in minor keys that resolve into major-key affirmations. Digital psalter apps offer curated lament playlists, prompting users to swipe through psalms of complaint and petition when anxiety strikes. Virtual reality prayer rooms immerse participants in immersive soundscapes—echoing temple acoustics—while text overlays guide them through lament structure. Youth ministries host open-mic lament nights where teens voice struggles with mental health, using psalmic frameworks to shape their stories. Liturgical designers create augmented-reality hymnals that highlight lament stanzas in red, ensuring that worshipers do not skip over sorrowful verses. Social-media campaigns share daily lament prompts—"Write one line of complaint and one line of trust"—fostering digital solidarity across time zones. By translating ancient cadences into modern media, the church ensures that lament remains a living, adaptive tradition for every generation.

12.2 Corporate Rhythms of Grief and Hope

12.2.1 "How Long, O Lord?" Services: Candle-Lighting, Silence, and Communal Weeping

In the face of chronic illness or community tragedy, churches convene "How Long, O Lord?" services to give space for extended lament. Candle-lighting rituals commence the service, each flame representing a narrative of pain—be it personal grief or collective sorrow over violence. Silence follows the candles' illumination, allowing participants to absorb both darkness and flickering light as tangible metaphors of hope amid despair. Soft instrumental psalms play in the background while congregants write confidential laments on strips of paper, which are then tied to a "lament wall" for symbolic release. Shared weeping is invited rather than shamed, normalizing tears as a legitimate response to suffering and echoing Job's own public grief. Trained pastoral caregivers circulate among attendees, offering tissues and gentle prayers, ensuring no one sobs alone. Theologically, these services affirm that the church exists not just to conquer but to accompany, embodying Christ's presence in Gethsemane. Following the lament segment, a brief responsive reading of Psalm 13's turn from complaint to declaration—"I will sing to the Lord, for he has been good to me"—points toward emerging hope. These events often conclude with a simple communal meal, where participants break bread in solidarity, transforming sorrow into mutual care. Over time, regular "How Long, O Lord?" gatherings foster a culture where grief is ritualized rather than repressed, weaving lament into the congregation's spiritual DNA.

12.2.2 Public Funerals and National Tragedy Vigils: When Sanctuary Becomes Town Square

When disasters strike—a school shooting, a natural calamity, or a pandemic's apex—church sanctuaries transform into public forums for collective mourning. Pastors open their pulpits to civic leaders, first responders, and survivors, offering space for testimonies alongside theological reflection on death's mystery. Hymns like "Abide with Me" and "Amazing Grace" anchor communal tears in holy refrain, while moments of silence honor those lost. Live-streamed vigils invite diaspora members to join digitally, expanding sanctuary walls to include global solidarities. Scripture readings shift to texts of communal lament—Lamentations 3, Jeremiah 9—acknowledging that corporate sin or cosmic events breed shared sorrow. Candles encircle the altar rail, each flame named after a victim, offering visible testimony to the breadth of loss. Journalists cover these services, broadcasting to the wider community that faith can lead the mourning and set the tone for public resilience. Clergy organize interfaith coalition vigils, reinforcing that grief transcends doctrinal divides and that the politics of compassion begins with shared lament. Ultimately, these public funerals and vigils reaffirm that sanctuary is not a private club but the heart of a city's grief and hope.

12.2.3 Communal Discernment After Disaster: Lament as Seedbed for Prophetic Action

Following calamity, lament opens hearts to both prayerful reflection and practical discernment. Churches hold aftermath forums where participants first voice grief, then transition into guided conversations on systemic causes—climate policy, gun violence, healthcare inequities. Facilitators ground discussions in Hebrews 4:16's invitation to approach "the throne of grace with confidence," ensuring that prophetic critique flows from prayer rather than anger. Small teams conduct site visits to affected areas, gathering stories that inform advocacy campaigns. Lament's raw honesty fuels moral imagination, driving congregations to partner with nonprofits on rebuild projects and policy reform. Youth groups compose lament hymns that double as protest chants at city hall hearings, linking worship with civic engagement. Through these practices, lament becomes the fuel for prophetic action, ensuring that tears water seeds of justice and mercy across the community.

12.2.4 Trauma-Informed Worship Spaces: Visual Simplicity, Sensory Safety, and Flexible Liturgies

Worshipping communities with significant trauma histories adapt space and liturgy to promote sensory safety. Visual simplicity—neutral color palettes, uncluttered furnishings—minimizes triggers for PTSD sufferers. Soft lighting options allow individuals to adjust brightness for their comfort, preventing sensory overload. Soundscape choices prioritize calm acoustics over sudden crescendos, and worship leaders introduce predictable order of service to reduce anxiety. Liturgies include "time-out tokens" that empower attendees to step out quietly when overwhelmed, knowing they can rejoin without disruption. Pastoral teams train on trauma-informed language, avoiding phrases like "God will never give you more than you can handle," which can retraumatize those in crisis. Children's worship areas include tactile corners with soft seating and sensory toys, supporting younger members with sensory processing differences. These trauma-informed environments exemplify the church's commitment to embodying Psalm 34:18's promise that God is close to the brokenhearted, ensuring that corporate worship becomes a space of invitation rather than intimidation.

12.3 Formational Outcomes of Suffering

12.3.1 Patience Forged in Delay: Waiting as Spiritual Weight-Training

Patience emerges not in moments of ease but in the crucible of unrelenting trial, much like a muscle strengthened under steady tension rather than sudden strain. In classes on spiritual endurance, mentors compare waiting on healing with the Israelites' forty years in the wilderness—an extended lesson in dependence and grace (Ex 16:35). When chemotherapy cycles stretch into months, patients discover that each delay deepens reliance on God rather than their own timetable. Support groups encourage journaling "waiting prayers," brief entries that track frustration one day and a small spark of trust the next, highlighting progress that escapes immediate notice. Pastors preach that the Lord's speed often mirrors His wisdom—He knows the ripest moment for relief better than we do, echoing Ecclesiastes 3:1's "To every thing there is a season." Families learn to reframe "waiting rooms" as "learning rooms," equipping children to recite Psalm 27:14—"Wait for the Lord; be strong, and let your heart take courage"—as a mantra in boredom or fear. Retreat ministries offer "waiting retreats" where participants practice silence and slow breathing, rehearsing Jesus's instruction in Mark 6:31 to rest even amid ministry demands. Nursing staff note that patients who cultivate active waiting—praying, reading, connecting—report lower anxiety than those who passively fret. Corporate worship sometimes includes extended silence after Scripture readings, embodying communal patience in physical form. Over time, congregants develop a theology of delay that sees God's pauses not as signs of absence but as invitations to deeper trust. As patience holds in tension the promise of healing and the reality of delay, souls grow resilient, ready for the next stage of formation.

12.3.2 Empathy and Advocacy: How Shared Pain Expands Moral Imagination

Suffering often opens eyes to others' hidden struggles, birthing empathy that fuels advocacy for systemic change. When a senior in a congregation faces mobility loss, fellow members grapple with wheelchair-access needs, leading the church council to lobby the city for curb cuts and ramp grants. Social-justice ministries spring from shared stories of chronic illness, as those who've known disability speak out against employment discrimination in local forums. Bible studies highlight Romans 12:15—"Rejoice with those who rejoice; mourn with those who mourn"—as a commissioning for practical solidarity, prompting members to deliver meals or drive to appointments. Health ministries hold empathy-training workshops where participants don vision-impairment goggles or use canes, simulating conditions that foster compassion. Youth groups partner with special-needs ministries, learning to communicate beyond words and to celebrate small victories in therapy sessions. Testimonies at worship services underscore how personal pain prompted reforms in church parking, nursery accessibility, or community counseling referrals. Over time, empathy ripples outward: congregations partner with civic health boards to address food deserts and mental-health deserts, advocating for clinics in underserved neighborhoods. Ethical reflection circles discuss how Jesus's healing of the centurion's servant (Matt 8:5–13) modeled bridging social distance and responding to unseen needs. By linking empathy born in suffering to public advocacy, faith communities expand their moral imagination, embodying justice born of compassion.

12.3.3 Eternal Perspective: Orienting Daily Decisions Toward the Coming Kingdom

Suffering can recalibrate temporal priorities, prompting believers to make choices that reflect eternal values rather than fleeting comfort. Cancer survivors often report reordering budgets—shifting from luxury spending to missions giving—echoing Jesus's counsel to "lay up treasures in heaven" (Matt 6:20). Patients in palliative care sometimes draft letters to grandchildren, investing in legacy that transcends their lifespan and underscores the kingdom's enduring relevance. Small-group reflections on 2 Corinthians 4:17—"This light momentary affliction is preparing for us an eternal weight of glory"— encourage daily practices like hospitality and prayer over frantic busyness. Families facing a dementia diagnosis create photo albums with gospel captions, ensuring that descendants inherit faith narratives more than material inheritance. Volunteers monitor Sabbath observance, reminding busy caregivers that rest anchors existence in God's unchanging presence, not in ever-shifting health metrics. Sermons on Revelation's new heaven and new earth paint future wholeness so vividly that present trials shrink into perspective, guiding believers to choose generosity over hoarding, service over self-preservation. Personal mission statements are revised to reflect kingdom impact—mentoring new believers, supporting community health initiatives—rather than focus on personal comfort. By embracing an eternal horizon, the formation of character prioritizes what lasts beyond the grave, infusing each decision with heaven's promise.

12.3.4 Testimony Circles: Storytelling Practices that Re-author Community Identity

Small circles of four to six believers gather regularly to share testimonies of suffering and grace, weaving individual stories into a communal tapestry that shapes identity. Each participant recounts a recent struggle—loss of mobility, a broken relationship, or chronic fatigue—and then speaks of God's sustaining presence, modeling narrative honesty and hope. Facilitators guide the group through reflective questions: How has this suffering changed your view of God? What new spiritual fruit has emerged? These questions turn raw accounts into theological insights and bless both speaker and listeners. Congregational video ministries record composite testimonies—blended from multiple voices—to screen in services, reinforcing that the body of Christ bears collective witness to redemption. Artistic "story quilts" hang in fellowship halls, each square emblazoned with a testimony snippet and symbolic artwork, making personal narratives part of the church's visual identity. Elder–young adult pairs collaborate on writing workshops to craft testimonies for digital platforms, empowering new generations to speak vulnerably online. When testimonies resonate, they spark further formation: volunteers initiate ministries for spinal-injury exercise or grief counseling, directly responding to needs revealed in circles. Theologically, these practices echo Acts 4:32's unity of heart and soul, transforming isolated pain into shared narrative that defines who we are as a community shaped by suffering and hope.

12.4 Joy and Gratitude Practices in the Furnace (Hab 3:17–19)

12.4.1 Eucharistic Thanksgiving with Tears: Receiving Bread When Appetite Is Gone

Amid physical weakness and loss of appetite, believers are invited to gather around the Lord's Table, tasting grace when earthly nourishment fails. Liturgies emphasize that the bread of heaven—Christ's body—sustains beyond physical hunger, echoing Habakkuk's paradoxical joy in drought. Chaplains bring communion elements to hospital rooms, laying a single wafer on the tongue of patients too weak for a full meal, affirming that spiritual nourishment precedes physical restoration. Audiovisual aids—soft organ music, candlelight—create sensory environments that foreground thanksgiving over gloom, even when tears mix with the sacramental juice. Worship teams adapt the eucharistic prayers to include explicit thanksgiving for small mercies—manageable pain levels, a good night's sleep, a visitor's presence—grounding gratitude in immediate experience. Families are encouraged to share one thing they are thankful for before reciting the Lord's Prayer, reinforcing that gratitude can bloom amidst suffering. Pastors reference 1 Thessalonians 5:18—"give thanks in all circumstances"—as normative, reminding congregations that eucharistic thanksgiving expresses trust in God's overarching goodness. Through these adaptations, the Eucharist becomes a furnace in which gratitude is refined, shaping hearts to praise in the midst of pain.

12.4.2 Daily Examen of Small Graces: Five-Finger Gratitude, Breath Prayers, and "Goodness Journals"

Daily examen practices help believers retrace God's footprints in the midst of suffering by pausing to notice five small gifts each day. A "five-finger gratitude" technique invites participants to list five blessings—sunlight on a window, a visitor's smile, a pain-free hour—each time candlelight flickers in evening prayer. Breath prayers like "Thank you…Jesus" synchronize heartbeat and thanksgiving, anchoring awareness in God's presence with each inhale and exhale. Goodness journals, small notebooks kept beside the bed, record entries such as a nurse's kindness or a moment of clear thought, creating tangible reminders of grace. Small-group "examen partners" meet weekly to share top gratitude entries, fostering mutual encouragement and accountability. Research in positive psychology affirms that focusing on small positives increases resilience, even when overall circumstances remain dire. Pastors incorporate short examen pauses into liturgy, dimming sanctuary lights for thirty seconds of collective gratitude reflection. Smartphone apps developed by church-affiliated teams prompt users with prayer and journal reminders, integrating spiritual practice into daily rhythms. Over months, these practices reshape perception, making blessings more visible and suffering less overwhelming. The daily examen thus becomes a spiritual gym where gratitude muscles grow, equipping sufferers to find joy in the furnace.

12.4.3 Festival-in-Exile: Retaining Holy-Day Rhythms During Medical Crises or Displacement

When illness or displacement disrupts normal life, congregations intentionally preserve key festivals—Christmas, Easter, Pentecost—as islands of rejoicing. Hospitals partner with churches to sponsor "festival carts" that deliver liturgy kits—candles, simple hymn sheets, small crosses—to patient rooms on feast days, ensuring that isolation does not eclipse celebration. Pastors record video homilies tailored to those in medical crisis, emphasizing that the incarnation and resurrection break into every human predicament. In refugee camps, faithful adapt festival feasts to limited rations, celebrating with small portions of symbolic food like bread and juice, echoing Acts 2's communal sharing. Seasonal drum circles and dance reflections, drawn from global Christian traditions, allow expressive joy even when bodies are frail. Nursing homes host intergenerational festival parties, where children teach elders new festival carols, reaffirming continuity amid loss. Sermon series on advent hope or paschal light blend ancient liturgy with modern testimonies of survival, creating a tapestry of rejoicing in adversity. By practicing festival-in-exile, the church proclaims that the sacred calendar transcends circumstances, forging resilient joy that testifies to God's faithfulness across all seasons.

12.4.4 Artistic Doxology: Lament-to-Praise Psalters, Mended-Clay Workshops, and Hope Murals

Art channels the soul's movements from lament into praise, as seen in workshops where participants sculpt broken clay vessels that are then mended with gold—inspired by Japanese kintsugi—to symbolize God's redemptive beauty in brokenness. Lament-to-praise psalters are created in writing groups, collecting paired psalm stanzas—one of complaint, one of trust—and arranging them in diptychs that guide readers from sorrow to joy. Community art projects paint hope murals on clinic walls, featuring images of sunrise over storm clouds, weaving scripture texts like Lamentations 3:22–23 into the design. Music ministries compose "lament-to-doxology" song cycles that move from minor-key blues to triumphant gospel, narrating spiritual journeys. Fiber-arts circles knit prayer shawls interwoven with ribbons inscribed with gratitude words, offering tactile expressions of doxology. Over time, these artistic practices saturate worship spaces with living testimonies of hope, providing visual and tactile reminders that suffering can give rise to beauty and praise.

12.5 Discipling the Next Generation Through Honest Worship

12.5.1 Children's Lament Liturgies: Stuffed-Animal Prayer Circles and Draw-Your-Psalm Exercises

Children experience confusion and fear when facing serious illness in family or community, yet are often excluded from adult lament rituals. Stuffed-animal prayer circles invite youngsters to bring a beloved toy that "knows their secrets," placing it in the center as a symbol of bringing personal worries before God. Leaders guide simple prayers—"Dear God, my teddy is sad because Grandpa is sick"—helping children articulate grief in accessible language. Draw-your-psalm exercises equip kids to illustrate imagery from a selected lament verse, such as a valley of tears, embedding emotional literacy through art. Sunday school rooms display these drawings as a "children's lament gallery," signaling that the church hears even smallest voices. Pediatric chaplains coordinate with children's ministries to integrate these liturgies into hospital playrooms, ensuring continuity of spiritual formation. Counseling psychologists note that naming sadness through toy rituals reduces anxiety and fosters a sense of agency. Storybooks adapted from psalms—with rhyming couplets and comforting metaphors—become part of bedtime routines, reinforcing that lament belongs in healthy faith life. Through these practices, children internalize that honest worship includes both tears and trust.

12.5.2 Youth Doubt Forums: Guiding Teen Questions without Rush to Resolution

Adolescents facing existential questions often meet silence or clichés in adult worship, stifling spiritual growth. Youth doubt forums create structured spaces where teens can air theological and ethical questions—"Why does God allow my friend's terminal illness?"—without fear of immediate correction. Trained mentors facilitate discussions grounded in Scripture, encouraging exploration of Job's wrestling rather than premature doctrinal answers. Journals and anonymous question boxes allow introverted participants to share deeper doubts, ensuring inclusivity. Debates on topics like suffering, justice, and the problem of evil integrate philosophical resources and pastoral sensitivity, modeling how to live with unresolved tension. Service projects for sick peers follow forum sessions, teaching that doubt need not paralyze compassion. Pastors occasionally join these forums as learners rather than teachers, demonstrating humility and mutual respect. When teens see leaders wrestling openly with faith questions, they gain courage to own their doubts without abandoning hope. Over time, these forums cultivate a generation adept at holding faith and uncertainty in dynamic tension, shaping resilient disciples.

12.5.3 Mentoring Programs Pairing Elders of Affliction with Young Leaders

Elders who have endured long seasons of illness or loss possess wisdom that can guide younger believers through emerging challenges. Mentoring programs connect these seasoned saints—who have written memoirs of perseverance—with youth via regular meetings where stories of God's faithfulness spark hope. Intergenerational pairs meet for tea and testimony, with elders sharing psalms that carried them through hospital stays and youth reflecting on current struggles. Retreat weekends include "story circle" sessions where both mentor and mentee write joint laments and praises, forging bonds that transcend age. Structured curricula include reading Ecclesiastes's lessons on seasons and decline, framing suffering in eternal perspective. Mentees accompany mentors to medical appointments when appropriate, learning compassion and medical-system advocacy firsthand. Programs invite theologians to train elder mentors in basic counseling skills, ensuring safe boundaries and effective listening. Youth report increased empathy and less fear of suffering when they witness elders living victoriously "through many dangers, toils, and snares" by faith. These mentoring relationships model Titus 2:3–5's vision of older women teaching younger to love and endure, enshrining suffering as a vehicle for communal formation.

12.5.4 Digital Worship Kits for College Students Navigating Isolation and Loss

College campuses often lack the close-knit supports of home communities, leaving students to face illness or grief in dorm-room isolation. Digital worship kits—downloadable guided liturgies, lament playlists, and breath-prayer video tutorials—offer portable spiritual resources. Students can project bedside candle images on laptops to create intimate worship corners, using psalm text overlays to lead personal lament services. Mobile apps send nightly reminders to journal gratitude and lament, bridging academic schedules with spiritual rhythms. Virtual small groups meet via video chat to read psalms together, pray for peers, and share resources for counseling centers. University chaplaincies collaborate with church tech teams to embed these kits in campus learning platforms, ensuring visibility. When friends experience campus health crises, these kits provide immediate frameworks for shared prayer on group chats, knitting dispersed students into spiritual solidarity. As college students move between classrooms, study sessions, and hospital visits, digital worship kits become lifelines, reminding them that lament, worship, and formation persist even amid isolation and loss.

12.6 Pastoral Care Architectures for Long-Term Sufferers

12.6.1 Rule of Life for Chronic Pain: Sabbath, Medical Stewardship, and Community Check-Ins

A Rule of Life tailored for those with chronic pain integrates rhythmic rest, intentional medical care, and structured communal support. Grounded in Exodus 20:8–10's Sabbath command, believers with persistent pain receive permission to observe weekly rest days, suspending medical appointments and housework to focus on spiritual renewal. These Sabbath pauses are scheduled in congregational calendars alongside worship services, signaling communal endorsement. Medical stewardship invites each sufferer to partner with a small team—nurse, physical therapist, and prayer partner—who collaborate on treatment plans, ensuring medications are managed responsibly while prayers accompany each dosage. Community check-ins are organized in triads: two fellow sufferers and one pastoral caregiver meet weekly, rotating between homes or cafés to share updates on pain levels, coping strategies, and devotional insights. These gatherings open with a brief liturgy adapted from Psalm 62:5—"Find rest, my soul, in God alone"—linking physical rest with spiritual trust. Participants then circle-share using a "pain-grace" format: one person describes a high-pain moment and a corresponding experience of grace, fostering honesty and hope. Chaplains train triad members in basic pain-management coaching—applying heat, guiding relaxation exercises, praying breath prayers—turning pastoral presence into practical care. Digital tools remind members of check-in times and track collective pain-stability trends, alerting the group when someone reports escalating symptoms. Congregations allocate benevolence funds to cover costs of adaptive equipment—compression socks, ergonomic chairs—demonstrating material care. Pastors preach periodically on the body as temple (1 Cor 6:19), contextualizing medical stewardship as spiritual worship. Workshops on Sabbath theology help families overcome guilt around rest, reframing pause as obedience rather than laziness. Over months, triads cultivate compassionate routines that buffer isolation and empower members to cohere as a supportive community. This structured Rule of Life transforms chronic pain from a solitary burden into a shared spiritual discipline, revealing that rest, stewardship, and solidarity together shape resilient faith.

12.6.2 Home Communion and Mobile Choirs: Extending Worship to Bed- and House-Bound Saints When chronic illness confines members to home or bed, worship must follow them. Home communion teams—trained volunteers including deacons and elders—visit weekly to distribute consecrated elements, recite Eucharistic prayers, and sing simple hymn refrains like "Jesus Loves Me." The liturgy is adapted for physical limitations: small gluten-free wafers, sips of juice administered by spoon, and lighting of battery-powered prayer candles to evoke sanctuary presence. Nurses assist by checking vital signs before and after communion, ensuring safety and documenting spiritual response alongside physical data. Mobile choirs of two to four singers—children, youth, or retirees—rotate through households, their voices carrying psalm stanzas door-to-door. Choir members learn to modulate volume for fragile ears and to hold hands for brief "laying on of hands" after each verse, creating embodied communion. Families are encouraged to join via video calls during each visit, restoring intergenerational fellowship even when distance separates. Congregational newsletters highlight these visits, inviting prayer support and volunteer recruitment. Training modules for home communion and mobile choir teams cover liturgical theology, infection-control protocols, and sensitivity to identity loss prompted by isolation. Pastors preach on the mustard-seed church (Matt 17:20), reminding congregations that even small gatherings in homes reflect Christ's expanding kingdom. Over time, these practices affirm that worship is not bound to building walls, but lives wherever the body of Christ dwells, ensuring that no sister or brother is cut off from sacramental grace.

12.6.3 Integrating Mental-Health Professionals into Prayer Teams Mental-health issues often intertwine with physical suffering, calling for integrated ministry that spans clinical and spiritual care. Prayer teams now include a rotating counselor or clinical social worker who co-leads intercessory sessions, addressing both prayer requests and cognitive-behavioral coping strategies. These hybrid teams hold monthly "Healing Hearts" gatherings, starting with a time of confession and prayer, then transitioning into psychoeducational workshops on anxiety, depression, or trauma responses. Licensed professionals teach simple grounding techniques—5-4-3-2-1 sensory exercises—embedded within prayer rhythms, ensuring that participants gain practical tools alongside spiritual support. Teams develop referral maps for specialized mental-health resources and coordinate with pastoral staff to follow up on critical concerns, such as suicide ideation. Confidentiality agreements clarify when mental-health mandates override clergy-penitent privilege, protecting vulnerable individuals. Congregational communications emphasize that seeking counseling is consistent with biblical examples of wise counsel (Prov 11:14), reducing stigma. Retreats include both silent contemplation sessions and guided group therapy exercises, merging monastic retreats with modern psychotherapy. Chaplains and psychologists co-author devotionals that integrate journaling prompts on emotions with scriptural reflections. As trust grows, individuals who might have shunned prayer rooms now attend therapeutic-prayer gatherings, experiencing wholeness in body and mind. By embedding mental-health professionals in prayer teams, churches embody Christ's holistic healing ministry, bridging sacred and clinical interventions.

12.6.4 Measuring Congregational Resilience: Surveys, Story Audits, and Exit Interviews To evaluate and refine pastoral care architectures, congregations implement resilience metrics. Quarterly surveys assess members' perceived support, spiritual well-being, and participation in care structures, using validated instruments like the Brief Resilience Scale. Story audits gather qualitative data: focus-group facilitators collect narratives of suffering and care, analyzing themes of isolation, hope, and community response. Exit interviews with those who leave care programs probe reasons—schedule conflicts, unmet needs, or confusion—guiding program adjustments. Data dashboards display anonymized resilience scores alongside participation rates in Rule of Life triads, home communion visits, and Healing Hearts gatherings. Leadership teams review these metrics in council meetings, asking hard questions: Are chronic sufferers staying engaged? Which support structures correlate with improved spiritual health? How can we reduce drop-off? Congregations involve academic partners—local seminaries or psychology departments—in analyzing trends and recommending evidence-based enhancements. Grants from denominational bodies fund technology like mobile data-collection apps and secure cloud storage for resilience data, ensuring confidentiality. Published case studies celebrate successes—such as a 30 percent increase in triad retention—and model transparency. By measuring resilience, faith communities demonstrate commitment to stewarding both resources and relationships, iteratively shaping pastoral care that honors long-term sufferers.

12.7 Eschatological Lament and Final Hallelujah

12.7.1 Groaning Creation and Spirit Groans (Rom 8:22–27)

Paul's declaration that all creation "groans" together resonates in the cacophony of natural disasters and personal trials, uniting human lament with cosmic longing. The Spirit's intercession "with sighs too deep for words" (Rom 8:26) assures believers that even when they cannot articulate pain, the Spirit is voicing their deepest cries. Liturgies incorporate collective groaning through extended silent prayers and low, resonant chants that echo primordial laments. Worship retreats offer "groan labs" where participants express unspoken fears through body movement and wordless sound, releasing pent-up anguish in communal vulnerability. Preaching on Romans 8 bridges individual affliction with global suffering—climate injustice, pandemics—crafting an eschatological awareness that personal tears link to creation's overall redemption. Prayer collects for Spirit groans are included in confessional liturgies, modeling that corporate church prayer need not be verbatim but can mirror groaning cries for justice, healing, and restoration. Theological reflections on Spirit groaning inform pastoral care: chaplains recognize when a penitent's silent tears are the Spirit's intercession rather than merely emotional catharsis. Artistic installations in sanctuary entryways depict swirling cosmic shapes and hands lifted in wordless yearning, inviting worshipers into the Spirit's groaning before any spoken prayer. Through these practices, congregations live in the tension of already redeemed and not yet restored, participating in the Spirit's redemptive travail until the kingdom fully comes.

12.7.2 Maranatha Spirituality: Yearning for the Appearing While Serving in the Present

"Maranatha," Aramaic for "Come, Lord," embodies a spirituality that holds eager anticipation for Christ's return alongside active service in the present age. Worship services integrate Maranatha chants, repeating the plea "Revelation's dawning, come now, O Lord" between psalm stanzas of lament and praise. Liturgical calendars mark "Maranatha Sundays" with extended readings from Revelation's throne room scenes, drawing connections between present suffering and future glorification. Small groups commit to Maranatha practices: nightly prayers for the Lord's return, brief fasting hours on the 29th day of each month, and mapping personal vocations to kingdom purposes while anticipating consummation. Sermons emphasize that longing for the appearing does not foster escapism but fuels compassion, as the early church's hope in Jesus's coming empowered deacons to serve widows. Community service projects—food-pantry work, refugee support— are framed as rehearsals of kingdom justice, bearing prophetic witness to the world that Christ is coming to right every wrong. Music ministries compose Maranatha anthems that interweave lyrics of redemption with minor-key motifs of current sorrow, reflecting the gospel's paradox. Retreat centers host "Already-Not Yet" weekends where participants oscillate between contemplative silence and hands-on mission work, embodying double-focus spirituality. In these ways, Maranatha spirituality cultivates longing that animates present ministry rather than postponing engagement until some hypothetical future.

12.7.3 Revelation's Tearless Horizon and the Practice of Hope Today John's vision of a new heaven and new earth where "God will wipe away every tear" (Rev 21:4) crystallizes the hope to which every lament points. Worship leaders project visual motifs of tearless landscapes—crystal rivers, verdant trees—during congregational singing of hope hymns. Pastoral reflections on Revelation's tearless horizon guide prayer groups to imagine future joy as a foretaste, using guided meditations that transition from current sorrows to eschatological celebration. Art therapists facilitate painting exercises where participants repaint scenes of personal tragedy into vibrant visions of healed reality, rehearsing hope through creativity. Testimony time in worship includes closing affirmations: "We will laugh again" or "We will dance without pain," transforming language of defeat into confessions of eternal victory. Sermon series on Revelation's healing imagery underscore that no grief endures into eternity, motivating congregants to steward present tears in service and advocacy rather than bitterness. Youth ministries dramatize Revelation's promise through short plays that end with scenes of reunions beyond the veil, offering imaginative hope for younger generations. By focusing on the tearless horizon, the church teaches that present laments are not ends in themselves but preludes to everlasting celebration, embedding hope in the very fabric of worship.

12.7.4 Preparing a People for Eternal Praise: Lament as the Last Lesson Before Glory The final lesson before entering God's presence is often lament, as scripture's last lines sometimes dwell on trials before culminating in promise. Worship education programs teach that lament prepares hearts to appreciate unmediated joy, much like a palate cleansed before a grand feast. Choirs practice "lament-through-praise" anthems that move from minor to major keys, reflecting the trajectory of redemption. Congregations host "final lament" services preceding ordinations or mission departures, inviting ministers to confess vulnerability before launching into confident blessing declarations. Retreat guides frame last-day gatherings around shared farewells, using psalms of ascents—Psalm 122's pilgrimage motif—as metaphors for entry into eternal praise. Visual art in sanctuaries transitions from stark grey tapestries during lament seasons to luminous banners on festival days, rehearsing the arc from trial to triumph. Pastoral farewells—such as hospital discharge or homebound assignments—are conducted as mini-rites of passage, blending lament for departure with commissioning into ongoing praise. Ultimately, lament as the last lesson before glory reminds the people of every season that God's consummating gift makes every tear a seed for eternal laughter, equipping hearts for the everlasting doxology that awaits beyond the veil.

12.8 Epilogue — From Wailing Wall to Wedding Feast

Worship leaders learn that crafting liturgies of lament requires balancing honesty with movement toward hope, drawing on psalm structures to give shape to communal grief. Counselors discover that integrating lament practices into therapy—journaling, psalm recitation, silence—enhances clients' resilience and deepens spiritual growth. Everyday sufferers find that expressing sorrow in community prevents hidden pain from becoming shameful secrecy. Service planners recognize the power of sensory environments—lighting, acoustics, tactile objects—to facilitate safe lament. Theologians deepen reflection on divine accompaniment amid suffering, reframing pain as a context for encountering Christ's solidarity rather than evidence of divine absence. Pastoral teams implement measured resilience metrics to track the effects of lament ministries, ensuring care remains adaptive. Educators infuse lament into discipleship curriculums, teaching that faith matures through both tears and trust. Small-group facilitators refine storytelling protocols to honor confidentiality while amplifying shared identity. Artists and musicians collaborate with worship architects to embed lament motifs—minor keys, broken clay installations—into sacred spaces. Hospital chaplains adopt trauma-informed lament liturgies, bridging healthcare and worship. Youth and children's ministries embrace age-appropriate lament forms, preventing generational faith erosion. Mission strategists integrate lament-in-action as prelude to advocacy, linking sorrow to service. Technology teams develop apps for communal lament tracking, ensuring digital inclusion. Financial stewards allocate budget line items for lament workshops, demonstrating institutional priority. These insights offer a roadmap for embedding lament as a transformative, formative practice across all spheres of church life.

Conclusion When a community learns to weep together, it becomes a wellspring of compassion, resilience, and prophetic action. Honest lament reshapes worship spaces, infuses discipleship with depth, and equips believers to bear one another's burdens across all seasons of life. As tears give rise to trust, waiting becomes spiritual formation, and shared pain expands moral imagination into advocacy for justice. By weaving lament into our daily rhythms—through prayer, art, and ritual—we shape a people ready not only to survive suffering but to sing its redemption. In the final chapters, we will carry this vision of wounded healers into the wider world, living out the gospel as communities that both mourn with and minister to the nations.

Chapter 13 – The Church's Vocation: Compassionate Community and Advocacy

The church's calling extends far beyond worship services and Sunday schools; it is summoned to embody the mercy of Christ in concrete acts of care and courageous advocacy. As God's hands and feet, congregations become havens where the lonely find listening hearts, the sick receive sacramental touch, and the doubting are met with honest companionship. This vocation draws on ancient practices—diakonia, bedside Eucharist, prayerful presence—and reimagines them for contemporary realities, from virtual chaplaincy to trauma-informed liturgy. At the same time, the church carries a prophetic mandate to speak truth to power, championing policies that protect the vulnerable and working in coalition for public health, justice, and environmental wholeness. In this chapter, we explore how faithful communities organize compassionate care, form disciples who serve and advocate, and cultivate an eschatological imagination that fuels hope-fueled activism in a broken world.

13.0 Prelude — Love with Skin On: Why Ecclesial Compassion Still Matters

13.0.1 The Triune God's Nearness as Model for Pastoral Presence

The Father's faithfulness to Israel in exile embodies a steadfast presence that never abandons a suffering people (Isa 43:2). The Son's incarnation demonstrates divine solidarity, as Jesus "dwelt among us," entering human pain to redeem it (John 1:14). His walking with the two on the Emmaus road shows that accompaniment transforms despair into hope (Luke 24:15–27). The Spirit's abiding comfort teaches that presence is not merely physical proximity but continual inner support (John 14:16–17). Pastoral presence mirrors this Trinitarian model by offering not just advice but shared space, prayerful attention, and empathetic silence. Listening without interruption or agenda allows congregants to feel the Spirit's voice working through the minister's ears. Just as Jesus paused at Lazarus's tomb and wept with Mary and Martha, pastors are invited to enter grief rather than rush to fix it (John 11:35). Hospital chaplains learn that presence in corridors—quietly sitting by an IV drip—can speak louder than scripted prayers. Rural pastors make house calls across miles, embodying the Spirit's nearness through travel and time investment. Urban pastors partner with community navigators to accompany refugees in processing trauma, reflecting the Father's care for the alien and oppressed (Exod 22:21). Seminary courses in pastoral theology now include field practicums in palliative units, ensuring students learn presence amid pain. Retreat centers train spiritual directors to hold space for penitent silence as much as for spoken counsel, aligning with the Spirit's wordless intercession (Rom 8:26). Digital ministries experiment with video "check-in" calls that maintain relational warmth when in-person visits are impossible. Small-group leaders practice "sacred pauses," inviting group members to sit together in silence for a minute before praying aloud. These practices guard against hollow consolation by rooting care in the Triune God's demonstrated nearness. Pastoral presence thus becomes a sacrament of the Spirit, offering tangible signs of divine compassion. As we shift from model to method, we now consider diakonia's ancient roots and modern vocations in communal service.

13.0.2 From First-Century Diakonia to Twenty-First-Century Advocacy

In Acts 6, the apostles appointed the first deacons to serve tables, ensuring equitable care for all widows—an early form of church-administered welfare (Acts 6:1–4). That service, or diakonia, fused spiritual devotion with practical mercy, setting a precedent for generations of Christian caregivers. The Rule of St. Basil in the fourth century formalized diaconal care in monasteries, integrating infirmaries and guesthouses under ecclesial oversight. Medieval guilds of charitable laypeople maintained hospices and almshouses, recognizing mercy as a communal responsibility. The Protestant Reformation recast diakonia as a vocational call, affirming that nursing and teaching are forms of kingdom service. In the eighteenth century, William Wilberforce and contemporaries engaged in social reform as an extension of gospel compassion. Today's churches carry that legacy forward by establishing community centers, food banks, and mental-health ministries. Nonprofit arms of congregations partner with municipal agencies to deliver winter shelters, reflecting Isaiah's call to loosen the bonds of injustice (Isa 58:6). Faith-based advocacy groups lobby for policies that protect the poor and vulnerable, embodying Micah's imperative to "do justice, love mercy, walk humbly" (Micah 6:8). Deacons negotiate rental assistance with landlords, while elders supply legal aid referrals for families at risk of eviction. Interfaith coalitions unite around clean-water and anti-trafficking campaigns, extending diakonia into civic arenas. Church networks convene annual advocacy summits, training members in issue-based lobbying and public testimony. Social-media ministries publish video stories of beneficiaries to humanize policy debates. Seminaries now include public-theology tracks, equipping students to translate biblical ethics into legislative action. As diakonia evolves into twenty-first-century advocacy, it preserves the early church's fusion of prayer, presence, and public witness. With this foundation, we turn to the core practices of pastoral presence in local care contexts.

13.1 Pastoral Theology of Presence

13.1.1 The Ministry of Listening: Silence, Empathy, and Holy Curiosity

Effective pastoral care begins with active listening, a practice grounded in James's injunction to "be quick to listen, slow to speak" (Jas 1:19). Silence creates space for the sufferer's story to emerge, freeing them from the pressure to shape testimony to expectations. Empathy means entering another's emotional world without losing one's own center in Christ (Romans 12:15). Holy curiosity invites open-ended questions—"What is this day teaching you about God?"—rather than closed yes/no queries. Training programs for new pastoral interns include hourly "listening labs" where they practice nonverbal encouragement: eye contact, nods, and gentle affirmations. Reflective listening techniques—paraphrasing the speaker's words—help ensure understanding and validate the person's experience. Cultural competency modules teach sensitivity to language barriers, avoiding assumptions about grief expressed differently in various ethnic traditions. Chaplaincy rotations in emergency departments emphasize how to listen to families amid adrenaline and trauma. Online pastoral care lines require practitioners to mirror tone and pace in text-based conversations, translating listening into digital mediums. Supervisory sessions for pastors include feedback on recorded counseling sessions, highlighting areas for deeper listening rather than quicker advice. Congregations form "listening teams" for newcomers, offering a nonjudgmental ear at welcome dinners. Retreat centers on "silent weekends" instruct participants in the rhythms of listening to God's voice through scripture and to one another through shared silence. Theological reflection on Hebrews 4:15–16 frames listening as entering the empathic ministry of the Son. Pastors who cultivate listening skills report reduced burnout, finding spiritual replenishment in the simple act of bearing witness. As the ministry of listening anchors care, we next explore the sacraments at the bedside.

13.1.2 Sacraments at the Sickbed: Eucharist, Oil, and Mutual Consolation

James's commissioning—"Is anyone among you sick? Let them call the elders to pray over them and anoint them with oil" (Jas 5:14)—remains a foundational warrant for sacramental ministry in illness. Chaplains and elders carry consecrated oil in portable kits, ensuring readiness to anoint with sacred intent and sanitizing protocols. The anointing ritual includes laying hands, praying scriptural benedictions, and gently marking the forehead with oil, symbolizing Christ's healing touch. Homebound pastors bring elements of the Eucharist from the congregation's service, reciting the Words of Institution at the patient's threshold. Portable communion cups and wafers are approved by infection-control committees to prevent cross-contamination. Families gather around the bed, forming a circle of mutual consolation as one minister administers the sacrament. The fragrance of oil—often unscented for clinical safety—carries subtle reminders of the Holy Spirit's presence. Medical staff note that patients who receive bedside sacraments report deeper peace, paralleling physiological markers of reduced stress. Seminary courses train ministers to integrate sacramental theology with respectful coordination alongside nursing procedures. After administering sacraments, ministers often stay in silence, affirming that presence continues beyond spoken words. Eucharistic meditations—such as the Agnus Dei or the Magnificat—are sometimes chanted at a quiet decibel, inviting contemplative focus. Chaplains document sacramental visits in pastoral care notes, tracking spiritual interventions alongside medical treatments. A rite of mutual consolation allows patients to anoint caregivers in return, fostering reciprocal care. These bedside sacraments embody incarnational theology, demonstrating that God's life-giving sacraments extend beyond sanctuary walls.

13.1.3 Companionship in Doubt: Walking with the Angry, the Numb, and the Afraid

Suffering often provokes doubt, anger, and numbness that resist simple reassurances. Pastoral presence honors these experiences as legitimate responses, mirroring Jesus's attitude in the Garden of Gethsemane when He expressed anguish to the Father (Mk 14:33–34). Ministers receive training in grief counseling to hold space without rescuing or correcting raw emotions. Group workshops on spiritual doubt encourage participants to articulate questions in safe environments, guided by leaders skilled in theological reflection. Departments of pastoral care develop "companion handbooks" that suggest appropriate responses to anger—listening, acknowledging the feeling, and offering to pray when the moment is right. Retreat curricula teach "lament drumming," where participants use percussion instruments to express rage in a structured ritual that transitions into silence and reflection. Audio-guided prayer walks prompt doubters to name fears aloud, then to pause for scripture prompts that speak of God's faithfulness. Pastors practice "emotional radical hospitality," welcoming any feeling without judgment, as Jesus's parable of the prodigal son welcomes back the wayward child (Luke 15:20). Mental-health liaisons accompany chaplains in session for those experiencing spiritual numbness, integrating CBT techniques with biblical metaphors. Anxiety workshops teach grounding techniques—breath prayer, sensory focusing—to the fearful, framing Psalm 56:3—"When I am afraid, I put my trust in you"—as a breath-synchronized mantra. Through patient companionship, ministers model the Reformation motto of simul justus et peccator—we are at once justified and struggling—offering solidarity rather than perfectionist pressure.

13.1.4 Boundaries and Burnout: Self-Care as Stewardship of the Presence-Gift

Ministers risk compassion fatigue when endlessly bearing others' burdens without replenishment. Mark 6:31's injunction to "come away...to a quiet place and rest" mandates sabbath rhythms for caregivers themselves. Pastoral leaders set boundaries on visitation schedules, ensuring that no chaplain conducts more than two hour-long sessions without a restorative break. Denominational policies require clergy to take annual retreats, subsidized by the congregation, to renew spiritual and emotional well-being. Peer supervision groups meet monthly to debrief challenging cases and to provide mutual accountability, preventing isolation. Continuing-education requirements incorporate self-care modules—mindful listening, body scans, prayer journaling—underscoring that the minister's wellness is a stewardship concern. Chaplaincy rotor schedules guarantee one on-call week followed by two weeks off, aligning with occupational health recommendations. Spiritual directors offer confidential pastoral counseling to clergy, modeling reciprocal care. Congregations celebrate a "Clergy Appreciation Sunday" with communal prayers for ministers to affirm their service and invite rest. Retreats include guided nature immersion—forest bathing and labyrinth walks—to cultivate contemplative rhythms. Leaders preach self-care as obedience rather than indulgence, linking Psalm 23's "He restores my soul" to practical restoration rhythms. In this way, clergy preserve their capacity to embody God's presence without succumbing to burnout. With these pastoral foundations, we turn now to how congregations organize systemic care.

13.2 Congregational Care Ecosystems

13.2.1 Visitation Teams: Training, Scheduling, and Story-Sensitive Protocols

Visitation teams extend pastoral presence by training volunteers in confidentiality, listening skills, and spiritual sensitivity. Each volunteer completes a curriculum covering HIPAA basics, active listening, and spiritual discernment, ensuring care respects both privacy and faith needs. Teams employ digital scheduling platforms to match visitors with the homebound, balancing geographic proximity and shared life experiences to foster rapport. Story-sensitive protocols guide volunteers to avoid leading questions that may re-traumatize, focusing instead on open-ended invitations like "Tell me what this week has been like." Role-play exercises teach volunteers how to respond to strong emotions—grief, anger, despair—without reacting defensively. Volunteers wear discreet name badges and carry pastoral-care business cards, making future contact easy for clients seeking further support. Monthly debrief gatherings allow teams to share successful approaches and to pray for challenging visitations. Volunteers document high-level visit notes—prayer requests and resource needs—in secure church databases, flagging urgent needs for pastoral follow-up. Lead pastors coordinate with visitation teams to integrate sacramental supplies—oil, prayer cards—so that volunteers can offer basic spiritual care. Quarterly training updates address evolving community needs, such as support for new diagnoses or bereavement protocols after communal tragedies. Retention strategies include appreciation luncheons and "care for the caregiver" Bible studies. Some churches equip visitation teams with small resource kits—granola bars, hand lotion, Scripture bookmarks—to meet practical and spiritual needs. Through these structured ecosystems, congregational care becomes coordinated, compassionate, and sustainable.

13.2.2 Meal Trains, Ride Shares, and Micro-Grants: Logistics of Everyday Mercy

When illness strikes a family, basic tasks like cooking and transportation can feel overwhelming. Meal-train platforms allow church members to sign up online to deliver home-cooked meals on scheduled dates, ensuring dietary restrictions—diabetic, gluten-free—are honored. Coordinators collect allergy and preference data from recipients and distribute "meal profile cards" to volunteers. Ride-share ministries partner with taxi apps or church-owned vehicles to transport seniors and patients to appointments, staffed by vetted volunteer drivers. A micro-grant fund, supported by congregation benevolence offerings, awards one-time $100 reimbursements for urgent needs—grocery bills, prescription co-pays—based on pastoral recommendations. An administration team reviews micro-grant applications weekly, ensuring transparency and fairness. Volunteers are trained in gratitude protocols—sending follow-up notes or making courtesy calls—to reinforce relational warmth. Annual summaries of meal-train and ride-share metrics—meals delivered, rides given—are reported in church newsletters to encourage continued support. Logistical manuals document standard operating procedures, allowing new teams to onboard quickly during crises. Children's ministries involve youth in assembling "care packages" with easy-to-prepare foods and encouraging notes, fostering intergenerational service. These everyday-mercy logistics turn abstract compassion into tangible assistance, reflecting Jesus's feeding of the hungry (Matt 25:35).

13.2.3 Support Hubs for Chronic Illness: Peer-Led Groups, Resource Libraries, and Digital Check-Ins

Chronic illness often requires long-term support beyond sporadic visits. Churches establish physical hubs—rooms stocked with medical texts, adaptive aids, and support contacts—where sufferers can access information and community. Peer-led groups meet weekly to share coping techniques, prayer, and updates on treatment advances, fostering mutual encouragement. Facilitators guide groups through curated curricula on topics like pain management, spiritual resilience, and navigating healthcare systems. Resource libraries offer books, DVDs, and pamphlets on specific conditions—diabetes, MS, arthritis—alongside directories of local specialists. Digital check-in programs use secure messaging apps to prompt daily wellness reports and devotional reflections, enabling pastoral staff to monitor well-being remotely. Quarterly "hub days" feature guest speakers—nutritionists, therapists, chaplains—providing integrated care insights. Financial stewardship workshops help members with budgeting for medical expenses and exploring insurance options. Hub coordinators collaborate with health ministries to retrofit church facilities with accessibility features—ramps, handrails, adjustable seating. Confidential prayer chains within the hub allow members to request immediate intercession for flare-ups or crises. Over time, these support ecosystems become lifelines that sustain sufferers spiritually, physically, and socially.

13.2.4 Trauma-Informed Worship Practices: Space Design, Language Choices, and Flexible Liturgies

Worship spaces can inadvertently retraumatize those with past abuse or medical trauma. Trauma-informed design principles advocate for soft edge furniture, neutral color palettes, and clear signage to reduce anxiety. Worship planners choose inclusive language, avoiding militaristic metaphors like "fight" or "battle" that can trigger trauma survivors. Liturgy outlines include "time-out" moments—songs or readings that allow for reflection—so attendees who become overwhelmed can re-engage gently. Ushers are trained to recognize signs of distress and guide individuals to quiet prayer areas. Visual cues—such as discreetly placed weighted blankets—are provided for those who benefit from sensory regulation. Music selections feature a balance of contemplative and celebratory songs, preventing emotional overload. Pre-service announcements invite newcomers to sample the order of service materials to reduce surprise triggers. Children's worship rooms include sensory kits—fidget toys and calming visuals—to support neurodivergent and traumatized youngsters. Safety protocols ensure cameras and microphones are used respectfully, protecting privacy. Trauma-informed practices transform liturgy into a safe refuge where healing rhythms can unfold.

13.2.5 Measuring Impact: Care Dashboards, Testimony Nights, and Continuous Improvement Cycles

To sustain care ecosystems, churches adopt metrics that balance quantitative data with narrative richness. Care dashboards display anonymized data on visitation frequency, meal-train participation, and support-hub engagement, enabling leaders to spot trends. Testimony nights invite beneficiaries to share stories of transformation, adding qualitative depth to dashboard numbers. Feedback surveys assess perceived helpfulness, timeliness, and spiritual impact of care programs. Continuous improvement cycles meet quarterly, where teams review metrics, celebrate successes, and plan adjustments. Data-driven discussions ask probing questions: Which neighborhoods lack access to ride-share? How can meal diversity improve? Leadership retreats include data workshops to train volunteers in interpreting dashboards responsibly. Partnerships with local universities provide analytic support, correlating care participation with church attendance and spiritual growth indicators. Continuous improvement fosters a culture of learning, ensuring that care structures evolve to meet emerging needs with agility and compassion.

13.3 Formation of Compassionate Disciples

13.3.1 Catechesis of the Wounded Healer: Integrating Lament, Hope, and Action

Catechesis of the wounded healer begins by teaching that every believer carries scars from personal or communal suffering, echoing Christ's own wounds (Isaiah 53:5). Instructional sessions invite participants to narrate their own experiences of pain, then to reflect theologically on how suffering can refine character (James 1:2–4). Small-group dialogues unpack the paradox that wounds both wound and witness, shaping empathy that compels action. Bible studies on Psalms of lament and New Testament healing narratives equip learners to move from raw grief toward hopeful service. Role-play exercises train disciples to respond compassionately in concrete scenarios—visiting a widow, comforting someone after job loss, or advocating for a neighbor denied medical care. Service projects follow catechetical classes: groups coordinate meal trains or transportation ministries to apply lessons immediately. Reflection journals guide participants to identify how God has used their wounds to cultivate mercy in their hearts. Mentors model self-disclosure, sharing personal stories of God's comfort, teaching that vulnerability invites divine strength (2 Corinthians 1:3–4). Workshops on spiritual disciplines—lament prayer, gratitude examen, healing meditation—anchor emotional experience in spiritual rhythms. Community art projects, such as collective murals of blessing and brokenness, offer tactile integration of catechesis themes. Retreats incorporate silence and guided imagery, helping participants internalize that God dialogues with wounded souls. Seminar courses on pastoral theology require students to design catechetical curricula for local congregations, ensuring direct applicability. Preachers weave catechetical elements into sermons, inviting congregants to practice lament publicly and to commit to serving one another. Volunteer coordinators partner with care ministries to identify opportunities for new disciples to engage their gifts of mercy and helps. Periodic "wounded healer" commissioning services dedicate those stepping into caregiving roles, marking transitions into compassionate action. Evaluations of formation programs ask participants to report growth in empathy, spiritual resilience, and service involvement. Ongoing support groups sustain formation, providing accountability and shared prayer. In this way, catechesis transforms wounded hearts into channels of Christ's healing presence.

13.3.2 Intergenerational Mentoring: Elders of Affliction Pairing with Emerging Leaders

Intergenerational mentoring pairs seasoned saints who have navigated long-term suffering with younger believers seeking to develop pastoral compassion. Each mentor-mentee duo begins with covenantal agreements: confidentiality, meeting frequency, and mutual prayer commitments (Titus 2:3–5). Elders share testimonies of how specific hardships—chronic illness, grief, financial crisis—shaped their faith and ministry calling. Emerging leaders listen deeply, recording stories in "spiritual formation" journals that track lessons learned. Monthly gatherings include joint study of biblical figures who endured suffering—Joseph, David, Paul—drawing parallels to contemporary contexts. Practical assignments invite mentees to accompany mentors on pastoral visits, observing presence, prayer, and pastoral listening in action. Debrief sessions after visits explore emotional responses and theological reflections, guided by questions like "How did you sense God's grace in that moment?" Mentor workshops train elders in active listening and coaching techniques, ensuring that wisdom sharing remains constructive rather than authoritative. Congregational leaders celebrate mentoring relationships during worship, highlighting their fruit in testimonies of restored hope and service. Youth ministries incorporate mentoring into confirmation and leadership-training tracks, giving teenagers early exposure to the wounded-healer legacy. Intergenerational retreats center on shared lament and shared gratitude, fostering mutual understanding across age divides. Digital platforms facilitate supplemental communication between meetings—sharing prayer requests, Scripture passages, and reflective prompts. Surveys assess the impact of mentoring on both parties, measuring increases in spiritual maturity, empathy, and ministry engagement. As mentees graduate to mentoring roles themselves, a multiplying effect embeds compassionate leadership throughout the congregation. This intergenerational chain of care embodies 2 Timothy 2:2's vision of truth passed faithfully through successive generations.

13.3.3 Youth Service Learning: Hospital Internships, Accessibility Audits, and Advocacy Projects

Youth service learning embeds emerging disciples directly in care contexts, teaching that faith without works is dead (James 2:17). Summer internship programs place high-school and college students in hospital chaplaincy departments, shadowing chaplains during rounds, prayer visits, and support groups. Academic-credit partnerships with local universities ensure reflection papers integrate spiritual theology with observed care practices. Accessibility audits become hands-on service projects: youth teams assess church and community buildings for ADA compliance, identify barriers, and propose improvements. These audits teach technical skills—reading blueprints, measuring door widths—alongside theological commitment to welcoming the "least of these" (Matthew 25:40). Teen-led advocacy projects address public-health issues such as mental-health awareness, hosting community forums with healthcare professionals and policymakers. Youth artisans design "care kits" containing comfort items (blankets, journals, Scripture cards) for distribution to hospital patients. Service-learning journals guide reflections on how youth experiences reshape personal values and vocational aspirations. Adult mentors accompany students, debriefing emotional challenges such as witnessing suffering and death. High-school chapels include "service testimonies" where interns share insights, inspiring peers to join future cohorts. Partnerships with nonprofits provide ongoing volunteer placements, transitioning students from short-term interns to long-term community advocates. Youth pastors integrate service-learning into discipleship small groups, connecting action with Bible study on justice and mercy. End-of-program celebrations bless interns and commission them for continued service, embedding a vocational sense of compassionate community. Surveys show that participants report increased resilience, empathy, and clarity of calling post-internship. Youth service learning thus forms compassionate disciples equipped to advocate for health and justice in the wider world.

13.3.4 Spiritual Gifts Discernment: Identifying Mercy, Helps, and Encouragement Charisms

Congregations facilitate spiritual gifts workshops that guide members in discovering charisms of mercy, helps, and encouragement (1 Corinthians 12:28). Interactive inventories help individuals reflect on past experiences: moments when they felt most alive, when others were drawn to their care, or when they felt a deep desire to alleviate suffering. Small-group discussions explore how these patterns align with biblical descriptions of specific gifts, grounding discernment in scripture. Gifted lay leaders model charisms by sharing stories—feeding the hungry, organizing care teams, or offering words of hope in pastoral encounters. Mentorship nodes connect those who believe they have mercy charisms with veteran caregivers for confirmation and coaching. Members experiment with service roles—meal delivery, hospital visits, administrative support—to test and refine their gifting. Periodic "gift of helps" retreats offer immersive experiences in community projects, such as building ramps or stocking food pantries. Encouragement charisms are practiced in prayer-line ministries, where volunteers phone or text isolated members to offer scripture and empathetic listening. Coordinators track volunteer deployment, ensuring that gifts of helps and mercy serve areas of greatest need without burnout. Spiritual directors provide one-on-one sessions for those discerning multiple or overlapping charisms, weaving vocational clarity with spiritual formation. Baptismal instruction for new believers includes modules on serving the body of Christ through spiritual gifts. Annual gift-celebration services publicly acknowledge those exercising mercy and helps, reinforcing the value of each charism. These discernment processes build a robust care culture, where each member contributes according to God's unique endowment.

13.3.5 Sabbath and Celebration: Rhythms That Sustain Long-Term Caregivers

Long-term caregivers require rhythms of Sabbath rest and corporate celebration to avoid depletion in ministry. Congregational calendars designate "Caregiver Sabbath Sundays" where those involved in care ministries are explicitly encour-aged to receive care rather than give it. Special services include blessing rites for caregivers, anointing them with oil of encouragement and committing the congregation to uphold them. Sabbatical policies allow deacons, pastoral counselors, and care-team leaders to take extended breaks—one month every three years—for renewal and retraining. Celebratory events such as annual care ministry picnics or retreat weekends mix fun, reflection, and worship, reinforcing team cohesion and joy. Financial stipends or honoraria accompany these celebrations, acknowledging the value of unpaid care work. Sabbath workshops teach spiritual rest practices—lectio divina, contemplative walking, creative arts—that nourish weary hearts. Group celebrations incorporate testimonies of transformed lives, reminding caregivers of the fruit of their labors. Children's choirs perform at these events, symbolizing generational continuity of care. Retreat locations often include natural settings—lakeside cabins, forest lodges—to facilitate deeper relaxation and spiritual recharge. Preachers emphasize Exodus 20's call to rest as gift rather than mandate, reframing Sabbath as divine grace. Bake-off or potluck lunches at celebration events honor culinary charisms and build community through shared hospitality. These rhythms of Sabbath and celebration sustain compassion long-term, ensuring that the church's vocation remains a joy-filled calling rather than a burdensome duty.

13.4 Prophetic Voice in Public Health

13.4.1 Speaking for the Voiceless: Biblical Mandates and Modern Policy Forums

Scripture repeatedly upholds advocacy for the vulnerable: Isaiah's call to "defend the fatherless and plead for the widow" (Isa 1:17) and Proverbs's warning to "speak up for those who cannot speak for themselves" (Prov 31:8) form the bedrock of prophetic public health engagement. Churches develop advocacy training that equips laypeople to testify at city council hearings on issues like healthcare coverage for undocumented immigrants or mental-health resources in schools. Policy-education seminars explain legislative processes, teaching participants how to draft effective testimony and engage legislators. Working with legal clinics, congregants prepare "amici curiae" briefs in public health lawsuits, lending faith-based perspectives to judicial decisions. Partnerships with academic public-health departments enable congregations to present evidence-based data alongside moral imperatives when advocating for clean-water infrastructure. Faith leaders speak at press conferences demanding equitable vaccine distribution, invoking the Imago Dei to frame health not as privilege but as right. Prophetic sermons integrate policy calls to action, encouraging congregants to contact representatives and sign petitions. Social-media campaigns amplify voiceless communities—refugees, the homeless, rural residents—using story mapping and video vignettes to humanize statistics. Interfaith coalitions lobby for expanded Medicaid, crafting letters that draw on diverse religious mandates to care for the sick. Church publications feature op-eds on harm-reduction strategies for substance-use disorders, advocating needle-exchange services as public-health necessities. By speaking in policy forums, churches transform biblical mandates into real-world advocacy that protects those who otherwise lack a platform.

13.4.2 Congregations as Research Partners: Data Collection, Story Mapping, and Testimony at Hearings

Beyond speaking, congregations can become active partners in public-health research. Community-based participatory research projects enlist church members to collect health data—blood-pressure screenings, nutrition surveys—ensuring culturally sensitive methods. Story mapping workshops train volunteers to document personal health journeys on geographic information system (GIS) platforms, revealing patterns of food insecurity or environmental hazards. Researchers co-design questionnaires with congregational input, respecting local knowledge and wisdom. Data dashboards generated from church-collected data inform policy recommendations, adding granular detail to municipal health planning. Congregants present these findings at public hearings, pairing statistical charts with personal testimonies that illuminate the lived impact behind numbers. Research partnerships with seminaries yield interdisciplinary conferences where theologians and epidemiologists co-author publications on faith-based health interventions. Ethical protocols ensure that participant consent is informed and confidentiality maintained, reflecting biblical ethics of respect. Youth involvement in data collection cultivates future public-health advocates. When city planners see church-driven maps of asthma hotspots, they allocate resources for air-quality monitoring in those neighborhoods. Over time, partnerships deepen trust between researchers and communities historically wary of external surveys. Congregations thus shift from passive subjects to co-creators of knowledge, enhancing both public science and prophetic witness.

13.4.3 Coalition Building: Interfaith Alliances, NGOs, and Government Agencies

Public-health challenges often exceed one congregation's capacity, calling for coalitions. Churches convene interfaith roundtables on pandemic preparedness, bringing together rabbis, imams, Hindu leaders, and medical directors to draft inclusive response plans. These alliances foster shared resources—vaccination clinics held jointly in sacred spaces—and unified messaging that transcends doctrinal divides. NGOs specializing in issues like gender-based violence or substance abuse partner with churches to leverage volunteers and venues for training and support. Government health departments invite faith coalitions to advisory councils, recognizing churches' reach into underserved communities. Memoranda of understanding outline roles: churches provide outreach, NGOs offer expertise, agencies supply funding and policy authority. Coalition summits align strategic goals—from childhood obesity prevention to mental-health crisis response—ensuring that efforts amplify rather than duplicate. Shared public statements signed by diverse faith leaders carry moral weight in legislative debates. Joint grant applications secure multi-agency funding for holistic health programs that integrate spiritual care with medical services. Coalitions also coordinate disaster-response exercises, simulating mass-casualty events in stadiums to test interagency collaboration. Through coalition building, churches live Luke 10:1–2's vision of sending laborers together into the harvest, pooling gifts in service of comprehensive public health.

13.4.4 Health Equity Campaigns: Vaccine Access, Mental-Health Parity, and Environmental Justice

Health equity campaigns tackle systemic barriers to wellness. Churches host vaccine-access fairs in under-resourced neighborhoods, providing not only immunizations but language translators, childcare, and transportation assistance. Faith leaders partner with mental-health organizations to launch parity initiatives, lobbying insurers to cover counseling and to include spiritual-care codes in reimbursement schedules. Environmental justice efforts focus on areas burdened by pollution: congregational teams measure air quality near factories and push for zoning reforms to protect schools and parks. Campaign toolkits equip members to run letter-writing drives to health plan administrators and to testify at regulatory hearings. Partnerships with journalists amplify campaign stories, framing equity as a moral imperative grounded in creation-care theology (Gen 2:15). Graduate students in public policy intern with church-led equity task forces, offering research support. Mental-health parity days include webinars teaching congregants to navigate insurance appeals and to advocate for state-level parity laws. Environmental-action Sundays dedicate worship to prayers for clean air and water, followed by stewardship commitments in local elections. Successes include municipal ordinances expanding Medicaid eligibility and EPA directives limiting industrial emissions. Health equity campaigns thus operationalize gospel justice in the public domain.

13.4.5 Media Engagement: Crafting Op-Eds, Social-Media Advocacy, and Compassionate Messaging

Effective advocacy requires mastery of media channels. Congregations train spokespeople to write op-eds in local newspapers, framing health issues in narrative form that connects head and heart. Workshops on social-media advocacy provide templates for shareable graphics, video testimonies, and hashtags that maintain respectful tone aligned with Matthew 5:16's "let your light shine." Podcast series produce interviews with pastors, patients, and providers, weaving theology with practical public-health guidance. Media-scrutiny teams prepare leaders for TV interviews, teaching concise messaging and empathetic delivery. Crisis-communication protocols ensure rapid, accurate responses to emerging health threats, countering misinformation with scriptural integrity and medical facts. Regular church blogs highlight policy wins and ongoing needs, fostering sustained engagement. Youth media labs partner with journalism departments to create short documentaries on community health initiatives. Press releases on care programs leverage denominational networks, expanding reach. Through strategic media engagement, the church amplifies its prophetic voice, ensuring that compassionate advocacy shapes public discourse.

13.5 Missional Partnerships for Holistic Care

13.5.1 Parish-Clinic Models: Shared Space, Shared Staff, Shared Sacrament

Parish-clinic models co-locate medical and pastoral services under one roof, embodying holistic care. Many churches renovate basement rooms into exam suites adjacent to prayer chapels, signaling equal importance of body and soul. Shared staffing arrangements employ nurse practitioners who also hold lay ministry credentials, bridging clinical assessment with spiritual presence. Medical record systems integrate pastoral-care notes, ensuring clinicians know patients' spiritual needs while chaplains understand medical contexts. Weekly clinic hours align with midday prayer services, allowing patients to attend both in one visit. Volunteers serve as clinic hosts, providing hospitality and facilitating transitions between waiting areas and worship nooks. Communion services for clinic patients occur at lunchtime, offering bread alongside blood-pressure checks. Joint governance boards—including physicians, pastors, and community representatives—set strategic priorities, ensuring sustainable operations. Funding streams blend insurance reimbursements, church benevolence funds, and sliding-scale fees, democratizing access. Parish-clinic partnerships demonstrate Acts 2:44–47's vision of shared resources, translating ecclesial community into tangible health ministries.

13.5.2 Tele-Pastoral Care and Digital Chaplaincy: Extending Reach to Remote or Home-Bound Populations

Tele-pastoral care uses video-conferencing platforms to connect chaplains with patients in rural areas or under quarantine. Secure, HIPAA-compliant systems protect confidentiality while enabling face-to-face spiritual encounters. Digital chaplains conduct weekly check-ins, prayer sessions, and scriptural meditations, offering continuity when in-person visits are impossible. Simple telechapel apps provide curated liturgies, breath-prayer timers, and psalm audio recordings for home-bound users. Training modules teach chaplains how to interpret nonverbal cues through video and to maintain pastoral presence across screens. Partnerships with telehealth providers embed pastoral-care referrals in e-visit workflows, ensuring spiritual care becomes part of standard telemedicine. Volunteers assist older adults with technology setup, coaching them in video call etiquette. Digital prayer walls allow remote communities to post requests and receive real-time intercessions. Telechaplaincy programs track engagement metrics—session length, repeat visits—to evaluate impact. Case studies reveal that patients who access tele-pastoral care report reduced isolation and improved coping, demonstrating the digital church's capacity to embody Christ's nearness.

13.5.3 Disaster-Response Networks: Rapid-Deployment Prayer & Relief Teams

When natural disasters strike, churches activate disaster-response networks combining prayer, medical aid, and reconstruction. Rapid-deployment teams include logistical coordinators, medical responders, mental-health counselors, and prayer volunteers. Pre-positioned supply caches—blankets, nonperishable food, hygiene kits—are stored in regional church warehouses. Prayer chains mobilize within minutes of crisis alerts, initiating continuous intercession alongside ground operations. Medical triage tents set up next to prayer spaces, enabling holistic care that attends to physical wounds and spiritual shock. Counseling hotlines staffed by pastoral and psychological professionals provide immediate telephonic support to survivors. Post-disaster volunteer training covers trauma-informed care, reinforcing sensitivity to cultural and individual variations in grief. Partnerships with government agencies secure access to FEMA resources, while church logistics teams coordinate shelter operations in congregation-owned buildings. After-action reviews capture lessons learned and refine protocols for future crises. Disaster-response networks thus incarnate Luke 10's model of neighborly compassion under pressure.

13.5.4 Global Companionships: Sister Churches, Medical Missions, and Reciprocal Learning

Global companionships pair congregations from different contexts—urban North American churches with rural African parishes—to foster mutual encouragement and resource exchange. Medical missionaries co-train local healthcare workers, sharing protocols for maternal-child health, infectious-disease control, and trauma care. Long-term companions engage in reciprocal visits: northern volunteers learn indigenous healing practices, while southern partners receive training in advanced clinical techniques. Joint virtual seminars on public-health challenges—water sanitation, malnutrition, epidemic preparedness—facilitate shared problem-solving. Scholarship programs support local seminary students studying public health, integrating theological training with epidemiology. Church-to-church grants fund sanitation infrastructure projects co-designed by both partners. Shared prayer calendars synchronize global intercession for pressing needs. Cultural exchange events—food festivals, storytelling nights—celebrate unity in Christ's body. These global partnerships embody Galatians 6:2's call to bear burdens one for another, extending compassionate community beyond borders.

13.5.5 Funding the Future: Benevolence Budgets, Grant Writing, and Social Enterprise Initiatives

Sustaining holistic care requires innovative funding strategies. Benevolence budgets allocate a percentage of annual giving specifically for health ministries, ensuring predictable funding. Grant-writing teams composed of pastors, development officers, and healthcare professionals submit proposals to foundations supporting mental-health programs, medical equipment purchases, and community clinics. Social enterprise initiatives—church-run coffee shops employing those in recovery or thrift stores generating revenue for benevolence—reduce dependence on donations alone. Financial transparency is maintained through annual reports detailing program expenditures and outcomes. Congregational workshops teach generosity as stewardship, encouraging members to direct part of their giving portfolios to care ministries. Partnerships with local businesses secure in-kind donations of medical supplies and professional services. Endowment funds are structured with spend-down policies that allocate returns to care initiatives while preserving capital. Crowdfunding campaigns highlight specific projects—wheelchair ramps, telechaplaincy platforms—fostering congregation-wide participation. By diversifying funding, churches ensure that compassionate community and advocacy remain sustainable callings into the future.

13.6 Eschatological Imagination and Advocacy

13.6.1 Justice as Foretaste of the Kingdom Banquet (Isa 25:6–8)

Isaiah's prophetic vision of a feast on the mountain where "the Lord Almighty will prepare a feast…with rich food and aged wine" resonates as an image of ultimate restoration (Isa 25:6). This banquet symbolizes God's justice and grace fully met, where death and mourning are swallowed up in victory (Isa 25:8). For the church, earthly advocacy becomes a rehearsal of that feast, as we work to ensure all have access to the "bread of life" and "living water" now. Campaigns for food security reflect the eschatological promise by feeding the hungry and restoring dignity. Initiatives to end homelessness mirror the invitation to the great banquet: "Go out to the roads and country lanes and compel them to come in" (Luke 14:23), compelling society to welcome the marginalized. Legal clinics for immigrants enact a foretaste of justice, advocating for those shut out of public tables. Efforts to reform criminal justice systems—seeking restorative rather than retributive approaches—anticipate the day when swords will be beaten into plowshares (Isa 2:4). Churches host community feasts that pair neighbors across social divides, practicing radical inclusion as if the eternal table were already set. Environmental cleanup projects honor creation's sanctity, stewarding the garden that will one day be fully renewed. Through these actions, congregations declare that God's kingdom is breaking into the present, turning moments of advocacy into glimpses of the coming feast where every tear will be wiped away and every need satisfied.

13.6.2 Hope-Fueled Activism: Maranatha Longing Energizing Present Work

"Maranatha—Come, Lord!" blends fervent longing with urgent action. The church's anticipation of Christ's return compels believers not to retreat into passivity but to engage the world with energy born of hope. Activists grounded in Maranatha spirituality carry petitionary prayers for justice into legislative halls, trusting that their labor partners with divine purpose. When congregations organize anti-trafficking coalitions or climate justice marches, they proclaim both a present mandate and eschatological hope. Training sessions in "Hope-Fueled Activism" combine biblical exegesis of Revelation's new heaven with workshops on grassroots organizing. Participants learn that the same Spirit who raised Jesus will empower their advocacy for the oppressed (Rom 8:11). Youth groups led by Maranatha visionaries work through summer to equip local schools with mental-health resources, fueled by prayer for the coming Kingdom. Churches integrate activism into worship by reciting "Even so, come, Lord Jesus" between petitions for policy change, linking liturgy with civic engagement. Mission trips to disaster zones include both relief work and prophetic lament services, reminding volunteers that their hope compels compassion. As Maranatha activists serve today, they live out the tension of alreadiness and not-yet-ness, finding strength in the promise that God's final victory transforms all struggle into celebration.

13.6.3 Storytelling the New Creation: Art, Media, and Public Theology

Vision-casting for a renewed world happens through narrative arts that imagine the tearless future. Churches commission mural projects depicting Revelation's river of life and the tree with leaves for healing (Rev 22:1–2), placing public theology on city walls. Drama ministries stage Passion plays that extend into visions of the restored creation, inviting audiences to see beyond suffering. Podcast series blend interviews with theologians and health advocates, weaving testimonies of transformation with eschatological commentary. In print and online, church magazines feature creative writing contests on life in the new earth, cultivating imaginative hope. Liturgical dance teams choreograph pieces that move from lament gestures—fallen posture and reaching hands—to upright praise, embodying the transition from brokenness to wholeness. Visual artists lead "New Creation Labs" where participants collage images of current suffering alongside future healing, crafting prophetic art installations in public spaces. Graphic designers create shareable infographics that map the arc of redemption from Genesis 3 through Revelation 21, equipping congregants to tell coherent biblical stories on social media. Public theology forums partner with universities to host art exhibitions that challenge onlookers to envision justice as love in action. By telling stories of the new creation through diverse media, the church saturates the cultural imagination with hope that shapes values and actions in the present.

13.6.4 Practicing Resurrection Economics: Generosity, Redistribution, and Jubilee Principles

Resurrection economics flows from the promise that in the new creation, scarcity and inequality are abolished. Churches experiment with Jubilee-based practices—canceling debts among members, redistributing unused resources, and establishing land trusts to ensure communal stewardship (Leviticus 25). Congregational benevolence funds adopt sliding-scale allotments that prioritize the most vulnerable, reflecting Christ's concern for widows and orphans. Time-banking systems trade services—tutoring, meal prep, transportation—without money changing hands, embodying an economy of mutual care. Generosity workshops teach families to tithe not only their income but also time and talents, expanding the concept of treasure laid up in heaven (Matt 6:20). Social enterprises—cooperative cafés, thrift stores, urban farms—integrate profit with purpose, feeding bodies and communities alike. Financial discipleship curricula include lessons on debt cancellation as an act of gospel proclamation, aligning with Jesus's announcement of the year of Jubilee (Luke 4:18–19). Partnerships with microfinance institutions fund small businesses in low-income neighborhoods, fostering economic empowerment rooted in solidarity. Churches host "Resurrection Economics Summits" where theologians, economists, and practitioners explore models of equitable wealth distribution. By living out Jubilee and resurrection principles, faith communities prefigure a world where abundance flows from God's gracious provision and where resources serve as instruments of mercy rather than sources of division.

13.7 Epilogue — Hands Ready, Hearts Soft: Becoming a People of Embodied Mercy

Pastors are reminded that preaching must integrate proclamation and practical care, modeling presence and advocacy as twin pillars of pulpit ministry. Deacons are called to refine their gifts of mercy and helps, coordinating care teams with compassionate logistical skill. Health professionals in the congregation learn to view medical expertise as a sacred trust, collaborating with spiritual caregivers to serve body and soul. Lay advocates discover that their civic engagement—lobbying, coalition-building, public theology—flows from baptismal identity as ambassadors of Christ (2 Cor 5:20). All participants must cultivate rhythms of lament, hope, and jubilee-based generosity to sustain long-term service. Intergenerational mentoring structures ensure wisdom is transferred from experienced caregivers to emerging leaders. Digital platforms expand the reach of prayer, pastoral counseling, and advocacy training, equipping members in remote or secular contexts. Trauma-informed worship practices create safe environments for all bodies, reflecting God's nearness to the brokenhearted. Sabbath and celebration rhythms guard volunteers against burnout, framing rest as service to the mission. Storytelling in art and media embeds prophetic vision of the new creation in public imagination. Data-driven dashboards and continuous-improvement cycles translate compassion into accountable ministry. Partnerships—parish-clinic models, telechaplaincy, disaster networks—demonstrate that no single congregation stands alone in the work of holistic care. These key takeaways form a toolkit for living out a vocation of embodied mercy in diverse contexts.

Conclusion When a congregation becomes a matrix of listening, caregiving, and prophetic witness, it reflects the Triune God's presence in a suffering world. Volunteers who deliver meals, mentors who guide wounded leaders, and advocates who lobby for vaccine equity all participate in a grand narrative of healing and justice. By integrating sacramental ministry with data-informed care, intergenerational formation, and global partnerships, the church fulfills its vocation as compassionate community and bold advocate. As we prepare to breathe our final benediction, we carry forward a vision of hands ready for service and hearts softened by grace—living signs of the kingdom where mercy reigns and every voice is heard.

Chapter 14 – The Eschatological Hope: New Creation and the End of Sickness

Every tear, every ache, and every groan of this fallen world points toward a promise that outlasts all suffering. From the earliest prophecies to the final vision in Revelation, Scripture paints a picture of a reality where death, mourning, and pain are banished, and healing flows like a river through a renewed cosmos. This chapter invites us to dwell in that promise—to see our present struggles as birth pangs of the coming new creation, to root our identity in the power of Christ's resurrection, and to live each day as pilgrims who have already tasted—but not yet fully received—the banquet of God's restorative glory. By tracing biblical visions, unpacking resurrection theology, and cultivating practices that anticipate God's future, we discover how hope reshapes our care for bodies now and propels us into mission with confidence that the story's final word will be redemption.

14.0 Prelude — Longing for the Last Word

The world itself seems to groan under the weight of sin, decay, and disease, echoing the apostle's observation that "the creation waits in eager expectation" (Rom 8:19). Every birth defect, every chronic illness, every hospice vigil reminds us that our world is out of joint, crying out for repair. Yet alongside that groaning lies a deeper, more resilient ache—an intrinsic yearning for ultimate restoration that no therapy or reform can fully satisfy. This longing shapes art, music, and worship across cultures, suggesting that humans are hardwired to hope for "the last word" from God. When we catch sight of the Bible's finale—where tears and sickness are swept away—we see that our deepest aspirations find their home in divine promise. The scriptures repeatedly point forward to a time when "God himself will be with them and be their God" (Rev 21:3), affirming that relationship, not mere relief, is the goal of redemption. This eschatological horizon gives shape and meaning to all our smaller hopes, anchoring present afflictions in a broader narrative of cosmic renewal.

Our present reality, however, is marked by the "already and not yet" tension. We have experienced foretaste of resurrection life in moments of healing, restored relationships, and glimpses of justice; yet suffering persists. This tension propels the church into mission, resisting both triumphalistic denial of pain and despairing capitulation to it. Faith that embraces the final chapter shapes pastoral care, theological reflection, and ethical action, reminding us that every tear has a purpose and every cry will find an answer. By holding together what has already been inaugurated in Christ and what remains to be consummated, the church becomes a signpost to the world: pointing backward to the cross and forward to the new creation. As we turn to biblical visions of total healing, we carry this longing as both anchor and impetus, trusting that the God who began this good work will bring it to completion (Phil 1:6).

14.1 Biblical Visions of Total Healing (Rev 21:4)

The book of Revelation climaxes in a vision of a city where the former things—death, mourning, crying, and pain—have passed away forever (Rev 21:4). This promise shatters the finality of any diagnosis, reframing even terminal prognoses as transient shadows before the dawn of divine renewal. The vivid language—God wiping away every tear—portrays healing not as a medical procedure but as an intimate, personal act of compassion by the Creator Himself. This passage aligns with Isaiah's prophecy of a world where the effects of sin's curse are reversed and the groans of creation give way to songs of joy. The imagery assures sufferers that their experiences are neither trivial nor overlooked; they stand at the heart of God's restorative agenda.

While the promise of no more death signals cessation of mortality, the vision of no more crying and no more pain encompasses emotional and physical healing in their entirety. Grief that lingers for justice delayed and bodies that bear the scars of oppression both find closure in the Edenic picture of restored paradise. In ancient Israel, healing was often partial and temporary, a signpost pointing toward fuller redemption. The prophetic hope of Revelation fulfills that trajectory, presenting a consummate healing that unites the spiritual and the material into a seamless new reality. In this light, the church's ministries of prayer, sacrament, and medicine become pilgrim gestures that anticipate and participate in the final banqueting hall where all needs are met.

The continuity and transformation of the body in this vision affirm that resurrection is not an ethereal disembodiment but a re-creation of flesh in glory. The same persons who suffered and died will rise, recognized by body and name, yet freed from weakness and corruption. Paul's description of bodies sown perishable and raised imperishable (1 Cor 15:42–44) resonates with Revelation's tearless city; our healed bodies will be both continuous with our present selves and radically renewed. This dual emphasis guards against Gnostic denials of the body and purely materialist hopes that neglect the soul's redemption. The biblical pattern promises a holistic healing that honors the goodness of God's original creation, elevates human dignity, and fulfills the Creator's design for embodied life in communion with Him.

Beyond individual healing, Revelation's mention of the tree of life whose leaves bring healing to the nations (Rev 22:2) extends restoration to a corporate and cosmic scale. Sickness and sorrow touch not just individual bodies but families, communities, and ecosystems. The promise of leaves for the nations underscores the global scope of God's redemptive purposes, uniting ethnicities and cultures around the banquet table. It envisions an ecological flourishing where human stewardship aligns with divine care—rivers cleanse the land, healed bodies cultivate gardens, and healed societies foster justice. This cosmic shalom echoes Isaiah's vision of the wolf lying down with the lamb (Isa 11:6–9), portraying a world reordered under God's reign. Taken together, these biblical visions summon the church to embody foretaste of the new creation now—working for justice, healing individuals, and reconciling communities—while trusting in the ultimate fulfillment of God's restorative promise.

14.2 Resurrection Theology and Bodily Redemption

The apostle Paul's resurrection theology grounds Christian hope in the historical reality of Christ's rising as "the firstfruits of those who have fallen asleep" (1 Cor 15:20). This designation as firstfruits guarantees that Jesus's resurrection inaugurates a harvest of redeemed bodies, affirming that our own resurrection is secure in Him. Just as firstfruits offered to God heralded the fullness of the harvest in Israel's traditions, Christ's resurrection stands as a pledge of total bodily redemption for all who follow Him. The theological weight of this image dissolves any notion that bodily healing is merely provisional or symbolic; it is a foretaste of nothing less than the transformation that awaits every believer.

Spirit-empowered transformation continues this logic: the same Spirit who raised Jesus from the dead dwells in believers, empowering present bodies even amid weakness (Rom 8:11). Paul speaks of the inner longing for adoption and redemption of our bodies (Rom 8:23), weaving Spirit-led renewal with future fulfillment. This pneumatological lens reframes current suffering—as painful as it is—as participatory entry into the Messiah's own labor pains (Rom 8:22–23). Believers thus find meaning in affliction, not as random cruelty, but as the birth pangs heralding the birth of God's renewed creation. This theological narrative enjoins the church to accompany sufferers with both compassion and prophetic perspective, knowing that pain serves a redemptive purpose in the Spirit's unfolding plan.

The "spiritual body" paradigm in Paul's explanation to the Corinthians establishes that resurrection bodies, though continuous with our present form, will bear properties beyond current comprehension—incorruptibility, glory, power, spiritual vitality (1 Cor 15:42–44). Identity, memory, and physicality find their highest expression in the resurrection body, ensuring that persons are recognized and relationships endure in the new creation. This hope preserves personal and communal identity beyond the grave, anchoring trust that those we love will rise, known and beloved, in transformed flesh. It also challenges the church to value bodies now—not merely as temples of the Spirit to be maintained for spiritual service but as bearers of eternal destiny, worthy of respect and care.

Finally, the implications for present suffering emerge from viewing affliction as "light and momentary" compared to the "eternal glory" it prepares (2 Cor 4:17). This comparative perspective does not minimize pain but situates it within a cosmic framework where God's redemptive work outweighs temporal distress. Pastoral care grounded in these truths offers both empathy for the immediacy of suffering and an unshakable hope that no trouble, persecution, or heartache can separate us from the love of God in Christ Jesus (Rom

8:38–39). As we bear one another's burdens, we practice resurrection solidarity—participating in the present gift of grace while awaiting its consummation. This eschatological hope transforms despair into expectancy, empowering the church to live as a community of healed witnesses in a world still awaiting its final healing.

14.3 Living in Anticipation

Eschatological hope is not a distant dream but an active lens shaping every Christian practice today. Baptism immerses believers into Christ's death and resurrection, signaling both cleansing from sin and participation in the new creation already inaugurated (Rom 6:4). When we gather for the Eucharist, we taste the marriage feast of the Lamb, as Jesus declared that His body and blood would anticipate the future banquet (Luke 22:18). Laying on of hands and anointing with oil become pledges of eventual healing and wholeness, reminding the sick that their bodies belong to a story far larger than current trials. Prayer uttered in "Maranatha"—"Come, Lord"—bridges our present fragility with the certainty of the coming Kingdom (1 Cor 16:22). Even hymns that speak of "hope that will not disappoint" direct our affections toward the enduring promises of God rather than the fleeting comfort of relief.

Mission work flows from anticipation as well. When a congregation sends medical teams to remote villages, they do so as ambassadors of the eschatological Kingdom, bearing signs of the new creation in womb-to-tomb clinics. Advocacy for health equity becomes an act of faith, proclaiming by deeds that in the healed world ahead, no one will lack care. Sermons on future restoration inspire laypeople to join disaster-response networks, not out of guilt for suffering, but out of joy for the coming shalom they embody. Even small acts—visiting someone in the hospital, offering a meal—become anticipatory rehearsals of a reality where death and sickness are banished forever.

Resurrection ethics infuse our daily decisions with eternal perspective. Generosity toward the poor, hospitality to strangers, and environmental stewardship reflect values of the restored earth. When we forgive debts, we enact Jubilee principles that look forward to a world where no debts remain. Schools incorporate gratitude and creation-care curricula to shape children's values in light of Revelation's promise of ecological renewal. Urban planners partner with churches to design green corridors, anticipating a city where "there will be no more curse" (Rev 22:3). Each such project proclaims that God's future shalom is powerful enough to transform the present.

Liturgy itself becomes a school of hope. Advent seasons teach patience and longing, while Easter celebrations affirm victory over death. Even in funerals, the language shifts from only loss to promised reunion: "We will meet again before the throne." Stanzas of "O Happy Day" remind mourners that the first word on the other side is "welcome." As congregations reclaim ancient liturgical rhythms, they anchor their souls in the steady drumbeat of eschatological expectation.

14.4 Pastoral and Practical Eschatology

Preparing the dying for home-going involves blending pastoral care with eschatological vision. Hospice chapels play hymns of resurrection while counselors guide families through narrative exercises that map loved ones' journeys into God's presence. Vigil services incorporate both the stanza "I'm going home to see my Lord" and silence for reflection on the "great cloud of witnesses" (Heb 12:1). Pastors coach caregivers to speak of the deceased not as absent but as "awaiting us in glory," affirming continuity of relationship beyond the grave.

Teaching children about hope requires creativity. Storybooks recounting the new creation with rhyming verse help young minds imagine tearless gardens where friends and pets greet them. Arts-and-crafts sessions let kids build dioramas of Revelation's river and tree of life, embedding truth in tactile experience. Memorial rituals like balloon releases or planting "hope trees" weave grief and promise into communal memory, offering tangible symbols of future reunion.

Artistic expressions provide windows into the new creation. Visual artists lead congregational workshops painting murals of healed bodies rising in light, channeling Paul's image of bodies sown in weakness and raised in power (1 Cor 15:43). Poets compose anthologies of "resurrection lyrics" that explore spiritual bodies with senses perfected. Songwriters craft "resurrection anthems" that ascend from minor chords of lament to triumphant major keys, echoing the arc of redemption. Such works become public theology, testifying visually and aurally to God's final restoration.

Yet many struggle when healing does not come now. Pastoral care must address "delayed miracles" with both empathy and hope.

Spiritual directors teach sufferers to live with unanswered prayers, offering lament prayers that model honesty before God. Small-group ministries focus on "lament drumming" or expressive writing to channel grief while holding onto future healing. Counselors integrate narrative therapy with biblical promise, helping individuals see their stories as chapters in a larger redemption plot.

Eschatological preaching stitches doctrine into daily living. Sermons on the new creation conclude with invitations to join community clinics, environmental projects, or justice campaigns, connecting impending joy with present action. Study groups trace biblical threads from Eden's tree of life to Revelation's restored paradise, reinforcing that God's redemptive plan spans the entire storyline. This pastoral work ensures that eschatology is not abstract theology but a practical framework for sustaining hope amid suffering.

14.5 Apologetics of Hope in a Skeptical Age

In a culture steeped in naturalism, defending resurrection hope requires historical grounding. Apologists point to multiple attestation of Jesus's resurrection in early creedal formulations (1 Cor 15:3–5) and to the willingness of eyewitnesses to die for their testimony. They engage historians' criteria of embarrassment and coherence to argue that the empty tomb and postmortem appearances fit the weight of ancient evidence. This historical credibility forms a bedrock for hope, showing that the firstfruits has already risen.

Philosophically, Christian hope counters despair born of materialist worldviews. By affirming that matter itself will be redeemed, the faith transcends dualistic pitfalls. The resurrection affirms that bodies matter and that goodness extends beyond physical survival. Philosophers and theologians collaborate to rebut notions that consciousness is doomed with the brain, articulating robust theories of embodied continuity rooted in personal identity over time.

Near-death experiences and reported healing miracles offer contemporary glimpses of foretaste. Pastors and chaplains gather testimonies—hearing stories of terminally ill patients who temporarily awaken with vivid visions of light, or of incurable wounds that inexplicably close—to illustrate that something transcendent interferes with medical expectations. While cautious about sensationalism, they support rigorous investigation where possible, inviting medical professionals to review case files and lab data. These testimonies, when credible, strengthen the Church's witness by showing that the boundary between this world and the next can thin in moments of crisis.

Public theology of joy offers a counter-narrative to culture's cynicism. Churches host joy festivals—events centered on music, dance, and communal feasts—proclaiming resurrection hope through embodied celebration. Art museums collaborate with congregations to curate exhibitions on themes of renewal, inviting skeptics into spaces of wonder. Academic-public church dialogues feature panels on faith and science, exploring how quantum theories of information preserve identity beyond death. Media engagements by theologians highlight hope's positive social effects—such as longer lifespans and greater charitable giving among hopeful communities—arguing that believing in resurrection shapes healthier societies.

Through robust apologetics—historical, philosophical, testimonial, and cultural—Christian hope shines as both plausible and transformative. In a world awash with despair, the resurrection faith proclaims a story whose final word is life.

14.7 Epilogue — From Alpha to Omega: Embracing the Story's Happy Ending

As we bring this exploration to a close, we stand at the threshold of the narrative that began with creation's dawn and will culminate in glory's consummation. The refrain "Amen. Come, Lord Jesus" (Rev 22:20) anchors our final benediction, uniting beginning and end in a joyful refrain. This concluding moment reminds us that every chapter—sickness and sin, ministry and mourning—finds its resolution in God's final act of redemption.

We are summoned to live as people whose story stretches from Alpha to Omega, whose present actions anticipate the final healing of all things. Our hands continue to serve in clinics and care homes, our voices rise in prayer for justice, and our feet move toward the marginalized, all with eyes fixed on the eschatological horizon. The feast that awaits is both guarantee and impetus, assuring us that no tear is wasted and no act of mercy is in vain.

In this epilogue, we affirm that God's narrative will not be thwarted by disease or death. His final word is a benediction of life, renewal, and communion. May our communities breathe that benediction now—in homes, hospitals, and halls of power—so that the world may glimpse the happy ending toward which history itself presses. Come, Lord Jesus. Amen.

Conclusion As this journey draws to a close, we stand between "already" and "not yet," holding fast to the assurance that what God has begun in Christ He will bring to completion. Our prayers for healing, our acts of compassion, and our advocacy for justice are all foretaste of the day when sickness and sorrow will be swept away forever. With hearts anchored in resurrection hope, we embrace the call to serve boldly, to comfort fearlessly, and to proclaim unwaveringly that God's final act will restore every broken thing. Let every ministry and every moment of care echo the triumphant refrain: "Amen. Come, Lord Jesus."

www.ingramcontent.com/pod-product-compliance
Lightning Source LLC
Chambersburg PA
CBHW070847050426
42453CB00012B/2084